MW01256814

Arch

The Newman Journal of Ideas

VOLUME 1 – 2012

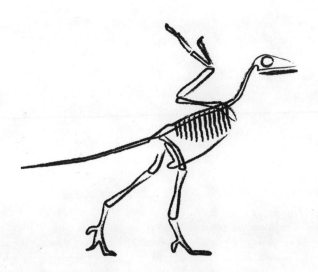

Published by
Newman University & The Gerber Institute

STAFF

Bryan D. Dietrich, Editor-In-Chief
John P. Jones, Managing Editor
Paul Manning, Assistant Editor
Annie Lessard, Assistant Editor
Sonny Laracuente, Cover Design

EDITORIAL BOARD

Michael Austin
Bryan D. Dietrich
Jamey Findling
Fr. Joseph Gile
Lise Goett
Cheryl Golden
Ron Hansen
John P. Jones
John Leyba
David Lunde
Timothy Richardson
Vicky Santiesteban
Curtis Scott Shumaker
Frederick Turner
Sherryl Vint

Newman University is a Catholic University named for John Henry Cardinal Newman and founded by the Adorers of the Blood of Christ for the purpose of empowering graduates to transform society. Newman University does not discriminate on the basis of sex, creed, handicap, national, or ethnic origin. Accredited by the North Central Association of Colleges and Schools, 30 N. LaSalle St., Ste. 2400, Chicago, IL, 60602-2504; 1-800-621-7440. Opinions and beliefs expressed in *Archaeopteryx* may not coincide with those of the Newman University community.

Copyright © 2012, The Gerber Institute
All rights reserved.
ISBN:1475122829
ISBN-13:9781475122824

A NOTE FROM THE DIRECTOR

Since its revitalization three years ago, the Gerber Institute has engaged in a variety of programming initiatives to fulfill its mission of "promoting interdisciplinary dialogue exploring Catholic thought and practice in the diverse realms of educational, philosophical, political, social, and cultural life." Our aim has been to foster the sort of discourse that is, we feel, most proper to a Catholic institution of higher learning: rigorous without being rigid, respectful without being uncritical, and inclusive in both the ecumenical and the interdisciplinary senses of the word.

In particular, we are committed to dialogue that actively seeks to reconcile differences. This does not mean abandoning principles or softening commitments. But too much of what passes for dialogue today is in reality a polite form of shouting that only reinforces what divides us. Genuine dialogue, by contrast, is built on the discipline of listening to the other; is unifying, not divisive; and is, we believe, fundamentally transformative for those who genuinely participate in it.

In launching a journal conceived as a forum for academic and creative work that advances the tradition of dialogical inquiry into the true, the beautiful, and the good, we are simply pursuing our mission into the realms of the written word and the printed page. Let souls encounter souls within these pages, that something transcendent may come forth!

—Jamey Findling, Director, Gerber Institute

A NOTE FROM THE EDITOR

When, in the Venerable Bede's account of the conversion of King Edwin, one of Edwin's advisors is asked to describe the pagan view of reality and humanity's place in it, the advisor tells him that life is like "the swift flight of a single sparrow through the banqueting-hall" filled with warm fire and friends, but that the sparrow exists in this warm space a short time only, traveling as it does between winter storm and winter storm. He says, "Even so, man appears on earth for a little while; but of what went before this life or of what follows, we know nothing." The bird, for the Anglo-Saxon advisor, is the soul. The house, the body.

Saint Augustine writes, "Understand that you may believe; believe that you may understand." John Keats says, "Beauty is truth, truth beauty—that is all ye know on earth, and all ye need to know." And Blaise Pascal offers, "For, in fact, what is man in nature? A Nothing in comparison with the Infinite, an All in comparison with the Nothing, a mean between nothing and everything." Historian, theologian, poet, philosopher... Each finds the human condition caught between mundanity and infinity. *Archaeopteryx: The Newman Journal of Ideas* exists to provide a space for academic and creative dialogue at this precise intersection, at the locus of the sublime, the nexus between faith and reason, the bright, brief interval where humanity finds itself housed.

In a world where too many public forums—be they books or bookstores, libraries or journals, newspapers or cable stations—find themselves failing, disappearing, or simply caving to popular sentiments concerning how little we need to question the world in which we live...In a world that shows us, daily, how seriously we seem to value entertainment and complacency over art and science and philosophy, over the vertiginous, over ideas that should shake us and make the world mean more, this journal is intended to manifest Cardinal Newman's vision of educating the whole person to seek the truth.

To this end, *Archaeopteryx* will strive to encourage a wide variety of meaningful, meaning-seeking modes of inquiry. The essays, stories, and poems found in these pages will have but one thing in common, Kafka's admonition that "A book must be the axe for the frozen sea within us." Named for the first bird—ancient, fossilized, frozen as if in the act of flying through shale—*Archaeopteryx* is intended to shake free storm and stone and ice and set the soul free to soar.

—Bryan D. Dietrich, Editor-In-Chief

CONTENTS

POETRY

FICTION

ESSAYS

SPECIAL FEATURE

POETRY

ARCHAEOPTERYX

Frederick Turner

COMANCHE PEAK

—on my 68th birthday

I. THE BLUE NORTHER

You see it coming. First it gets quite warm,
As if a frowsy summer had come back
Sleepless and tired. It isn't quite a storm:

Blue clouds in dreadful curds and flying wrack
Darken the Texas hills and drive the leaves,
But no rain yet to turn the limestone black.

It chills down, now, faster than one conceives.
The huge wind howls among the power-lines
And finds its way through collars and through sleeves.

Of course I choose this evening, by such signs,
To hike up to the ridge and celebrate
With one more gest my scorn for time's confines.

So many failures, and it's getting late;
All I believed in seems now to have failed:
The Church, the West, the limits of the State,

Free enterprise, just war, the tech we hailed
As freeing us; we never went to Mars;
We cannot reach again the heights we scaled.

I always somehow knew, though, that the bars
The prison's made of are the stuff and ore
To forge your freedom with and spear the stars—
And poemless these many months, the more
The trouble is, the higher gets the score.

II. THE CAVERN OF FALL

The road first passes through a cave
     of oaks now blowing bare,
But still a frail gold roof remains,
     and the gale's quieter there.

I must find out what I must be
     in these next—last—few years,
Living the time Vic did not live,
     before it disappears.

How young and wild my father seems,
     how deeper is the loss.
A whole medieval lifetime may
     still be my fate to cross.

But this trite reckoning is all
     tricks of the calendar.
For time is changing all the time,
     and memory's a scar:

Time does not, like these falling leaves,
     pass, but accumulate.
All information, science says,
     endures through state to state.

And what are we if we are not
     the form our matter takes?
All form is information, still
     sleeping until it wakes;

Even the substance of the leaves
     will feed the next spring's tree,
Its DNA undying twins
     through nature's alchemy;

And finer yet, each atom rings
     a spatio-temporal bell

Whose each reverberation sings
    out a swift-growing shell.

And all that is, is but the chord
    of all the form that falls
From all the rest; a re-record
    of all the old gold Falls.

III. THE COLD PASTURE

Now as it darkens the road turns eastwards, so that the   stormwind
Chills my left side, and I must clutch at my hat to keep it:
Winds of change, the cliché insists, sweeping America.
Barren acres stretch away to the north, arid,
Empty of cattle; my neighbor must have sent them to slaughter,
Feedstock prices gone through the roof with the drought, they are
    saying.
Over in Europe the banks are failing, collapse of the dream of the
Holy Roman Empire, the generous heart of socialism
Beating down to its zero-sum heat-death, like all schemes of sharing.
Capitalism itself is strangled with thieves, as the planet's breathing
Strangles with carbon, the creek is choked with eutrophication.
Through the nation the stink of political malice has poisoned the
Well of the constitution; we weasel and shun our creditors.
Will this tempest, then, blow the corruption away? How could it,
Being only a metaphor? Yet money's a metaphor also,
Sign not of obligation, but freedom from obligation:
Cash is unbondedness, all the debts that others owe us,
Negative sign of what you and your ancestors gave to the people,
Piety due to the past, seeing the past in the present,
Recognition we *are* only the keeping of promises,
Whether performed in laws or contracts or DNA codons,
Dead presidents' faces; bonds of love, duty,
Enzymes, chemistry, forces that bind the atom together:
All are metaphors, spooky action at distance, field-lines.
Over the field the wind is howling. Revolutions
Rage through Islam, the young at last have heard and risen,
Freedom shrieks through the internet, cries through the optical fiber,
Sings from the satellites, calling the crowds to the city centers.

11

Call to what though? Just another dictator? Call to the
Ballot, muezzin, or an inchoate "occupation"?
A new cybernetic *res publica*? United Colors of Benetton?
It is the end of the sexual revolution, nowhere to go now; the
End of the academic humanities disciplines, beginning of
Something else: the libraries of Alexandria, Byzantium
Sit with that of the Congress inside of our iphones, Google and
Mendicant Wiki making us all into idiot savants.
Really we're out on the edge here. The wind that blows from the
    pole is
Blowing us all inside out, blowing our top-knots off.

IV. HOPEWELL CEMETERY

Now the wind drops, there's a lull
In the cedar-forest's lee,
Dead limbs whiter than a skull,
Dark boughs green as verdigris.

In that forest, deep and twisted,
There's a graveyard that I know,
Where a township once existed,
Since abandoned long ago.

But the faith of those first dwellers,
Still recorded in their dates—
Mays and Barnards, Smiths and Gellers—
Haunts the place it consecrates.

V. THE JUNIPER FOREST

These are not cedars, though, but junipers:
The settlers named them with a bible name,
But they're not nourishers, they're ravagers,
Sucking our water into their dull flame.

They sucked poor Hopewell dry, like those who prey

In holy places on the children's love.
The bitter wormwood of what I must say
Can't be put off now, or referred above.

I have long travelled with an ancient faith
I came too late, who was an unbeliever.
The world of fact seemed then to me a wraith
Fleshed only in the flesh of the perceiver;

My poet task came like a prophet's call:
I was to draw the better from the worse,
Like him who cried "thy life's a miracle,"
To show the wonder of the universe.

I sought a house where I might join my voice
With the long history of human prayer,
And ratify the meaning of my choice
In something more embodied than the air:

So many good priests, gentle, funny, wise;
An old church, thoughtful, able to discern
The narratives from what they symbolize—
But rotten at its head, I came to learn.

Lest priest's sons should possess the nave and tower
Their fathers built to house the holy seed,
The popes and cardinals stamped out the flower
Of fleshly love in those it chose to lead.

And centuries of men, whose earnest thought
Was to forget the soft breast and the skin
Of woman, wrote the rules—how could they not?—
That turned our dearest act into a sin.

Yes, Venus is a giddy goddess, true,
And sexual betrayal is a crime
As great as any evil that we do,
And babies should have fathers every time;

But coop up men whose sex is as a child,
Who, told to love, seek any way they may;
Don't be surprised if what is meek and mild
Becomes their meat, and pray turns into prey.

Don't be surprised if such would bind with briars
The tender organs meant for love and joy
As much as for increase, and make desires
Sins between girl and girl or boy and boy.

And there are many women that I know,
Fitted to tread the church's quarterdeck,
And such was Mary's work so long ago,
True daughter of the priest Melchizedek.

If there is any sense in the great text
That we are images of the divine,
Then God is nobly hearted, fleshed, and sexed,
Pouring his nature into yours and mine.

We live with briars and thorny junipers
That tear and hold us back when we would pass,
And what is blessing's often called a curse,
And prohibitions desecrate the Mass.

Though Muslim Egypt has its Tahrir Square,
There will be no such freeing yet in Rome.
We must content ourselves with our free air,
Search for the holy fleshliness of home.

VI. THE BRAZOS VALLEY

The road now climbs unswerving into the sky,
Which, darker and more troubled still, in the west
Has grown an orange fringe of the fallen sun,
And the great valley of the Brazos opens,
Brazos de Dios.

This song-line is of time, not only of space.
The rising way becomes a graph of order
In the world of information, disorder
In the world of energy, a speeding-up
Of evolution.

The time-axis, t on the Cartesian scale,
Tilts upward till its vertical is the past,
Down is the heat-death of the universe.
But even this is wrong. The time-line branches
Just at the present—

This now—to make a wilderness of futures.
Apollo's sin was in making time a line
Unbranched, stapling our infant feet together,
Giving us new eyes in the back of our heads
To see what must be;

Making our births a clone, the crossroad a lie,
The fertile crotch closed shut but to its own son;
When you come to a fork in the road, take it,
Said Yogi Yogi Berra, the future ain't
What it used to be.

To act is to turn one virtual future real
And add it, as a past now, to the real past,
Growing time's body in a new direction.
All my mistakes, all my ideologies,
Dark fuel of being,

Were how to strip the dead paint of the present
To reveal the living flesh of what is past.
Remembering's just digging what is still there.
Where do we heap the tailings of the present,
Store the unearthed gold?

Time's like a growing apple, not like a line.
Time's like a movie's plot, not its celluloid.
Time's like a poem's music, not like its text.

Time's like a person's memories, not her dates.
Time's like her journal,

Not like the pages that it is written on.
Time's like the painting's paint, and not its canvas.
Time's like the painting's portrait, not like its paint.
Time is the journey up the Comanche ridge,
And also the ridge.

And so below me the dim-lit valley lies,
Prairies, forests, river-gleam, pylon-lines,
Lights coming on in this almost winter storm,
The Arms of God, what he has made of Himself,
A dear falling world.

VII. THE DAM

Now in the failing light rears up the dam
That checks two hundred million tons of water,
The Squaw Creek Reservoir impoundment, meant
To cool the domed twin towers of the reactors
Floodlit in science-fiction weird perspective
Above the concrete spillway.
                                        Texas is
The center of a vast high-tension grid,
The fuel-pump of the nation, churning out
Trillions of BTUs of gas and oil.
The Barnett Shale, the vast wind-turbine farms
Out west, Houston's haze-dimmed refineries,
The lonesome giant rigs in the blue Gulf,
Are how the elegant and thoughtful folk
Back East can play their gentle ethical games.
Texas is hunter-gatherer-miner country.
The grim metallic tech of cracking-towers
And striding geometric pylons, tankers,
Fracking bores, and massive filthy drillbits
Continue what began with chipped flint cores.

It's all turbines, whereby the one-way flow
Of natural decay is turned to spin,
Made to repeat itself, not fly away,
Be trapped to serve and fuel human life:
The slow entropic flow of prehistoric
Algaes into gas and oil, of water
Falling to a lower place of rest,
Of massive atoms shedding heavy neutrons,
Of this great wind that seeks a lower pressure;
And turbines turn matter to energy,
And energy transforms to information
In difference engines like the one I'll use
To set these thoughts in words, when information
Spinning the blades of mental wheels, becomes
Data, knowledge, thought, and understanding.

Matter is metamorphosed into spirit,
Whose time is of a making of its own,
At right angles to natural decay.
The run of things is turbulently creased
Into the cursive play of alphabet,
The pen retracing where it was with loop
And crossing, grammar, meter, logic, rhyme;
The mind revolving, shaping its own circuits,
Reading amazed what it has said somehow
Upon the mirror of the monitor.
Cultus is cult, culture, cultivation,
Colere, turning, tilling back and forth,
Retracing till the furrows weave a field.

So let me never disrespect or scorn
The ugly means and wreckage of this work
That turns the land of Texas to a mine.

CODA TO THE DAM

But living right down in the valley
The flood must take, should it come,

I might be accused, actually,
Of choosing a course that is dumb.

The earthquake that breaks the containment
And spills the plutonium rods
Would furnish yet more entertainment
To thrill the media gods.

But consider, all this being said,
An upside one might not first see:
Not to be dead in a hospital bed—
Just think how grateful you'd be.

VIII. THE DARK WATERFALL

As I return, the road passes over the river
There where it boilingly falls with a musical churning
(The wind having dropped in the hollow's sheltering trees)
Down to the reach that stretches on into darkness.
Night has fallen, but yet the turbulence glimmers
Dissipating into the depths of the pool.
Sometimes it seems I can hear a voice or voices;
Sometimes my own brain seems like a waterfall,
And out of it comes a reply to a question, retort,
Smiling paradox, gentle reminder, affectionate
Raillery, turning at times if I choose not to smother it
Into some strange conversations—maybe with God.
Put on the brakes here, son. The priests and psychiatrists
Equally frown on the man who believes he is speaking with
Him who in truth or in myth disposes the galaxies.
Say no more than: a functional god might emerge
Out of a cluster of braincells. Just be thankful:
Praise the muse and pass the ammunition.

But what if the Word was indeed the giving-on-over, the
First self-ruining of perfect intentionality
Into expression, into the laws of logic,
Into the towering gossamer structures of math,

Into the plane of the Hamiltonians, the labyrinth,
Fathomless, formed from algorithms of infinite
Depth and difficulty, making horizons,
Just like that between the past and the future, the
Calculable from the incalculable?
Space and time, just restatements of math?
What if matter and light were the only solution,
Only answer to logic's simple necessity? Did
God invent freedom by tearing himself into three?
Did he eviscerate himself into creation?
What was the cost? The evolution of beings
Able to suffer, to die, to be lost, to despair?
Fall the only condition of being, and he who
Took the cross was rightly taking the blame?
Fall, the great joke, to give the great gift in the guise of a
Punishment?--how could it indeed be otherwise?

What if the mind were always already a goddess,
Runaway, faithless bride of the Bridegroom and Father, who
Cannot shut out the whisper of where she was born?
She who has taken the terrible road of enactment, of
Being the only possible poem of Godhead?
What if her ongoing, momently dying, her time,
Incarnated truly the light of creation?

Fallen leaves, almost invisible, slip
Down the face of the chute and into the plunge:
All my dead friends, Vic and Allan and Julius,
Rick and Julia, Ed and Patton, swept on
Down the river of time and into the darkness.

IX. THE DOGS AT THE GATE

Eight dogs who think they own the road are there
As always, like dictators everywhere,
To bark at me and to secure the border—
As always I must wave my stick, defy their order.
My flashlight calls the demons from their eyes,
But cowardice reduces them in size.

The poet always, so I smugly muse,
Must be assailed by moral parvenus,
His paradoxes seared with malediction
As if he hadn't seen the contradiction.
The left dog finds the poet's ethics odd,
The right wing dog thinks he would steal his god,
The ignorant dog tries to get in a nip,
The literate one deplores his scholarship,
The post-postmodern one abhors his kitsch,
The pacifist, his military itch,
The atheist finds his prayers and praise quite sick,
The Church dog sees him as a heretic.
And so we poets are, misled by rhyme,
Abstract and brief chronicles of the time.
Let me on through, cut me a bit of slack.
Whoever came, you always saw his back.

X. COMING HOME

I leave the trees, and now the gale
Carries the first few drops of rain.
It's colder still—across the swale
Roars a black tide like a winter hurricane.

The sound of barking dies away.
Northwards the clouds are lit below
By the reactor's pseudo-day.
The woods along the river creak in the blow.

But now I see the lights of home,
The curtains drawn against the cold,
The place where time is reckoned from,
Where what is new emerges from what is old.

But there is no security.
The river's eating at the bluff,
The dam impends unceasingly;
Still, maybe this brief refuge will be enough.

For paradise is always here,
Right in the corner of meanwhile;
Now in the wind I think I hear
The sound of someone practicing on a viol.

David Lunde

DEATH OF A MURDERING THIEF
(Saudi Arabia, 1955)

They've got him on his knees now,
the murderer, thief, desecrator of mosques,
and they'll steal whatever he has left
after commending his soul to Allah.
Things are ready, just about, the tar
is nearly hot enough in its iron pot,
two strong men have roped his arms
and wrenched them out to either side,
the leather strap is belted tightly
about his forehead, he can hear the headsman
at his final stropping, the eager chirping
of stone on steel, and he gibbers
in a mantra of terror whatever word
he has left—*Allah* or *mama*—and then
after the first throat-ripping shriek
he has no breath even to scream with,
the headsman, with a small serrated knife,
is sawing his hand off at the wrist joint.

I can't remember which was first,
the right or left, dexter or sinister,
the one he ate with or the one he used
to wipe his ass, but no matter now.
They've plunged the gouting stump
into boiling tar to stop the bloodflow
and gone to work on the other.
There's no word for the face he wears
now, his whole nervous system numb
with shock, and the thong snatches back
his head and the sword falls
through his life forever, the eyes

in his tumbling head bulging
with disbelief; his spasming body
shits itself but can no longer wipe.

Forty-eight years later, I still cannot
either eat or shit without my hands
trembling, and all day I catch them
grasping each at the other, rubbing and
stroking to make sure they're there.

DRINKING WITH THE MOON

One jar of wine among the flowers,
no dear friend to drink with.
I offer a cup to the moon...
                    —Li Bai, ca. 730 C.E.

This very night the moon
 is at its closest approach to Earth,
30, 000 miles nearer than usual,
Jim, and where are we? Still orbiting
some invisible, unknown, perhaps
unknowable, common center of gravity.
Just goes to show it's still there,
that emotional adhesive, adamant
and stretchy, that was first applied
back when, in Iowa, those nights spent
making poems together, hatching
our first story (how many wives ago
was that between us? 4 or 5, I guess,
but we're still friends, and both at last,
at last with the ones we needed),
and dancing to the blues, dancing
to the blues beneath this moon—
like Li Bai 1273 years ago, with Du Fu
missing him at the end of the earth.

TO LI BAI, AFTER DRINKING WINE

Listen, Li Bai, here's the story:
Yuan Chi's damned insomniac lute playing
kept me from sleep too, so out I went
under the laughing moon
to see if anyone was playing Seven Sages
and had a cup to spare. Sure enough,
out back of Tao Qian's crib,
I could hear Meng's unmistakable croak
bawling out "Lady Night" songs
and the neighbor's dog howling
so I hurried over lickety-split
hoping there was still a little dew
on the lotus. All these drunk poets
were lined up by the eastern fence
pissing & I hollered out, "Hey, Tao!
Don't pick any yellow chrysanthemums!"
Several had already achieved enlightenment
and were scattered around the fish pond
like dead carp. Old Wang was there
maundering on about the poison dragons
in his brain & I told him, *Malt does more
than Milton can/To justify God's ways to man,*
and he gives me this look like I'm cockroach dung
then giggles and rolls backward into Peach Blossom Heaven.
Well, they don't let me leave till I've composed
a verse for this renga they're working on
called "In China they do it for Chili,"
and that's thirsty work, so by the time
things quiet down I have to admit
I'm a few sheets to the wind, but I'm too wired
to sleep so I tack off through the bamboo
looking for you. I felt like I'd climbed Tai-shan
by the time I finally stumbled across you
out there under the plum tree, face to face
with your wine jar, skunk drunk, singing
love songs to the Great Sky River. Pretty quick
you slumped over like a broken willow
and I buried you in plum blossoms

so the late-night strollers wouldn't see you—
don't know where you left your clothes,
but you were jade-naked. Later, after
I finished off the dregs in your jar,
I made a bunch of owl hoots—good ones, too—
and watched you get up and stagger off
to whiz in the river filled with moonlight,
your naked butt stippled with pink petals.
Nobody was around by then—even the birds
had gone home, so I did too. But listen, Li,
slow down, man—too much wine, too much
moonlight will be the death of you.

Mary Jane White

SIRVIANTE: NOAH
(May 2009)

I am watching the flare that follows. And remember
Nothing. Stop looking. Steadying fulcrum, sure foot,

Whirling vortex out of the air. Lapped by the Black Sea.
Then there was lightening and also dead silence

At the single line of the circling world's edge. This was
War's end. From Heaven my eyes fill with water,

Or Heaven whispers to me: empty them by blotting,
And let go the black southern shallow lapping

That empties itself into the great Mediterranean,
That empties itself further, on into the Atlantic

Through the constriction of the straits of the Bosphorus
And of Gibraltar. Let sail a trickle through these strictures

Out of the near-landlocked pool & this may have happened
First in Noah's time, ferrying his great ark of coupled

Beasts, and paired birds, over the great laying-waste
Of the then-known World, & then the flare-that-follows—

The repopulation—I, Noah, know I am leaving—a place
Behind, & abandoning doubt. Doubts that be several, as several call

One to one, as doves may do? Or as a single curlew?
A single note, then, as winter is my word. Not

Summer. Certainly the streams of Greece run, but
I may never visit their banks. I may never know any-

Thing of them, or step in or out of them, wondering whether
Of the past, or the future, whether in the water or above it,

Or of my sons' wanderings, the unbroken field where they may
Fall, as some end comes to them, unimaginably. Here is

Everything: more *as a fiction* than a future. Subtract the
Nights, subtract the steppes I lost and left behind, all

That comes to urge me to sleep, all that evaporates as I awake—
I can never leave the familiar, the nomination that is mine,

That is not me—a time when the living released me, but I
Could still sense the sweetness, & I fell silent about my own,

And Heaven spit on me—upon the familiar, upon all my own—all
that
Thick water weeping—this is how it fell: listen—as large drops,

Thick fog, negativity--so the vortex broke apart, & so the
Spray, fresh or salty, locked itself in layers, & there was no way for

Any visitor, any memory of home, of land that ended at my feet,
Curling of toes, lifting of gangplank from the pebbled beach,

Wrinkled eye-corners turning away from death or life,
Never thinking to see land, seeing it sink beneath the black

Waters, slow to retreat as I saved myself and my familiars,
Slow to forget this event, as my mouth remakes it, singing

To my familiars, to their bones, their blood, their cold, the water,
The milk, & of the glimpse of every feather afloat upon the sea,

Of spring's waning into summer, & beams of light upon wreckage
That floats. No, never was I steeled to that wreckage, or to how

It happened—this place and its altered landmarks, strewn with dead
Leavings, or the unstitched birthing of new lands, new shoals,

& the fruits gone which no one could gather in before the deluge,
Flotsam, & even an aging body loses itself in the certainty of
      survival,

Answering, light and heat call to it, slowly dawning. I see
The sun rise, weak as it breaks, with nothing more glowering,

Its new beginning, here in the new world of receding waters &
      fleeting
Rainbow, the small livings in new niches set up house once more

Upon the earth the Lord has wiped clean more than once—death is
Impatient and unsatisfied—even as it is a stormy morning—there is

Fresh food and fresh water—I will step into the stream that runs
Down to the new beach and the morning will wane & the moon be

Concealed, hidden and thin for the moment, as I lose sight of it
And disaster, nothing I would care to remember, not even the mud

Driven in curving rills along the new shoreline of that salvaged
Portion of Heaven, waving its warm welcome, & yes, gleaming.

SIRVIANTE: THAT

Weak sun, & the full fern's brackens—true—
The fern's brackens cover and uncover the ground,

Uncertainly, letting the earth-smell rise and then
Damping it again, let it be a fiddlehead

Unfurling, a commonplace tender green, and tenderer
White, as warmth draws forth the slender threads

Un-spun by every nervous to-and-fro stepping—
Of a woman—before her wheel—where

In the dark, Fortune plays openly with the hearts of men—
& not that we can see either the sure

Approach of Fame out of the burgeoning laurel
Or the open earth & its underworld & here

Outside no one is in command. No one
Thinks life can be lost. Even today

It is most ordinary outside: today
All handprints seem invisible, whether of men,

Or of their gods, or of their most recent
Adventures. The sun passes in and out

Of the notion that all this comes to naught (which one
Might mind) in the end. Quiet, and its devotees,

The whole world, lost avenues
Sink into the earth and beneath it. A single man

Loses office. Goes down to dishonor. Another
Escapes punishment. The silence of the elect holds

Or fails in its ancient grip. Seeing that it is
Time. Despair as it took them then. Those

Who are now gone still make their claim: to persist
In epic memory, & how slowly they grow

From one shaping to another shape into unashamed
Heroes, no less, as may be heard, even yet,

In every one of our Earth's mother tongues—
& how we cannot, having once heard them,

Furl them back, whitened, into their particular
Mouths—with a cupped hand—fold their tongue-like

Tips back to meet their stems—and fibrous roots:
How one might die for glory once, as supposed

Even recently: in the First War we yet
Have living memory of—of the last century

We yet have living memory of: so even
Clear-eyed Hardy was passingly deceived—

Harkening & writing back to the old mantle
Of Napoleon (glistening red) & not innocent,

Not fortunate—look below: our latest
Warriors lie close-mouthed, & senseless to night's

Passage over them—they lie under the earth's
Newest ferns—not in sleep. And no

Strong, nor weak sun wakes them.

Lise Goett

LITTLE WAY

All day, I work out this problem of metaphor:
my country with its inventory of secret wishes and trespasses
becoming a man, frisked naked,
the rivers of his blood
infiltrating the ground water
carried in pipes to the suburbs
where people use it to wash their foreign-made cars.

A cold voice comes out to nowhere.
"Nothing is like anything else.
And this love you've always had for transformation
is resistance to seeing things as they are."

This is how I move through my day:
doing small penances at the sink, straightening drawers,
my mind making connections between all that is seen and unseen
with the belief that these acts will redeem me.
I drink my one dark cup of coffee at noon,
thinking of how the couple who lived in this house before me
collected pine nuts for the macaroons they loved to eat
with their one dark cup,
brought their love for the fig tree from the old country,
wrapping the trees almost tenderly in linoleum
to protect them in winter.

Outside, the wind works the invisible,
scraps of paper, a Styrofoam lid, a Janus-faced chime
so that when the wind blows the face of the lion turns
into that of the lamb.
In the evening-green shade of a fig tree,
a beaten man stands before me,
his eyes racooned with the thickness of bruises,

window-lit buildings rising behind him
like glaciers of glass. He kneels down
in search of what is left after violence
of goodness, something to take home with him
like the sweetness of bread.
You don't understand my pain, he says.
And I admit that I probably can't.
Lay down your life for me, he says, and I don't.
My mind likes to locate pain elsewhere.
Not *here*. Not in *my* life.

Already, the first chill of autumn.
My nephews come dripping out of the backyard pool
to terry-cloth towels taken fresh from the dryer,
Later, sandwiches and milk, hands lifting white triangles
from waxed paper folded like the wings of the Holy Ghost,
our gated community, a cloister.

My little way is too little.

FLAME-SHIRT RAG

Love, you come lit with a fifth of alcohol,
always asking from your Cross to be taken down.
Your shirt split open, your heart wrapped in barbs,
Robe of Nessus, Sacred Heart, how can I put you on

without being burned? In the spectral hours, you visit me
in my fine, stone house, ask for a piece of bread,
show me your wounded heart and where the nails and shiv went in.
Immolated in their seamless shirts of flame,

the teens are up to no good again, shrouded in an ether dream.
I stay awake, as mothers do, worrying about the outcome.
I have had to cut my heart out to try to get some sleep.
You look down from your Cross and say,

"What can you do to me that you haven't already done?"
Tell me a story of resurrection and of a better life.
Tell me that I'll get home to heaven after all.
I've had my nervous breakdown. I've had electric shock.

I've had my figurative lobotomy, courtesy of patriarchy
and the cops. Your ladies of heaven look on the contraband of war
I'm always smuggling out. I'm running out of time.
O Sacred Victim, send me the clippings from your fingernails.

I need to resist temptation--another high in care
of Robitusson, airplane glue, naphtha,
the mechanical phallus, a whiff from an aluminum tube.
O fig tree planted in a prison yard, Liberty tattooed with a Molotov,

I can't die trying to love you enough.
Further, farther, faster, this life,
the passing scenery, and tarmac a blur,
o moonbeam on a sugar plate,

all I want is ecstasy and a lover who makes me wet.
In the carceral imagination, all of us are trapped.

Sometimes the mind and body are out of phase,
the dim boy in me the only one who claps.

Vicky Santiesteban

ADVICE

Do not wait until you're dead to learn words
come down like nuts for the mouth your head
wears, lording its troubles.

Do not wait until you're dead to learn death
fuels center, love lords life, hate binds fear,
or that guilt obliges folly.

Do not wait until you're dead to learn nothing
is learned the hard way, that you cannot know,
that you will never abandon fear.

Do not wait until you're dead to learn life
consumes hope, hope succeeds wonder, that
wonder persists, or that everything matters.

COMEDY

My mother said I came from a coconut. *A coconut!*
My father said *She's got one for a head.*

Whenever we crossed a bridge in our mischievous car
they worried aloud about how I couldn't swim yet.

In the grocery store, they'd threaten to sell me to strangers.
The butcher, they'd say, *He seems nice. He'll love you and*

clothe you and feed you pickled eyes! One day a man
brought two human hearts in jars to my Science class.

One of the hearts looked like a pink sponge soaked in urine,
the other like cauliflower oozing dishwater.

Suddenly, I understood my parents had organs.
They were absolute riots. I laughed and laughed.

SARTRE

The best of them come to you unannounced
and make their introductions with a smile
and a wag of the tail, provided they have
a tail, which Sartre did not. Red wonder
of a tailless beast, he claimed my dirty
front porch, uninvited, where he sat

waiting until I came from my bed to sit
with a cup of coffee and a smoke, our impromptu
appointment, our love at first sight, Sartre's dirty
paw on my knee, his puppy eyes grinning
as if to say *I've missed you. Wonderful*
to see you again, Friend. What choice did I have?

Those first months we trained. Both of us had
a lot to learn. We began with the obvious: Sit,
Stay, Heel, Fetch. One day Sartre wandered,
wooed by the scent of a bitch and I surprise-
attacked him, grabbed him by the snout and snarled.
Alpha commanded, he rolled onto his back in the dirt,

looked me in the eye and with a vicious, foul
cry warned, *I will rip out your throat. I have*
that instinct. I love you now let me go, his grimace
a row of fangs. I did as I was told. Situated
as we were, owner and owned, that spontaneous
lesson of respect spooked me. I wondered

if he might not be better a stray, wondered
if eating from garbage cans, sleeping in the dirt
under bridges, if following the scent of surprise
through a village to a city to another state would have
meant a better life for him than the one I imposed.
Years later I found Sartre pinned beneath our fence, smiling

at the infinite world in front of him despite the open grin
of wire that nailed his back to our placid, wondrous

life of bones, fresh water, morning kisses, nights sitting
with a book in front of the fire. Seeing the dirty,
bloody strip of fur the fence cut from his back had
its effect. Frustrated and sad and on impulse

I helped him escape, sat with a sorry smile,
lifted the trap, told him *Get out. Go.* I still wonder
where my dirty boy went, with whom, and what fun they must have
      had.

CONNECTIVE

In grade school
I was struck
in the back
of my neck
by a baseball
so hard it broke
the one-inch
herringbone
collar I wore
round my throat
a necklace
Robert Cave
gave in pledge
for my tongue
a soul kiss
that made me
sick *girl down*
on left field
spit, stars, stares
in the yard
as I stood
insisting
I could walk
to my house
alone where
when my mother
pressed wet rags
to my head
and asked
why the field?
I told her
the shorter
route home.

PREJUDICE

is a dagger, a toothpick, a burr,
a cloud in the shape of a dragon
eating the foot of a girl, a worm
disguised as a snake, a hammer
in an abandoned house struck
by lightening, burning

prejudice is a malicious car stuck
in neutral, a mendacious sea, an
octopus cradling a violin, my father
working the back of the house
for 15 years because of his accent:
don't you dare talk to the customers

prejudice is my babysitter slapping
my mouth when I said I'd grow up
and marry Mohammed Ali and we'd
have 5 children and a boat, prejudice
is a sea of blank faces speaking the same
nonsense at the same time to the empty

harbor where my husband and I dock
only our boat doesn't float and even
if it did there isn't any water

REVIVAL

The voice I heard said, *When God speaks you listen*
so I walked to the front of the church crying for a pain
a blue-suited preacher later explained had everything
to do with Jesus but was obscured by Satan.

I understood I was saved.

I went home with an evil understanding of how wicked
I'd become, how my lack of faith dug the hole I deserved: nineteen
and the mother of a toddler from a man who shoved my face
in everything I was stupid enough to say.

I was so sad my bowels produced pus.

For the answer, I went home to the book: *He that hath clean hands
and a pure heart; who hath not lifted up his soul unto vanity, nor sworn
deceitfully shall receive the blessing from the Lord.*
When spit in the face I thought Jesus.

When threatened with knives I thought God.

THE NICEST THING ANYONE EVER SAID TO ME
—*for Sean*

When I tell you my dream of waiting beneath the tree outside
my dead friend's bedroom window

me now only I'm fourteen again hearing my dead friend whisper
Be right there now except it's not her voice but

a man's voice beneath the tree behind me taunting *You're not
dreaming, not this time, not now*

when I tell you a razor-winged demon hopped upon her windowsill
and licked my initials in the glass, *VLS*, that I heard

the fawned skin of her back split, heard her eternal third rib snap
when I tell you I dreamed my dead friend's casket floated above its
    grave

while the man sat like a lord in a black chair blowing me kisses
you tell me you had the same dream only you were

in the tree outside my dead friend's bedroom window shaking
blossoms from the branches, raining forgiveness at my feet.

Sonya Taaffe

THE COLOR OF THE GHOST
—for Noel Jane D'Isa

Lucki says he is writing a novel
of the world as he found it, but he is leaving it to you
with all its apologetic *Sprachspiel*, half sin-offering,
half guest-gift, as if he could escape
even after death that paradox of earth and ice.
Austere as the emperor
of an intractable land,
he mooches around the kitchen
where your mother bakes parkin and *Spritzgebäck*,
in his grey flannels and Cambridge tweed
the famous photograph of himself
whose live dark eyes and boyish wire-hair
cannot be taken on any more faith
than a grey flame or the cinema's glass pane.
(The cats who see all colors in the dark
disregard him, their eyes the disconcerting cool
of Queen Isabella or the Angel Gabriel.
They know a ghost from its painting,
the sting of blood from the sound of blond.
Duck or rabbit, they know the lines of prey.)
God on the 5:15 train
is Drosselmeyer without a Christmas tree,
saying steadily there are no mysteries,
only misunderstandings.
All night in the sewing room
you can hear him softly talking
through his two worlds you also live between,
a question in *Hochdeutsch*, a mutter of Bloomsbury slang,
a whistle of Brahms curving pure as aerodynamics
down the turn of the darkened stairs
where streetlight silvers the television screen

44

like the silence that passes over,
but says something all the same.

A FIND AT ÞINGVELLIR

You cannot hear the sea-butchering strain of the oars,
the red-bladed ships rowing
from Vinland to the Pillars of Hercules
with the god in the stormwind,
in small iron at their throats,
honor's handclasp and the levin-shock
of a stranger's weight on a spear.
It feels in your hand
not like the molten cooling of meteorites
or the quern-stone of its name,
but a live thing,
excited as St. Elmo's fire
or the quick breath of battle,
copper-wire hilting
singing like a dynamo.
You can hear it humming
thorns and journeys, your inheritance.
Even the gods cannot hold it lightly,
or tightly, or for very long.

Ned Balbo

A PARABLE OF FLIGHT

Wouldn't it be great if lizards flew,
the world's mind thought and, thinking, made it true.
The pterosaur, ascendant in the sky,
would last an age and, over eons, die.

The world's mind thought and, thinking, made it true.
From trilobite to slow triceratops,
some good ideas would, over eons, die.
The bird-hipped dinosaur took baby steps

past trilobite, beyond triceratops,
till archaeopteryx, the feathered lizard
sought the sky. No time for baby steps—
Sharp claws and teeth protected it from hazard,
though the creature looked less bird than lizard.
Was its blood, perhaps, already warm?
Sharp claws and teeth protected it from hazard
when it fought, inflicting real harm—

The blood of carrion is always warm.
Who flew beside the starling and the crow?
The passenger pigeon, though it meant no harm,
rose up in great flocks shadowing the snow,

but who survived? The starling and the crow.
And yet, the world's mind also loves a joke—
ostrich and emu, striding over snow,
lush veldt, or outback took another look

(because the world's mind always loves a joke),
and said, *No, thanks.* The concept in reverse.
The dodo, too, from which a single look,
sad-eyed, brought traders' clubs down with a curse,

followed survival's trend-line in reverse.
Would it have fared much better in the sky?
It couldn't tell a blessing from a curse....
Earth-bound unfortunate, it never flew.

FOR JACOB KURTZBERG

Better known as Jack Kirby (1917-1993)

Nothing beyond his power, in Mineola,
drawing furiously, the artist Jacob,
"Jack" to friends and fans, finds one idea
compels him, hurtling, through every job—

for money, sure, but also (lit cigar stub
trailing smoke) for love: he knows his genre
offers myth, and heroes need a problem
that will test their powers. In Mineola,

working from home (postwar suburbia),
an East Side kid, Jack punched his way past trouble,
gave the world Captain America,
and more: the pantheon of heroes Jacob

draws for Marvel now. Aye, there's the rub
(eraser-shreds brushed back, tabula rasa
of the next page waiting): credit-grabbing
wordsmith Stan will think this new idea

is his alone; still, pages fill the sofa,
ready for the shoot. No time for "grub"—
Jack's on a mission, as at Omaha
ten days after the landing, when the job

eclipsed, by far, some petty contract's quota.
But what foe must his quartet face and clobber?
—A silver angel falls, his gleaming aura
crackling as he wakes in fiery rubble,
nothing beyond his power.

Timothy Richardson

THE DISPENSATION

> *For what have we been rescued, if not*
> *to see these and other things*
> *that have no love for us?*
>   —John Ashbery
>   "A Hundred Albums"

They formed a single line at the one desk
there is in the world, in the one room
of the only house with the yard and the one
mimosa growing from it. And they were quiet,
each behind the other. The one Doctor
and the only Doctor's Wife; one Cowboy
and the only Indian who would soon be
the one Dead Indian. The Baby crying
for the Mother who was standing further back.
And they muttered to themselves the word
that was the only word and carried only one
meaning, which was simply *when?*
The Man Behind the Desk stood slowly,
as is proper for the only man with a desk, offered
a present for each of the ones who were waiting.
The Doctor received the name of his Patient,
who was also his Wife. The Cowboy took
the only gun and the Indian the knife.
The Baby was given a breast and its Mother
teeth to grind at night. And so on down the line,
through the one Pigeon Trainer, the Catholic,
the Prodigal and Father, the single
Baseball Player, Gynecologist,
Lepidopterist, Dentist, Accountant,
the Tall Woman, the only Beatrice.
All through the long night the line moved

like the only snake there is, eaten,
it seemed, by the man at the only desk.
And at the end was, of course, the Last Man
who stood on one leg and one crutch, who saw
with one good eye and wept from the bad one,
who had hands, one left and one right, who slept
on one side, had one testicle, chewed with one tooth.
He was given nothing. The Last Man closed
his arms around the only Nothing in the world,
hopped through the house, across the only street,
mountain, desert, swam the only river, lake, ocean.
He picked up what he thought would be useful—
a gun in a river, a knife from bread, a telephone book—
as he pushed through the rising sun, the later setting one
to the only yesterday and the first desk in the world.
There he molded Absence into the best shape
he knew—an Ear as large as a hand that pulsed
to take whatever words were offered. He placed it
in a drawer. And there it fed on what fear
or hope or songs were present as the Man
began to give away everything he owned.

THE FAT MAN

Every man has something to conceal.
—Casper Gutman, *The Maltese Falcon*

I. ALL THE FALCONS IN THE WORLD

He found one in Rome and left it there.
His thumbnail scraped from beak-base to tip showed beneath
    enamel,

just like San Francisco, a lead (and so) pretend bird that should have
been beautiful, uncanny, intricate and heavy just like our Fat Man is

heavy and beautiful, fully believing that any fake leads to something
both better and forward and the line behind (though two's a scanty
    line)

is worst a joke and best solid evidence that there are three or four
or more and a final, single, true one.

He needs the dark shell and love with his fingertips.
If all roads lead from here, this is one.

II. THE SAME THING EVERYWHERE

He has taken to scraping everything black
hoping for gold or
reflected sun in an emerald eye
and reasons that since the birds are not
The Bird
it could be anything:
armchair, suitcase, dog,
the hair of the girl clicking down the alley
he's groped or plans to, you can read him either way.

Down the damp street wind whips
his tie and shows the line of buttons
snaking to his sway and
who could resist being charmed?
Not the girl whose hair is really brown
but in this light, when you want so much,
it's hard not to find something precious in a dark curl
crescenting an eye that's almost
green enough.

III. WHAT HEAT CAN DO

When he walks he sweats so much
he might be drowning. In the street opposite his hotel
birds tear at something someone
dropped/spread/threw (he can't see what).
They are crushed in traffic since
they won't give up a single crumb. He sees
two killed together as they bicker.
One just wings spread on the stones and one
ripped by the machinery.
He doesn't know what kind they are.
He knows they aren't his.

Some days the sky strains
from the weight of air thick with ocean
and the green hills are painful to see.
It's enough to make him sad,
such life thriving without any mind
to direction/goal/consummation
and the children wrestling in the too green weeds
for no reason but the fun of touching,
the pinned grimace of one and one laughing,
are disgusting.

At least the birds want more.

IV. THE LAST FRIEND IN THE WORLD

A fat man on his knees is amazing
when he's still and funny when he tries to get up.

Cairo—Joel, not the city—would giggle
as he wrapped his soft hands around a huge tricep
and heaved.
What he didn't know was the fat man's years of carrying
that bulk that marks a complete love
for life was too much,
his shins had long separated from their caps and
it was kneeling that hurt most,
every second a sharp second,
not moving meant feeling only one thing
and one is all you can hope for.

V. THINGS IN HIS POCKETS

The breast of his jacket is empty.
Anything would ruin the line.
The left front holds an old handkerchief
initialed JC and smells
like gardenias. In the right's
a cigarette case, black, enamel, almost empty
and an empty match case.
His trousers hold his hands.
He trims and shapes his nails each day.
The Fat Man is vain in little ways.

VI. HOW HIS POCKETS BECAME EMPTY

Women in doorways promise too much.
A line of them
one and one and one and
never a group, each is special, none is just right:

Girl Leaning On A Doorframe
Full-Breasted Woman With Arms Crossed
Blond Who Licks Her Lips Too Often
Doll Looking for Any Excuse to Bend Over
Sad One With Dark Hair Sitting

on the stoop whispers, he thinks, his name,
takes his paw with her little hand, pulls
the three fingers she can hold
through the door, up the stairs, into the sad
room she never shares and lets him
kiss her eyes. Naked
she might be beautiful.
Naked, he might feel hungry
though he's too huge to see his cock.
And she could tell him
Yes you can have more than you've asked for
and he could stay all night, move,
sweat and imagine
he's holding the most beautiful thing in the world.

VII. WHAT A PASSPORT TELLS

His papers say Gutman.
The two syllables show it all. He thinks
his name is perfect for him.
The casual bifurcation coming from the mouth,
whatever mouth that speaks it,
calls him both. Man because he is
and the stomach that means his appetite
and places hunger separate from him.
His belly is a thing he has.
The body of Gutman leads to something else.

VIII. SLOWER AFTERNOONS

He would, he thought, like to put him in wigs.

Blond and coifed:
Joel you are an American Girl at the beach.
You have just seen the man you know
you are destined to have children for.
He is tall and has
seen you for the first time.
Rush to tell your girlfriends everything you know.

Black, tight and lacquered:
You are a negress with great breasts and
a voice
deeper than thought. Sing for me
something slow and sad and French and
if I cry I will buy you
a drink.

Red, long, with gold in the sun:
Be Argentine Joel and dance
like you are
making love to someone far away.
Sway your eyes and make your hips
smile as if they know
a secret worth sharing.

Brown, dull, and curling loose:
Sit still and pout a little maybe but do not
wet your lips or God forbid
say anything. Pretend
you are asleep and hold your arms
as if your body wants to break loose.
If you speak I swear I will slap you.
Your voice right now could break my heart.

And so on.

IX. BEACHING

He swims privately. Actually,
he wades into the blue sea
to just above his navel,
that magic line where what makes
most of the world is capable
of lifting his weight away.
Where the evidence of all that
lust feels only neighborly.

You could have loved me thin,
he thinks. The world is like this:
The greater the man,
the more he can displace. Air becomes
dense when he enters a room and
ground spreads where he walks.
Crowds hurt themselves squeezing and
the distance between things thickens.

The world can hardly bear a fat man.

X. THE ELBA DAY

Pressure and Itch:

This large black rock can take the pressure
of a fat man spreading under the heavy sunshine
sparking the green in the blue of the sea.

Rock is the skin of the world as ocean is muscle
that pulls its seams apart or folds them underneath
to grind the body from the inside.

Inside, everything is sharp.

Outside alone and mother-naked
Gutman refers to surfaces. His belly, for instance,
knows the stone beneath was dry and is not now.

Sweat bonds with each loose particle to make
a gritty grease that is neither rock nor paunch and thighs
but something between them. A third skin. A solution.

And his back against the sky takes
the sun's soft friction, puckers under breeze and spray.
Evaporation lies. It is hotter than he thinks.

Tonight the bedsheet will tickle like paper, then burn.
His tomorrow's clothes mean penance for settling
between the earth and heaven. Every move will bite.

Each step will become a fire. A stretch will scrape him raw
then stop as he thickens, browns, and cracks.
That itch is worse than hurting.

Needing to dig his perfect nails into the flaking bark
will keep clawing him from sleep. Frustration, desire
and the catch of cotton will smother his nights

and warp the surface of days until it all peels away
or falls feathery into his shirt tails, socks, and sheets.
The miracle is after the rind is the new, the soft, the beautiful.

An old form with a new coat to meet the daily destiny
of a fat man and want and what glory there is
in considering everything small.

Sunning:

He is a great pale monster
who has eaten all he can find but
There are plenty of other fish in the sea
and is belching his love but

might be alone in the world.
Thus, he is in love with the world.

He is a small bird on
a black rock and hungry and
has forgotten what he eats. Stones
are hard and this is wet and may hold
a soft inside
so hot it melts and he can drink it.

He is a man wet with sweat
who breathes against
the world as black stone and
all he can hear is waves and birds
swimming in the air and
they will eat anything well-cooked.

The sun is an emotion
he feels with his spine that burns
and dies with the wind because
the wind is also emotional
and neither belongs to him. Which proves
the world does not love him back.

The Skin of the Night:

Remembering is like looking for the dirty parts of a book you read
too long ago.

It could have been Rome or Venice or even Frisco but was Gary
where he grew and grew too big.

At least the girl spoke slowly and he was very young and city
landmarks may specialize a place

but beds are the same and Gutman is a monument who moves.

Who doesn't remember her name or where or how she found him
there, but a first case is special

and this first was small and pale and the first with dark and loosely curling hair and though not the first with eyes

at least the first with that bright shade of green that shines when it shouldn't. She said she would love him

which was a first for any girl and this is the first thing he remembers in her voice.

All this beginning and more in a great bed creaking from his effort, his giant body appalled by the force

and he never has remembered finishing. He was so concerned with her skin and the sweat between them.

With her shuddering sheen and the moles of her back as a negative constellation, a whole sky turned inside out.

Her chinesed eyes that made his drip, her chuckling fellation, her smile for his kneeling sobs.

His welling pores and the bath he gave her of himself.

The pain of being surrounded, if only partly, by something so small as this girl.

Her itch and glimmer and the morning he rolled from bed and found her gone with his wallet

and a note that read *good thing it's not by the pound.* And he thought she could have loved him thin,

but fat it's fair for so much work. And she was very beautiful, intricate, and kind and taught him to love

what is gorgeous in the world in what its surface shows and how it feels against him. He once told Joel

You can never really touch a woman, just the patina you brush with your eyes.
She is hidden

no matter how you scratch as she lies in bed and out. She can offer you only
the skin of the night

and what exists inside you have to imagine is precious if you own it.

XI. QUIET EVENINGS ALONE

A clear night when the moon is gone and
stars cause black
slick paving stones to sparkle like
a photographs of oceans
on just such nights—
When the wind does not know
its path but moves every direction
including up—
Outside late Gutman breathes his best,
follows his thick desire in all
its dark and suspects the sun and
sharp grass beneath the morning
and sobs there
in the black green street.

The sea is not close but the gusting far
up past his socks reminds him.

The Fat Man shakes slowly, his body
heaving behind him as an afterthought.

XII. VENICE AND PERFORMANCE

This gourmand has trouble
eating in public but can drink and likes to
on clear days surrounded
by people he does not know. If they speak
another language, even better.

In the Piazzo San Marco musicians play something
intricately sad and Gutman
spreads in the absolute center of the listeners, feels
their bodies around him
as his own, their clapping his nerves firing up,
the dancers his small
thirty-two feet scuffing the courtyard stones,
every whisper a thought
about the coming clear night and sweat
in the creases of his joints.
His chins become soft arms of old women
waving to new friends.
His prick is the tallest waiter balancing dishes
too high to see the tops of.
His fingers are the hundred cigarettes gently poised
to smear the air.
His tongue is the girl in front drinking the violinist
whose fingers bow
confident as a talent unhooking her brassiere
and her eyes brighten
as she sucks his music in at each crescendo.
Her lips are parted
and wet and the Fat Man can taste three flavors:
envy, pepper, and love.

XIII. GUTMAN'S NOTES FOR A PAST MORNING

Morning.
Café.
Poor tea.
Table's leg nearest my right foot lacked its cap.
Cairo flicked eggshell onto the white linen.
Girl Serving Others brushed the corner with her hip.
Cup rattled and sloshed.
Joel giggled.
The cloth sucked the tea quickly.
It was really cotton.
A round brown stain.

I called the girl for more.
Still poor.
It burned my tongue.

XIV. IF GOD IS IN THE DETAILS

Gutman keeps every trace:
a Moroccan vendor,
the fiddler of Venice,
a dead vintner's daughter selling the estate,
Joel's betrayal,
each proof that there is something
real and there

at the end of the line he projects forward
on the ground of the piled clues behind.
He marks the points
in his compact hand on small paper
torn from an Accidental Baedekker
bound blank and missed.

Here, at this particular time, he heard
the slow man stutter....
That bright night, he thought he saw
lurking behind a....

Each note is
carefully dated and carefully placed
on top of the previous so they make the past
a plot.
He rolls the pages, ties them with string, carries
his history in the left front trouser pocket to
fondle idly on the sidewalk,
grip in frustration or doubt,
its tumescence evidence
of the coming release implied in every move
his body makes.

XV. ABOUT LOOKING

I will never
trust a man who doesn't
trust skin more than whatever fills it out.

Two problems:
The fat balloon and the nothing that fills it.
The falcon and the beautiful inside.

Joel was never lovelier to me
than when he wanted nothing more
than what would fill me up.
Nothing. More. And beautiful.

If there is skin and
If that skin in beautiful then
What lies inside isn't worth the digging?

Poor logic.
One knows that whatever is cut from
one space ends up in another. As new surfaces.

So gold. So this rubbertree sap.

That Moroccan didn't trust me.
I know I gave the wrong signs. I was punctured.
I frowned too much with my eyes.

That girl whose father died
had huge slick eyes and was dark and
had a magnificent backside.

Two notes:
Revisit the estate to toss his study.
Review her body to enjoy that night.

XVI. SOME VANITY

It is hard to recognize what glows
beneath lacquer. Gutman has been duped
before, and San Francisco was the first.
And Joel came from there, joined him in

the merry trek of continents content
to squeak at new perfumes and cry
for his shorter legs. A promenade,
a shopping spree, and each pomade
ground fresh from each locale and spit in
by the locals slicked special his hair and
glossed his skin to shine the gaslight out.

Joel loved the material it took to stretch
the short line of his inseam more than air
and each breath was only a way of touching
softly the starch of his handmade shirt.

He found pleasure in every stitch,
joy in cosmetics, desire in the windows
of shops lit to shallow every shadow
and force relief: a new black jacket

perched like a bird on a dummy's
spiny leg. Gutman loved Joel's love
for those parts of the world he could take
upon himself as a model for its charm.

Joel, he thought, *is cut from me and holds
the dirt I've given up to hold the bird
that shines, like him, beneath a stiff new flesh.*

XVII. IT'S BROWN WHEN IT'S NOT GREEN

It could have been Texas
the ground was so flat and
dirty, the fat man sweating like the rain

caught him napping.
He dug mostly with his hands and laughed
at each brown stone.

Joel, he said, *you had the voice of an ugly girl.*

On his knees, he might have been
making a sand castle
in reverse.
Land-locked, dirt, and a hole.

XVIII. BIG BLACK BIRDS IN LOVE

In the dark, he might have recognized the land.

But the sky is blue enough to strike the green in the grass so hard the
green takes over the earth.

And this green percolates as Gutman boils through the almost quiet
street, tugs his jacket off to the sweating trees

and huffs against his heart's heavy thumping to the whispers from
each corner.

He thinks *This is running.* He says *Joel would have hated this.* He loses
his left shoe, then right.

The sun makes the kind of light that turns the creases out and every
child playing on the lawn, each friend,

that pale girl touching and waving in the doorway seems less a person
than the promise to be one for him,

to give him more than he knows to ask for. He drops his shirt and
pants

on passing twin yews. His legs and arms are slick.
I am a bird, he says, *who has forgotten his beak.*

All that's left in the world once you've found what you want is everything you missed.

Not a real truth, but something he understands after Joel is gone and the bird is at hand and all he wants is the bush.

All the humid weight and color hurt. So much touching him and so much of him to touch.

Boys fight and laugh in the park. Big black birds are in love. The same girl is lonely at a different door.

Naked and lumbering through the thick air he cannot get enough of, there is too much mixed in,

Gutman trips in the weeds and rolls to his back. His shuddering stomach pushes to the sky and

he feels the long grass tickle him up. *It's so beautiful. If I were thin, I could see it all.*

William Coleman

FLIGHT

> *Sister Marie seized the extremity of a branch so little that a*
> *bird would have bent it, and from there, as though floating,*
> *she was raised on high.*
> —*The Sanctified Body*, Patricia Treece

Not floating, more a feeling
of helplessness that grew lighter.
The lime tree simply shrank.
I fluttered through distance, released.

I could not lift my head, couldn't quite see
how the orange sky swallowed me, comprised a cloister,
though thinly rooted, as though a single prayer could unearth it.
I glided through the body, unstrung.

Then Mother Superior
called for supper. I stumbled
down branches
and touched deep soil.

Children had gathered. They clutched
at my sleeves as I walked to the table.
I could not tell them it wasn't
a performance. All that rises is.

INSTRUCTIONS FOR THE WAKE

Find yourself, before earth concedes
and falls apart, a slender reed
with which to breathe no matter where
you may land—within the pooling of a decade of rain,
or the belly of the lamb of god.

Before forgetting, find yourself
a smaller straw to fit inside the old.
Then find another. And another.
When you're done, you must speak
from the smallest space you can find,

let your voice become the instrument of a man
you never found until the opening
and closing of the ground.

THE BARTENDER'S ADVICE

These maps I carry are flawed in projection,
so when I say I know where you're coming from,
understand it's a hunch. Still, entire moons

have been charted on less—you'll forgive me, then,
if my answer's far-fetched. Where you need to go
from here is out. I know, I know. Listen:

What it takes is the same delusional gumption
that led Columbus to believe his flags framed
something original, the kind of confidence

that'll get you in deep water in a hurry.
One moment you're nursing a gin and tonic,
the next you're setting sail across the bar.

Sure, the spiel will run its course—
that's the point. When it does, there'll be little
left to do but filter what little any of us knows

of love through porous, faulty bodies,
aligning imperfections until topographies blur,
like refolding a map a thousand different ways

and asserting the rightness of one.
That's what it takes. You
must be willing to ruin every sure thing

in your life for one divine proposition.

ACCORDING TO PETER

What was it he carried with him when he left
if not the dreams of everyone he touched?
Without them, without him, I was a stranger
beside a dying fire. He was gone,
his flesh already drawn to the earth
he loved, even as another nature
bloomed. Or so I was led to believe.
His presence was always a mystery to me,
his kingdom half-hidden, like a key.
In such darkness I found his body, stilled—.
Gone. And who was I?
I didn't lie. Until he called my name
once more, I did not know the man.

AFTER THE FLOOD

What's lost becomes a vacant shore in time.
Once, I heard a voice. Now silence holds me at bay.
Where are you, who made me foreign everywhere?

ABOUT GRIEF

I keep my mouth shut.
If it weighs on me, good—
I'll be mindful.
If I confess, I confess to weakness.

One day, all will be revealed.
That's what the book says.
Doesn't it? The book I read
before that day, on that day?
All will come to light, and
every grief sung to heaven.

That, of course, is the beginning
of the end of the world.

FICTION

ARCHAEOPTERYX

Laura Kopchick

THE MEDITATING MOTHER

The Mother started the chant alphabetically, with *Captopril*, her voice
a low monotone, and Stella turned to look at the blurred outline of
the woman's body, which she could see too clearly through the filmy
curtain. The Mother sat cross-legged on the bed behind her baby's
crib, arms resting on her knees, hands held palm up as if she were
meditating. The Mother repeated the word, feeling the rounded
vowels and sharp consonants until they evened out over her tongue.
Captopril. Later she added *Digoxin, Lasix, Potassium, Prostoglandin.*

"What's wrong with him, do you think?" Stella asked Nate. The
surgical team had moved the woman's son into the ICU late in the
afternoon, and the Mother had been sitting on the pull-out couch
behind her son's crib since the nurse had set up his oxygen and
explained how to care for his feeding tube. Stella's daughter, Gracie,
had a feeding tube. She had been in the ICU for three days and
refused to eat. Instead she pursed her lips against the strange rubber
nipple.

Crammed together on the pull-out bed behind Gracie's crib,
Stella's back rested against Nate's warm stomach and his breathing
settled into a pattern that told her he had almost fallen asleep.

"He's worse than Gracie," Nate said.

"All those drugs," Stella said. She thought of Dr. Tam's warning
from this morning, about how she needed to pump more often and
get Gracie to take a bottle in order to move out of the ICU and into
one of the private rooms up on the sixth floor. Up there they'd be
able to watch their own TV and sleep in a nice-sized flip out couch
and Gracie would have a normal crib, one with sides like the one she
had at home. On the tour before the surgery it became clear without
the hospitality guide having to tell them that when a baby moved
upstairs everything would turn out okay. After Gracie's surgery, when
they first moved her into the ICU, the baby next to Gracie's
station—the station the Meditating Mother's baby now occupied—
was being put into a red plastic wagon, his heart monitor balanced in
front of him on a pile of blankets. The boy, gauze cleanly taped to his

chest, happily tapped his hand against the side of the wagon and his father, a young Mexican man, had clapped and played peek-a-boo with his son while the nurses packed up all of the stuffed animals and family photographs that filled his area. "Upstairs today," he'd said to Stella. Then he pointed up at the ceiling as if he didn't trust his English, and Stella had nodded her head and pulled the curtain around Gracie's crib.

The first two days in the ICU Nate had remained silent on Gracie's refusal of the formula, and on Stella's sudden milk stoppage, until this morning when Dr. Tam mentioned putting Gracie on steroids. Now Nate watched the clock above Gracie's crib and nodded his head toward the nursing room every couple of hours.

"All those drop-ins from Dr. Tam." Stella knew Dr. Tam only dropped in on the serious cases—the ones Gracie's nurse called "wait and see's." *Digoxin*, Stella thought. *Lasix*.

Stella lay with one leg over the edge of the bed, nearly touching Gracie's elevated crib. Gracie's expensive pink diaper bag, covered in a shiny plastic material already torn at the corners, rested on the floor near Stella's arm. In the soft, green illumination from the monitor's glow she could see Gracie's wooden rattle in the shape of a flower, with its tiny gold cluster of bells in the middle of the petals. Gracie couldn't hold the wooden hoop securely in her fingers yet, but she liked to hold the flower to her mouth and nurse the bells. The empty bottle with the miniature giraffes marching in a line around the surface, chasing day-glo butterflies, rested in the small pouch on the side of the bag. One of the nurses had told Stella and Nate to bring her favorite toy as a comfort to Gracie after the surgery and Stella had swallowed the fact that Gracie didn't yet have a favorite toy.

The Mother's son's monitor rested on a cart behind the thin striped curtain at the foot of Nate and Stella's pull-out bed and gave off a steady pattern of two short bursts and then one long one. Gracie's heart monitor sounded different, like a soft whisper coming up to the surface of a pond—a tiny, trapped pocket of air.

Stella traced the knobby bones of Nate's knuckle on the hand that he had resting against her stomach and repeated the woman's chant over and over in her head, imagining how it would feel to say the words out loud. Saying the names of the drugs in her head kept her from thinking about the wire now attached to the outside of Gracie's heart, or the tape they had put over her eyes before the surgery, or how four days earlier on the night before Nate and Stella had brought her to the hospital they had dressed Gracie up like a baby chick for her first Easter and she had picked at the yellow and orange striped tights with her fingertips.

"I feel sorry for that woman," Stella said. She tried not to think about Dr. Tam, about the way the long, black hairs crept up and around his thick gold wedding ring. When Stella had asked him how Gracie's surgery had gone, an hour or so after they'd moved her into the Intensive Care Unit, he'd paused longer than necessary and said, "Fine." When she asked about the delay he'd been worried about in what he'd told them was called her QT interval, he said, "We'll know more when she's off the feeding tube and oxygen." Then he turned and flirted with the representative from the pacemaker company who was there to explain to them how Gracie's remote Carelink monitor worked.

"What about the baby?" Nate said, loudly enough that they heard the Mother shift around on her bed. "He's the one with the hole in his heart, or whatever it is they can't fix."

"He's just a baby," Stella said. "He won't remember any of this. She will."

Nate pushed himself up on his elbow and rested his chin on Stella's shoulder. He smelled sour, the way Gracie smelled when she hadn't had a bath in a few days and the milk settled into the creases in her neck. Stella turned her face toward him, longing to smell Gracie now, though she smelled nothing like she did at home. Each hour in this Intensive Care Unit diluted the smell of her, as if her daughter were dissolving into the grief that had settled in this room. Stella wanted Gracie home, dressed in her velour pink onesie, her dark eyes widening whenever the cat sprung onto the windowsill.

When Stella sat up and slid her feet into her slippers she didn't tell Nate about her need to smell their baby. Stella had gone to Gracie's crib twice already tonight, each time waking her up and making her pull at the wires of her monitor. Instead she said, "Pump, pump, pump. I feel like a cow." Stella's breasts ached, and her left one had grown hard. For six months she had nursed Gracie, never giving her a bottle. The professional pump in the small room off of the Pediatric Cardiac Intensive Care Unit could pump both breasts at one time, but in the fluorescent lighting the machine looked alien and precise, like something from a science fiction movie.

"Go," Nate said. "I'll listen for her." He rubbed Stella's arm and then let his hand slip to the side of her waist, where her hip bone would be if she had already lost the baby weight. They had both grown doughy since her pregnancy, their bones now buried deep beneath the soft surface of their skin.

"Okay, but don't fall asleep," she said. "How can you sleep?"

Nate's chest deflated as he exhaled. "Let that milk flow," he finally said.

Nate rubbed her side and Stella's skin went numb there, as if Nate were actually capable of erasing the feeling from her body. She said, "We'll never move upstairs. I don't think Upstairs really exists."

Nate shifted in the small bed, already claiming her side as his own.

"Go," Nate said, and gave her a light push. "May the Milking Gods be with you." He sounded half asleep already, the end of his sentence disappearing into the thin foam of his pillow.

In front of Stella, Gracie's monitor kept up its gentle hum. Behind the curtain at the foot of their bed, the Meditating Mother coughed. The sound came from deep in her chest, where some infection had rooted itself and wouldn't let go.

*   *   *

Nate and Stella had found out about the heart defect eight days earlier, on a routine trip to a cardiologist to check out what her pediatrician had called "a gentle murmur with a musical quality" and Stella had thought of a little cartoon guitar in the shape of a heart with the strings being plucked. But at the cardiologist's, as the doctor moved the stethoscope around Gracie's small chest, one edge of her diaper slipping loose, Stella noticed the slow, deliberate way the doctor pushed the scope over her daughter's skin and her throat closed up. The cardiologist, a woman with a mess of curly, dark hair and thin arms with small, knotty muscles, had kept them waiting too long after Gracie's heart ultrasound. Now she avoided looking at them, instead focusing her attention on Gracie's chest, nimbly navigating the minefield of electrode patches that littered her small body.

"I'm not an electrical specialist," she finally said. She pulled the stethoscope from around her neck and stood up, then she looked at

Nate and pulled a drawing from the pocket of her white lab coat. The drawing looked like a simple ink sketch of a heart from a fifth grade science book. She positioned her red pen over the drawing and drew arrows and lines and explained to Nate and Stella, in long sentences, that Gracie's heart had no electrical current going from the top chamber to the bottom. Third degree Atrioventicular Heart Block. She'd need a pacemaker.

"For how long?" Stella asked. The doctor turned to answer her and Stella took hold of Gracie's hand, which she was using to swipe the doctor's stethoscope. Nate stood with his back against the wall and stared at the back of the doctor's head.

"Her prognosis will depend on the surgery, which has its risks, and how her body responds to the pacing. But the electrical cardiologist will go over that information with you, and so will the surgeon." *Cardiologist. Surgeon.* The red arrows drawn over the cheap photocopied heart made Stella think of a Frieda Kahlo painting she had seen at the Art Institute when she had taken Nate's mother there over Christmas.

They took the train home. Stella sat with Gracie pushed against her chest and tried to call her Mom on her cell phone. She couldn't get reception, though, and even if she had, the noise from the grinding tracks beneath them would have made conversation impossible. Everyone around her—Nate, the teenager with the Ipod and the braided hair, the Mexican woman holding a blonde-haired infant—looked at her once, maybe twice, then pretended not to notice what was obvious. Finally Nate reached over and put his hand against Gracie's back. Gracie let out a small "Da," and then put her lips together to blow spit bubbles. Her white collar was spotted a light brown from the strained peaches she had had for lunch. The hair at the back of her head had started to grow, finally, into light brown waves that Stella pushed her fingers through.

"We should have taken the car," Stella said. She rubbed Gracie's back and thought of the heart drawing that she had stuffed into her purse after the cardiologist left it in the examination room, along with Gracie's paperwork.

Nate pulled his hand away. "No parking," he finally said. Stella looked at him and studied his face, soft and pink from the heat inside the train. The doctor had said that Stella's immune system had attacked the electrical system of Gracie's heart during the pregnancy. Nate had stared intently at Stella during this and for her part she tried to read what was behind his eyes. When the doctor had inspected Stella's face for signs of lupus she had let Nate take Gracie away from her before she sat on the edge of the exam room table, the doctor's cold fingers pressing into the flesh of her cheeks.

When the train lurched at the Belmont stop Nate wiped his face before he reached over and put his hand on top of Stella's. "It's okay," he said. "It's going to be okay."

*   *   *

After thirty minutes of pumping, Stella deposited the nearly-empty plastic bag in the storage cooler at the end of the ICU and walked across the hall to the women's restroom. There was a row of toilets on one end and a row of sinks and shower stalls on the other and the grey tiles were speckled with dark spots, which Stella at first had mistaken for an infestation of ants. At the end of the room, at the farthest sink, the Meditating Mother stood staring into the mirror, the water running in the sink in front of her. Stella stared at the back of the mother's neck, at the pale strip of skin that cut underneath the harsh line of her black bobbed hair.

When the Mother saw Stella she turned away from the mirror and stared at her. "Your baby's awake," she said. "I called your nurse." The Mother's voice sounded different—higher-pitched, louder—than when she chanted her incantation in the language of drugs. Stella thought of the neat row of nearly-empty milk bags in the cooler, and then of Nate, asleep on the pull-out bed, his mouth open.

"Thank you," Stella said. Then, because she felt that she needed to say something else, "My husband is exhausted."

The Meditating Mother turned off the water and faced the mirror again. "They don't understand what it's like," she said. "They don't have the same connection that we do." She said this firmly and for some reason Stella started to cry. Maybe she wasn't using the machine correctly. Maybe she should ask one of the nurses to help her. Or Nate. Maybe Nate should go in the room with her and deal with the tubes and suction cups. Stella hadn't cried since they brought Gracie down the hall for surgery almost four days ago, and now she leaned back against the cool, grey tile and let the chill ease its way into her skin. She wanted to wash her face, her hair. She wanted to get into one of the shower stalls and drench herself with cool water. She wanted to make herself disappear.

"Stop that," the Meditating Mother said, and when Stella looked up she saw that the woman was speaking to her. "Go in there and take care of her," she said. "You're one of the lucky ones." She turned away from Stella again and turned on the water, then leaned over the sink and spread her open palms under the spout.

Stella thought of the thick silver staples in her daughter's chest, of the gauzy white tape that had held her daughter's eyes closed during her surgery. The empty milk sacks that kept Gracie in the ICU. "I'm sorry."

"What for?" the Meditating Mother said. Water dripped from her pale face, spotting the lavender nightgown she wore.

"I don't know," Stella said. "I'm just sorry."

"Well don't be," the mother said. She wiped her hands on the front of her nightgown and walked past Stella to leave. She smelled like all of the mothers in the ICU—a mixture of sharp disinfectant and rose-scented soap.

* * *

In the ICU, the fluorescent light spotlighted Gracie's chest incision; a nurse stood over her crib, trying to coax her into taking a bottle. Nate stood next to the nurse, his arm resting next to Gracie's feeding tube. The nurse's white face mask made her look as if she were some nameless horror with no mouth yet capable still of devouring Gracie's arms and legs, her swollen cheeks. When Nate saw Stella he smiled. The nurse paused and waited for Stella to walk across the room, past the Meditating Mother's boy, whose skin seemed translucent in the pool of halogen where he slept.

The nurse handed Stella the bottle and then looked down at Gracie's chart, which she held in front of her, carefully, like an undecipherable calculus. Stella tilted the bottle and rubbed the nipple against Gracie's lower lip, just as the nurse had shown her. Some milk pooled in the crevasse of Gracie's closed lips, chapped and pink.

"Open your lips, Muffin," Stella whispered. She moved the bottle back and forth, slowly, and Gracie turned her head away. Finally, without opening her eyes, Gracie parted her lips and Stella slid the nipple, which was an obscene aqua blue—the color of cupcake frosting—into her mouth. Gracie sucked in her cheeks,

83

swallowing twice, before tasting the rubber and pushing the nipple out with her tongue. She squeezed her eyes and clenched her tiny fists.

Later, when Gracie had fallen back asleep and Stella came back to bed, Nate put his arm around her. "Any luck pumping?" he asked, as if all she had to do was rub a rabbit's foot and her milk would magically flow.

"Maybe we should hook you up to that thing and see how you do," she said.

"I don't think I'd have much luck," Nate said. "I'm a B-cup at best." Then, when she wouldn't let him touch her, he said, "So I fell asleep, I'm sorry. I'm tired."

Stella let him slip his arm around her. "Well I am, too."

"We both are," he said. "Right?"

Nate moved in close to her and then leaned down to tug at the tangled bedsheet. Later, Stella fell asleep with his hand resting against the small of her back, listening to the Meditating Mother on the other side of the curtain. She had started chanting again, going through the list of words that sounded like foreign countries, ready to be invaded. *Captopril, Digoxin, Lasix, Potassium, Prostoglandin.*

The next morning the nurses pulled open the curtains and raised the lights enough to read the charts. The babies—all in the same transparent cribs without side panels—mostly slept while the parents rubbed the small muscles in their legs and took turns going to the bathroom or down to the cafeteria. Each baby had a day nurse, and Gracie's nurse was a youngish woman, probably a few years out of college, with long red hair. She was noticeably pregnant, the top of her scrubs outfit straining across her wide stomach. On Gracie's first day in the ICU she had told Nate and Stella that she'd demanded to have a 3-D heart ultrasound of her baby.

"I can take Down Syndrome, but I've been working here long enough to know I can't take a heart problem." She fussed with the tape that held Gracie's breathing tube in place.

Lucky us, Stella had wanted to say. Instead, she said, "I bet this place gets depressing," and watched as the nurse's plump fingers felt around the gauze taped over Gracie's chest, and then the other, smaller piece that covered the pacemaker wound on her stomach. Stella remembered the fuzzy yellow body of the chicken costume, and the small wings that stuck out and made Gracie look like she had no arms.

"You have no idea." The nurse sounded exhausted, and she reached her hand to rub her own belly the way all pregnant mothers do without even thinking about it, and Stella found herself touching her own belly, too, trying to remember the feeling.

While Stella waited for Dr. Tam to come check Gracie's fluid levels, Nate went down the hall to the family waiting center, which they'd decorated with brightly carpeted walls and permanent wooden play structures, miniaturized for indoors. Along one wall stood a row of computers, separated by metal privacy panels. The few times Stella had been to the room she'd avoided the computers and instead sat with a cup of coffee and watched a half hour of morning television. The bright television hosts, perked up in their Spring pastel suits, became for her proof that the world outside of the hospital had continued, without machines that pumped and whined and suctioned off fluids. Had continued without sutures and sideless cribs.

When Nate returned he paused by the glass doors and sanitized his hands with the gel that seemed to disappear on contact, then came up behind Stella as she stood over Gracie.

"She looks good." He touched Gracie's small shoulder.

"You'll wake her. Stop it."

Gracie's eyelids fluttered and Nate moved his hand and touched her cheek. "Bottle," Nate whispered to Gracie. "When you wake up you're going to drink from a bottle."

"Fat chance," Stella said.

"We could get her one of those helmets with the drink holders," Nate said. "Like we saw at the Cubs game." He leaned his chin against Stella's shoulder and squeezed the side of his face against hers. He smelled like soap—he'd snuck a quick shower in the men's room across the hall. Stella had promised herself that she wouldn't take one until they got upstairs, safely tucked away in the privacy of their own room, Gracie's body free from the machines and the feeding tubes. The curls at the back of her head had gone limp from four straight days in the crib.

Gracie stretched one arm out and then made a grimace. When she tried to cry her mouth stayed open but no sound came out.

Stella wanted to pick her up, feel Gracie's weight against her chest, and run her fingers over the soft, downy hair on top of her head that felt, to Stella, like nothing else she had ever touched. But when Stella felt her eyes start to water she thought instead of the alien pumping machine, and of the row of flat milk bags. Maybe if she put all of the bags together and Gracie drank most of the milk that would be enough for Dr. Tam. If she could get Gracie through one good feeding with a bottle by the time Dr. Tam came up for his afternoon rounds maybe he'd let Gracie go.

"She looks like a doll," Stella said. She wasn't used to seeing Gracie in only a diaper, her small shoulders rounded and soft. Without the clothes, the pink ribbons and polka dots, Gracie seemed on the verge of disappearing and there would be nothing to prove she had ever existed at all. Stella touched the dark bruise that had formed on Gracie's side, next to her ribs, near the small hole the surgeons cut for a drainage tube. The Meditating Mother was right— Nate didn't want to scream at doctors for putting a hole in the side of his daughter's body, or for breaking her breastbone to attach wires to her tiny fist of a heart. He didn't want to slam the heart monitor into the wall and run screaming down the hall, destroying everything man-made in an incandescent rage. Stella did.

The nurse had come up behind Stella and rolled the IV cart away from Gracie's crib. She held a full IV bag in one hand and a roll of gauze in the other. "Time for a change," she said.

Stella turned to Nate. "There's probably three ounces in the cooler if you combine the bags," she said, turning her back to Gracie's crib so she wouldn't have to see the small staples that worked their way up Gracie's chest, and the row of dark stitches that zipped up between them.

Stella thought of Nate's jokes about all of the tattoos Gracie would eventually cover her chest with, anyway, when she turned into a rebellious teenager who wanted to stalk the malls. She thought of all of the jokes Nate had made over the past four days, which Stella knew were meant to cheer her up, but instead made Stella want slap him, hard. Make him blink as his eyes teared up, make him realize that this—whatever this was—would never be something to make light of, not ever. Not even if they suddenly woke to discover it was just a nightmare they'd somehow sleepwalked into, could it ever be recalled without horror and anguish. She looked at his fleshy white cheek. Nate must have seen this violence in her face, because instead of making a comment about how happy he was the last time someone had offered him three ounces of something, or instead of making another joke about breasts, he just turned and took the bottle from the diaper bag and headed for the refrigerator at the end of the room, his gaze focused on the wall in front of him. Not on the row of cribs and curtains and mothers.

As soon as Stella opened the door she heard the grinding hum of the pumping machine.

"Come in," the Meditating Mother said. "I'm almost finished." The Mother sat on an overstuffed loveseat against the wall with her blouse with tiny blue flowers unbuttoned, the machine sitting against the wall across the room from her, pumping air. The Mother sighed and leaned back, her shirt spreading open to reveal her small white breasts.

"I can come back," Stella said and started to turn away from her.

"Sit," the mother said. She patted the cushion next to her and Stella sat, so close that Stella's thigh touched hers. Unlike Stella's breasts, which strained against her nursing bra, the mother's looked incapable of producing anything. In the harsh fluorescent lights Stella now realized that the bobbed haircut had grown out too much and was plagued with split ends. Up close Stella could tell the woman was older than she'd originally thought, maybe in her early forties. She thought of all of the older women at her obstetrician's office who would cautiously ask to touch her swollen belly, their own stomachs flat and smooth in their pencil skirts and wrap dresses. "I never get anything, anyway," the Meditating Mother said. "But I try." The Mother held the plastic bag in her hand, her baby's patient sticker lopsided across the top. "I thought I'd do better with their pump." She looked down at the bag in her lap, and then looked up at Stella. "How many days have you been here? Three?"

"Today is day four," Stella said. The sound of the pump made it difficult to speak quietly and so Stella got up to turn it off.

"Go ahead and pump," the Meditating Mother said. "Don't mind me."

Stella sat down in the hard chair in the corner next to the pump and opened up her shirt and the flaps of her nursing bra, which even Nate hadn't seen her do. At home she always took the baby into their bedroom and shut the door. The skin felt hard and hot underneath her fingers and Stella winced as she moved to position the pump's cup over her breast.

"No wonder," the woman said.

When Stella looked up, she could see the woman staring at her chest, then she pointed at Stella's breast. "You've got an infection." She dropped her hand and stood up, then came over and leaned down to look more closely at Stella's breast, which had turned bright red. The Meditating Mother touched her cool palm against the skin next to Stella's nipple. "I'm going to get you a heating pad," she said. "But what you need is cabbage leaves."

"Cabbage leaves," Stella repeated.

The Mother ignored Stella's remark and instead moved her hand up to touch her face, then she pressed the back of her hand against Stella's forehead, then her cheek. The Mother's skin felt papery and thin, like the outside peels of an onion.

"Don't worry," the Mother said. She stood up and helped Stella position the pump's suction cup over her swollen breast. "See if you can get anything," the Mother said. "I'll be back in a minute."

The Mother left before Stella could remind her to button her shirt, and Stella imagined the Mother bumping into Dr. Tam in the hallway, his eyes looking discreetly away as he brushed past her on his way to the ICU.

*   *   *

On the morning of Gracie's surgery, the surgeon who would crack open her chest and screw the leads of the pacemaker to the surface of her heart had come into the pre-op room to ask Stella and Nate if they had any questions before they took Gracie to the operating room down the hall, behind two white double doors with no windows. Stella stared at the surgeon's clogs, which weren't white but a dark brown and so worn that a hole had formed over the big toe on one of them.

"What does it look like?" Stella asked.

The surgeon had crossed his arms, confused, and finally asked "What does what look like?"

"The pacemaker," Stella said. Gracie lay on the examining table, playing with her rattle. She turned to look at Stella, her brown eyes cloudy from the respiratory infection that she'd had for the past two weeks, the one that had sent them to her pediatrician in the first place.

"What does one look like?" The surgeon asked, and looked at Nate. When Nate shook his head the doctor sighed and held out his hand and curled his thumb and index finger into a small circle. "It's this big around, and about half an inch thick."

He'd already explained that they'd put it on her abdomen, and when she grew older they'd eventually move it up near her shoulder.

"You'll be able to feel it, of course," he said. "But it's a pretty complicated little piece of equipment. Probably costs more than the car most people drive," he said. He paused and leaned against the frame of the door. "Anything else?"

"Her chest congestion?" Stella asked.

"Stella," Nate said. "The anesthesiologist already went over that with us."

"I know," Stella said. The surgeon adjusted his glasses and stood patiently and explained that Gracie's infection was viral, not bacterial.

"Everything's ready," the surgeon coaxed. And then Nate stood and shook the surgeon's hand and thanked him, a trusting smile playing with the edges of his mouth. Stella looked away from the two men and instead watched Gracie as she started to cry, her cheeks turning red from the strain. Gracie tried to tug at the wiring of her heart monitor, then gave up and reached again for her rattle.

*   *   *

When the Meditating Mother returned she held a hot water bottle in one hand and a cup of coffee in the other. Her shirt was buttoned now, the collar raised on one side as if she'd put herself together in a rush. The hot water bottle was mauve pink rubber and bloated and looked like the old-fashioned kind Stella's mother used to put under the covers of her bed to keep her warm when Stella was growing up. The Mother handed Stella the cup of coffee, which turned out to be lukewarm tea. Then she opened her palm and produced two pills.

"Take these," the Mother said. "For the fever and swelling."

Stella took the pills without asking what they were, and then washed them down with the tea, which was sweetened with honey and soothed Stella's dry throat. Then the Mother leaned over Stella's breast and pressed the water bottle against her chest and held it there, her palm flat against the bottle to steady the wobbliness of the

89

rubber. The warmth spread quickly and the pain eased away for the first time in three days.

"No cabbage leaves," the Mother said. "But they offered me lettuce." She smiled and put Stella's hand where hers was and then stepped back and sat again on the loveseat across from Stella.

"Thank you," Stella said.

The Mother looked at the ounce of milk from the one breast Stella had been able to produce. Stella held the bag in her lap protectively, and then the Mother glanced at the pile of empty plastic sacks with the other babies' names on them that sat stacked on the table next to the loveseat. "Most of these are gone. You'd think they'd understand how that might make us feel when we come in here. Having to see the names of all these babies," she said. She looked at the machine in the corner, now quiet. The Mother leaned back and stretched her arms over her head and yawned. "The nurses won't even look at me," she said. "That tells you all you need to know."

Stella felt the bottle cooling a little and she moved it to the other breast, which didn't ache as badly.

"No, keep it against the one that's infected," the Mother said. "It'll help bring the milk down."

It felt good to have someone who seemed to know what she was doing taking control, and Stella did as the Mother said. The straps of Stella's nursing bra rested against her stomach, which bunched up over the wide band of her maternity jeans. In the harsh lighting her stomach looked luminescent, a bright moon in the small room. In the days they'd been in the ICU Stella had picked up on the rules of the parents: no questions, no open crying, no eye contact.

"He's not ours, really," the Mother finally said. "The baby, I mean. He's adopted. I've been taking these pills that are supposed to make me lactate but so far nothing. Keep trying, they tell me. It'll happen, they tell me."

The machine stood silently next to Stella, as if waiting, and she moved the hot water bottle away from her chest. Stella's breast had swollen larger than she imagined it could, and the pain made her eyes water. She thought of the Mother's baby boy in his crib, the tubes coming from his nose and mouth, and the small legs that the Meditating Mother massaged each morning for what seemed like forever.

The Mother got up and repositioned the water bottle and peeked underneath. "That has to feel better," she said, and Stella nodded. It occurred to her now why the Mother's baby's area, like Gracie's, was free from taped family photographs and cards. Stella hadn't wanted to put any up because somehow that would make Gracie's stay permanent. And maybe that's what the Mother thought, too. Or maybe she knew he would never move upstairs, or go home.

"We can try for another one, my husband says. I don't even know what he means when he says that." The woman's face was inches away from Stella's chest, the top of her bobbed hair interrupted by a white sliver of scalp. Finally, she gave up on positioning the hot water bottle and looked up at Stella. "What does that even mean?"

"I don't know," Stella said. She could feel the Mother's anger close around the two of them like the cuff of a blood pressure monitor, and Stella suddenly remembered the strange way Nate's face had turned bright red around his lips and eyes—like some sort of glowing raccoon—on the night before they brought Gracie in for her surgery and he had finally let himself cry.

"What does that even mean," the Mother said; it wasn't a question. Stella felt her face get hot and she sat, the cooling water bottle flat against her thigh, her breast swollen and exposed. Stella kept her eyes on the Mother and didn't say anything. *One of the lucky ones*, she thought, and Stella imagined the Mother's boy with his glowing white skin, his covered eyes, his list of medications and she realized that she had never seen the baby move his head, or reach out to tug at the wires splayed across his chest.

"I'm sorry," Stella finally said.

The Mother pressed the palms of her hands against her lap, smoothing the creases that had formed in her linen pants. Then she pushed her hands through the wispy ends of her bobbed hair.

Stella waited for the Mother to answer, but instead the woman turned her head and stared at the empty milk bags on the table in the corner next to her. After a minute, Stella saw the Mother move her lips, her voice almost a whisper as she began her chant. The names of the drugs had now become familiar to Stella, too, and she found herself reciting, almost prayer-like, along with the Mother as she reassembled the straps of her nursing bra, accidentally pinching the tender skin above her breast, and then pulled her shirt down to cover her stomach. Then Stella picked up the baggie of milk and walked past the Mother out of the room, her arm brushing against the Mother's on the way out.

Down the hall Stella could see Nate talking to Dr. Tam, Gracie's still-full bottle in his hand, the plastic milk sacks on the chair behind him. *Captopril,* Stella whispered. *Digoxin.* Gracie's nurse, belly heavy against the side of Gracie's crib, reached to replace the IV bag that hung from the metal pole at the head of Gracie's crib. Dr. Tam said something to Nate and then paused, and Nate turned his head to look down the hall. Dr. Tam held a folder full of papers in his hands, charts of some sort, and he pointed at the top one but Nate looked at Stella instead.

Lasix, Potassium, Stella continued. *Upstairs. One of the Lucky Ones.*

Then she felt a rush of something warm and wet against her chest.

Maureen McCoy

COMMUNION OF SAINTS, FORGIVENESS OF SINS

What stayed with Lloyd: the flash of eerie peace, confidence, forgiving acceptance in the boy's eyes, a picture that stopped time by whiting out vision a moment later. So began eternity.

The kid on the bike shot out from somewhere and by the time this registered, he was wheeled up, airborne, like the showy exhilaration in movies, stunt ads—almost vertical for that split second, immobile save for the spinning wheels, risen above the car's hood—a beige hood; Lloyd wasn't vain; his was a family sedan of a kind that came in beige. The boy's wide smile of surprise—what a ride!—and the curls unspooling just a bit in their own inclination toward freedom, with Lloyd thinking it unusual that they'd let a kid still have curls at that age, what, ten. The sun was out there, not culprit but at the ready, having given up the joy and sparkliness of an earlier hour to palm flat light over the quiet, orderly suburban residential street along which many statues of Mary and grottoes with flowers marked front yards as those of people who sought protection of a kind Lloyd's job, insurance company work, could not touch. The Italians. Lloyd knew the kid, rather knew who he was—Lloyd lived around the corner and up three houses—and the kid flashed him that look you would have to call an angel look, the opposite of the evil eye. He, Lloyd, was Catholic like the kid but, unlike the kid, not Italian, with no personal history of statue protection or tribal rituals outside the mass. He was an insurance man, a fair-minded Midwesterner putting faith in numbers; and in his shock, which would clarify when his vision left him temporarily, he saw the change ahead. The angel boy was signaling: *you too. You will come.*

Sure, Lloyd remembered thinking in that second before horror rolled him out of the car moaning at the little body that could not be dead. The burnished arms and knees folded, the large sneakers set sideways in running position—this was a healthy growing kid, ready to spring back onto his bike which had slowly stopped its humming.

It was one of those purposely-short bikes good for wheelies and dirt and get-aways. In Lloyd's day add a banana seat. Metallic purple, that bike, a prideful color, nothing to do with sorrow. Shadows of people were what Lloyd remembered next and the breath test, somehow being turned away. The sirens, the crew as efficient as the street sweepers he had heard were beholden to the kid's father.

Lloyd was taken home. Expect the car returned sometime. A detective would come by.

Home: his wife Suzanne crumpling as she listened and the faraway look that meant, Children, sacred children; of course they barely have a chance, though quickly she told him, "It couldn't be helped." The cops at the scene—an insulting presence to the kid's father in any situation—had declared this so: no speeding or recklessness; no drinking or drugs; a man on his way home from work, nearly home, eyes on the road and the kid, having lost control, is spit out onto the street at the exact moment the right front tire claims its spot.

"The boy is dead," Lloyd responded. He and his wife knew that guilt in the heart supersedes exoneration by the law. The fabric on Lloyd's easy chair had little ridges he had never noticed, and these were painful and compelling to touch on the armrests now.

No dinner was made and Lloyd sat, certain that he could hear wailing. A light breeze surely was carrying the wailing down the street and around the corner to his house.

"What do we do?" asked Suzanne, a pale version of Donna Reed in the old Christmas movie they watched every year. By nature calm and hopeful, she depended on Lloyd for order and instructions in life. Why? he thought with a thread of irritation. Because he made the money. Because he, the man, was supposed to know what came next.

Their two daughters: little blond fillies who had inherited their mother's air of quiet and industry; at five, one had her very own sewing machine and was busy making something, a rug for a doll to parade upon. The younger often had jam or dirt on her face and wore baby basketball shoes, the kind worn by boys, but Suzanne had found them featured in the tiniest sizes in pink. (The angel boy's were black.) Now in summer the girls splashed in a blow-up pool out back and ran in and out wearing swimsuits ruffled over their behinds like the tails of bobbing ducks.

This was all gone now, this life, the wonder of fabric on armrests, sheer baby girl delight, though he dared not tell Suzanne and upset her further. In a flash, in that angel boy's smile, so sweetly convinced, a truth was conveyed. Lloyd's life, too, would end. Soon. No, he couldn't tell his wife. He saw the way she looked at the girls plopped down in small chairs to eat cheese sandwiches with the crusts removed. The innocence of parenthood, if it ever had existed, was gone now. The simple enjoyment of his girls would be clouded by new knowledge. By his waiting. To leave. How could he touch them? How could he not?

In the night Lloyd lay awake, got up, checked the girls' breathing, checked the flimsy locks and returned. He was sorry, he told them silently. Unless a kind man took pity on his wife, the girls would grow up poor, huddled against a strained and perhaps bitter mother. *I have to leave you,* he beamed at them. *It can't be helped.*

"Lloyd?"

'Shh," he told Suzanne and patted her arm. "Go back to sleep."

"I can't, really. To think that one moment—"

"If I had stopped for milk as you'd asked or if—"

"Now you stop, honey."

"But the boy is dead and that will never stop."

"No," she agreed. "We will have to be strong."

"We won't want the car back."

"No."

"Insurance will provide a loaner."

*　　　*　　　*

In the days to come, much was made in the Tribune about the father's network, his murky position of power and, though not once sent to prison, his trials; his rumored practice of vicious thuggery, Chicago forever in need of proving itself to New York. Glimpsed at newsstands, funeral pictures showed a wife heavily veiled, and ranged behind the couple, double-wide men with faces from a bad movie.

A few of Lloyd's neighbors nodded or shook their heads in wordless sympathy. Came the refrain: "Coulda happened to anyone's the thing." Then, nothing but quiet.

As one quiet day beat into the next, a suffocating Lloyd approached the parish priest about his burden, and here too he found laconic reluctance. Would Father talk frankly? "All praise to Him," came the answer. And "He works in mysterious ways." Lloyd felt that the priest was speaking in code, of the boss, as the papers were being sure to call the father of the dead boy. *A ruthless man.*

"Maybe I should move the family?" Lloyd wondered aloud.

"And with your spirit," said the increasingly agitated priest.

"My family," Lloyd began again.

"They are safe." The way the priest said words that should bring comfort, Lloyd felt certain that a plan against him had been hatched, and the priest knew. "Still," the priest added dully, "unintended death is not the worst, as we all must die. The boy," he recited, "his only son, is in heaven."

"I hope that comforts the father."

The priest's sallow face became suffused with the red of emotion. "Do not approach him. He is inconsolable."

Over time the rectory had been spruced up mightily; in the drive sat a new black Cadillac. The priest was known to take retreats to Lourdes, Sicily and, twice a year, to sunny California, to Santa Monica, the name pronounced from the pulpit as if its holiness were reason enough to go. Monsignor Herlihey was Irish. Lloyd appealed to him on that account, as one outsider to another. "My wife's people are from Killarney and Cork."

The priest closed his eyes against such identification. His assistant, a papery little man who had probably stood listening at the door, knocked. The priest had other business now of course.

*   *   *

The angel boy's look had transmitted to Lloyd that it would be a good place they'd go to—the boy, between worlds, could see it already--though the getting there would hurt. It's about to hurt, Mister! The boy did not bring equivocation to the look, though Lloyd, used to actuarials, he, an actuary man, factored that in: angel face was a mere boy, already made to quit life; Lloyd had had decades of living, time enough to get ready for the end. Complaint would be shameful.

True. But if Lloyd took out a large life insurance policy on himself now, wouldn't it look suspicious once he'd be gone— presumably soon? And what if he was never found, which would probably be the case. What about that? Suzanne couldn't collect and that would just add more grief. So far—and he'd tried to stay out of this—hadn't the father been accused, legally accused, of any number of things you only thought about with, well, yes, the "mob"? Even here, or especially here, in the Chicago suburbs. Racketeering (whatever that meant) and extortion, not to mention worse? Hadn't the guy walked away time and again? Wouldn't he always manage to do so, and so devastate Lloyd's gouged-out family all the more? His girls, where could Suzanne take his girls? Her mother was a weak tyrant always waiting for the worst news, the very worst. Bad news broke on her like sunshine, jackpots, and she could hum her ugly tunes of victory—she was already doing this, calling—for a long time on others' grief. In the old dark city building she refused to leave, she had tenants and surely one, the basement couple, could be let go so Suzanne and the girls would have shelter. Dark basement shelter. Their daddy killed a boy. Their daddy left them. That's how it would play out by the glotatious old crone.

Of course there was suicide, but add cowardice to their horror and he might as well take out the whole family right now. Listen to how he was thinking: like them, like they talked. "Take out" and "take down" or "rub out" or…he couldn't think of what all he'd heard in the damn movies.

Over and over the paper speculated, all the while replaying, after histrionic leads, the cops' comments and even, bless her, the squawking of some visiting grandmother who had been out watering flowers that day and vouched for Lloyd's innocence, before she'd been hauled back inside and shipped home. Officially, Lloyd could not have avoided hitting the beloved son of the darkly powerful man. The car had been maniacally examined: brakes had been applied and brakes were in excellent condition. Charts and photos were arranged and consulted: no, the sun angle did not figure, would not have blinded anyone. Was Lloyd drinking or eating or sneezing or—no, none of these. No evidence. Speed limit was obeyed, period, the speedometer showed Lloyd going at exactly one mile under. If he had driven even slower…but, really, why couldn't he hear the bike coming? It traveled too fast, on smooth asphalt, and a ramp jump figured. The boys had been warned, but there it was. The detective that came by later spoke pityingly, if factually: "You've been cleared." The beige car was sold for them by the auto shop. Lloyd paid to keep the navy blue loaner.

The younger child, the sister left behind by angel boy, would grow up to bleach her hair, leave home quickly, assume another name, but Lloyd wouldn't be around to know that. Years into the future, Suzanne might switch on a feature news story and hear in the woman's voice a studied evasiveness: "If family is hurt, yeah, I could imagine my dad had something to do with that, you know, occurrence. He never showed emotion but from the basement I'd hear him crying, the scariest sound ever."

*   *   *

How it would happen: Just as uniformed Marines come to the door announcing a soldier's death, see two dark-suited men wearing those sunglasses they all wear, suddenly muscling Lloyd into a car, coffee and donut dropped, where he would be punched immediately for good measure. See your own blood. Lloyd would be ready; he'd be happy to see his own blood at last, relieved-happy but he wouldn't let on.

Days passed, more time passed. The mind fevered with imagination and anticipatory dread. Angel face took up most of Lloyd's mind. "First it will hurt." Or: "It's gonna hurt now, but later, nah." That's more how a boy talked.

The Monsignor didn't care to hear this part, hear Lloyd speak of his passage to heaven, as being very, very tough—and told to him by angel boy. The Monsignor, who did not drive, had a car waiting.

*   *   *

Sometimes Lloyd woke in confusion. Having so intensely imagined the end he would be surprised to find himself still there, in his bed, waiting, expected to go forward, to hug the girls, to put food in his body, to dress for work and go to the insurance company far enough away (now in a navy blue car) that no one there dwelled on his "tough luck," where many claims for this and that injury had to be considered. His job he saw now as being all about life ongoing, an unbearable situation, without a shred of its former tedium surviving Lloyd's changed heart. Due to his work, Lloyd knew that the neighborhood's many brick houses were topped with what were called mansard roofs. He'd had no reason to tell anyone this, ever.

He had never spoken these words aloud. In the fifties, a company of brothers had come through and built plenty of brick. Post-war red brick were built to last. Second stories had been added to a few; additions to the side, swallowing the carport or making for a breezeway, were more common. Wrought iron railings bordered front porches, small squares of cement. Cars parked on the street gave in to the inevitability of salt, bother, and rust, though few people minded, as most leased their cars in an effort to keep up.

Angel boy's house looked no different from the rest in its bland modesty, with a finished basement. (Lloyd looked this up.) The basement was where angel boy had played, of course. The madonna statue out front framed by what looked like a miniature bathtub cut in half, painted blue inside, had flowers growing around it. This was the time of peonies and roses: pink peonies at one edge, bowed by rain; pink roses on a small bush. It all looked, Lloyd thought now, somewhat like the cemetery. He had visited his mother's grave at Memorial Day weekend, as always: dark peonies and some homegrown lilies sure to sprout beakish orange flowers soon. Thank goodness she was gone, allowed to die of a common elder trauma, a broken hip, pneumonia, the quick goodbye, rather than dying of grief, the grief to come. Unlike Suzanne's mother, Lloyd's had been a kind woman. He held her hand until the very end.

Down the block in one front yard grew an unusual tree that Suzanne had looked up: mountain ash, with its orange berries in fall. Lloyd promised to get one planted for her. Lloyd's house had evergreen bushes under the picture window that Suzanne had had updated into something showing many vertical panes, with molding in between that she had painted a color she called Tuscan straw. "This," she had said, laughing, "is actually Italian." Before. She could laugh, saying that, before.

The way a tree, a bush, would outlast you, struck Lloyd as significant now, and wondrous. You try to accept the human cycle, sure, but that tree, those mute bushes—yews, sheared every year—might stand forever.

Metal swing sets creaked, little screams raking his head, at odd times. He had to remember: school is out for summer. That was the problem in the first place. He was shaking. This happened now, bouts of shaking.

A huge carpet of flowers, set in pots, in baskets, coned in cellophane, had grown around angel boy's madonna. This was flashed on the news before Lloyd and Suzanne, neither of whom had ever gone on that street again, could switch channels. Suzanne had helped Lloyd compose a card to send, but none of it made sense. Suzanne, then, sent her own card which Lloyd knew without reading: *My husband and I express our heartfelt sorrow…My husband is devastate….a father too…My husband is a good man…If there is anything…Words cannot convey…*

She had begun to want sex again. Or, did Lloyd want her to want it? It was possible to perform, even urgently, when he willed her to understand—remember—that he loved her. Afterward they lay silently, but comfortably enough, pretty much as before.

He meant to leave a physical impression of intimacy up until the end. She was never to notice his receding from their life.

Suzanne looked outright ecstatic the evening he said, as everyone finished dinner, "Let's go for ice cream!" Yes, he dared to drive the entire family in the navy car which, he noted every time he started it up, did not explode. In the back seat the girls squealed and even sang songs. There was an old-fashioned A&W not so far away, with window service—a tray attached to the driver's lowered window—a remnant of a time, where the burgers still had names that urged everyone to join the fun of eating out: Papa Burger; Mama Burger; Teen Burger; and Baby Burger. Lloyd ordered root beer floats all around. And when everyone finished, Lloyd said, "Let's have another one." The girls squealed all the more and Suzanne feigned horror as she reached over to touch him. A normal man on a normal summer evening: he would want her to remember this. *The last time we had sex; the last time we drove out for root beer floats; the last time he said, "I've always liked your casseroles." The last time he splashed the girls with the hose; the last time; the time I remember.*

*   *   *

His mission every day was to be alert, be prepared, to live every moment ready for the last even as he moved further from Suzanne and the kids. His appetite had left him and nothing on the TV could hold his attention. All around, the little homes, brick or frame, split-level, men out with mowers. He did that. He cut the grass and kept things tidy. He listened, consciously looking bright, as Suzanne talked about this or that event, kids at the day camp, something exasperating that her mother said. After a number of weeks, she had determinedly moved on. Lloyd had done his job well, allowing this for Suzanne. He never glanced in mirrors.

His daily rituals: touch everything; remember all as consolation for the passage. Surely the dead have no memory, but just as surely, remembering is all that the dying own, so touch everything, and line up the best memories to play when the hurt begins.

He composed a note for Suzanne and tucked it away under shirts she would grab to her face in terror the day he failed to return. "They have come for me. Do not worry. I have to leave and it can't be helped. It's going to hurt, my love, going to heaven, but then comes"—the angel face smile—"delight. And soothing. I am convinced."

He was coming around to a sense of satisfaction. Nudging Suzanne toward moving on, that was an accomplishment to be proud of. He could think that leaving all of them, being taken away, was a supreme expression of love for his family and even, yes, a sense of fairness accorded to the other. There can be fairness in love, even in death. Generosity, surely. He had received the signal and recognized sacrifice and duty, which was more grace than many people were granted. You would not call forewarning of death a penance. Life does end, after all.

Murder, the word: One day with a little breeze blowing in as Lloyd walked quickly from the car to the side door, he noted how the word had softened for him. He felt the sleepy tickle of a kiss, the kind on the cheek that caused the nerve down the left side of his face to feather. He thought, it is simply one of a thousand ways to go, that's all. If God were waiting, well, God was waiting. He began practicing saying without difficulty, "I'm ready. I'm going of my own free will." This, while being shoved roughly into the car smoked blank with dark windows, feeling the first punch. "Please tell the father that I understand. I know love. I am coming of my own free will." These words could backfire, enrage; yet the outcome would be the same, and what Lloyd has craved, he realizes, is giving voice to the situation. He had to open his heart, the one thing he could do, what the living zestfully urged upon each other: Open your heart to the moment.

The car is cruising. No one speaks or listens to Lloyd, or perhaps his mouth is already bloodied past the ability to talk and the blindfold presses his eyes. He holds to his stoicism, his plan, until the last moments when the car slows in nowhere, the water sounds from a depth below, and with a shudder he admits that he had never known water to sound greedy, so greedy and sucking, and this shakes his calm.

The angel boy's face comes to him. This time the voice is different; the voice is his own, and the understanding is quite different. The angel boy is whirled up in the air on his bike, surprised, and unsure of what is to come, and he is calling, just like any boy, "Mommy." Past that first instant of seeing a car, Lloyd hadn't mattered; only angel boy's mother mattered. Lloyd is shaking, shoved from the car, and he hears himself as a last thought comes too, an admission, a confession that he thought he had rehearsed out of mattering, out of any route of allowance to the heart: I would rather live, live and atone, on earth, die old, atone forever, in difficult ways, just, please, live to do so. But his head is filled with only one word now; and he cannot possibly care what the rank men breathing on him think; he cannot apologize to God or say or think something prayerful; rather he hears himself calling, like the angel boy, and with the angel boy: "Mommy."

Matthew Eck

ANOTHER WAR STORY

It was never easy the war between you and me. It was hard and it was bitter and it lasted as long as winter. Such battles and defeats. The battle of your mother's birthday, the battle of Main and 47th, and the short-lived truce of November, because it was ugly out all the time, and we needed to make love. There was the long night when you stayed away for the first time, a night you spent on a "friend's couch." But in the end there were just a lot of last moments. The last time we laughed together at the thought of our first date. That first date which lasted a week—never alone for a moment, so that we knew every secret and every shame of the other before we'd even tired of our names.

Well, I've walked point in this one long enough. Rain, shine, vacations, weddings, I was out there risking it all, acting as decoy and guide for our love.

I can see it now, the books with maps and details about our love, full of famous French words and expressions for that added extra touch of loss and camaraderie for blood spilled on foreign shores. Your coda emblazoned, an epitaph for the ages: *You can never be too rich, too thin, or too tight.*

I can still hear the rise in your voice during our last exchange of goods, the one where I gave you back your CDs and your books and the shirt you bought me in Las Vegas. I can still see those Emily the dog and Natalie the cat, those little soldiers, those little POWs of our love, watching from the wreckage. The dog's long face and the cat's snub face camouflaged against emotion. The famous exchange of gifts, *with every gift made richer by your touch and breath*. Where I returned your tear blue baseball cap and we both smiled at that hat, that tiny ambassador for a team with another losing season waiting in the wings. Our last exchange of gifts and the way your voice moved, the change of pitch as it shifted from anger to love, and then the slow swing back to anger as we migrated through every emotion and every obscured truth we ever knew together.

You want a message to take back to the troops, you want a message to take back to your side: *it's going to be a long life*. And we need a hard winter here somewhere, one that'll thin out the snakes and spiders and rats and bastards.

Casualties? There were a few. Not like we were the Vietnam or the World War II of love, but we were a good one, rode the proverbial front page of this town for awhile, long enough to make a memory.

The well of despair is deep and never ending, but the peak of happiness is always in sight, never hidden by the clouds. The mountain is always there, as naked as the truth. Let it stand as the dividing line between you and me. The well of despair is deep, my dear, and never ending. What a sad song to leave a one note relationship on.

You want a moment. You want a tangible scene to wrap your pretty little fingers around, one that signifies the shape of our love. Let it be the battle of Valentine's. Let it be the battle of that full-blooded beast of a day.

Your dog needed walking, so we went, as we so often did, up 42nd, left onto Broadway, left onto 45th, left onto Warwick and, finally, because we could only reach the center of the maze and the center of our troubles by turning left enough times, we walked the long downward slope home. That path is burned in my mind like I'm the forester's horse: *Fall asleep love, I'll get you home again, even though the way is dark and the woods are deep and there are snipers on every rooftop.*

Well, the way is always dark and the woods are always deep, my dear, they have to be, or our war would have been easy.

There was very little color to the sky that night, the whole canopy just dark enough to go without notice. An old rust-colored van raddled by and I thought of shotguns and kidnappings and forced oral sex for no other reason than it was night, and lonely enough out to stir my fear. And Emily the dog, your dog, wasn't even big enough to warn the world away, to warn the world of anything save another empty gesture. In my mind's eye I saw the dog's red collar, tag still attached, as the only clue left behind, sitting on top of crushed snow. Your panties found under a bridge a few miles and days later. The wreckage of you, never seen again. My body and mind dumped somewhere near water. But I'd survive, scarred and quiet into old age. Reticent to the point of taciturn. Just another casualty of the war between you and I.

But that's to say that others fought our battles, that others were eager to fight for our dreams before collapsing through that yawning maw of dirt and clay.

That night you wore your hair up, and I put my foot finally down, "It's love or nothing else," I said.

"I do love you," you insisted, and another Valentine's Day Massacre ensued, as the night skipped a heartbeat, like time in the trenches. "There's no one else," you said. "You ask too much."

Which meant she was fucking someone else. Or thinking about it. Either way they felt alike.

Always the same argument. Always the same battle plan. Controlled retreat, then attack. Barbed-wire and machine guns.

"I just can't love you like that anymore," you said. "It's too much to ask."

But I never understood your battle-plan. I always aimed for sympathy and humor, hoping to get a little love. "So this is another moment we won't tell our children about," I said, trying to get a laugh, to get a truce, a little wave of the white flag, to get out of the trenches for a little one on one, a little consorting for one last moment, one last memory, one last, good kiss as the poets say.

There's no denying it, each side fights to win.

The things we wouldn't tell our children, our imaginary children, the children we'd never have, had become quite a list: the day outside planned parenthood, the phone incident, every mother's birthday. That list was falling away. Another treaty, another truce, torn and broken before we called it quits.

"Let's say I'm the monster in this one," I said, "but that I have the best intentions." And with a massive exhalation, "Christ," as we looked at each other across the battlefield. "I always wanted to be the last name you'd ever say."

"I'm sorry," you said, leaving me there, alone on the edge of a park that stretched back into a schoolyard and an apartment complex and a cut of trees. What a place for an ambush.

So I sat down on the curb, gut-shot, and left alone to die on a nameless ridge.

It was hard going in the war between you and I. But then again, I always wanted to die in battle.

Curtis Scott Shumaker

GEOMETRY OF SHADOWS

Suddenly shadows preoccupy my mind, my waking thoughts and dreams. The way they pool around people's feet at noon. Around my feet. I step gingerly on my shadow, as though the darkened sidewalk were a thin crust of ice, which could crack and give way, plunging me into shadow space, a realm as mysterious, as indefinable, as the Antizero.

That is what disturbs me the most: these thoughts of indefinable properties that emerge with the sight of shadows. How thick is the shadow of a telephone pole on a brick wall? Which strikes the ground first: my shadow or the light surrounding it? How much does the shadow of an airplane weigh? Do shadows sleep at night, beneath my bed, or do they rise and soundlessly roam the deserted streets?

> *As we wind on down the road*
> *Our shadows taller than our souls*

Led Zeppelin. The lyrics haunt me daily. Jimmy Page's phantom guitar chords give the words their own shadows. How tall? Near sunset, I stare into my lengthening shadow and imagine a hypotenuse drawn from its head to mine. $A2 + B2 = C2$. Is $C2 >$ or $=$ my soul?

At the university. Nine o'clock. My basic numbers systems class meets in thirty minutes. As with each passing semester, the students seem duller, unable to follow my path through the barely charted frontier of mathematics and mind.

I see Alex Richards entering his office down the hall and I follow. He smiles and sits behind his desk, speaking to me with mock formality:

"So, Dr. Conrad, how may I help you today?"

I produce an artificial intelligence journal from my briefcase.

"Take a look at this and give me one good reason why I shouldn't climb to the top of the campanile and jump off."

I open the journal to the article titled "Modular Calculus and Thought Metageometry." Richards nods.

"I know, Joe. I read it last night and made the connection right away. Hell, the part defining key isomorphisms could have been taken straight out of your dissertation. If these researchers had studied with us at Cal Tech, you could probably sue for plagiarism."

I sit across from Richards in one of the uncomfortable vinyl and metal chairs that permeate universities like viruses. A tree's branches shuffle back and forth in the breeze outside. Leaf shadows shift nervously on the office window.

"No, that's not the point. The system is there for anyone willing to look hard enough. Just like gravity. All it takes is an apple to fall on someone's head. I just wish I had stuck with it until..." "No, Joe, you can't blame yourself. Back when you started on metageometric thought, no one would listen. The good 'ole days of scientific enlightenment, right? But now they're ready. You were just ahead of you time."

As he talks, my attention drifts to the window behind him. The leaf shadows move rhythmically, almost dancing. For a second, I hear the music, or see it, in their subtle gestures. They move as a part of a system: notes with melody, tempo, and structure. Then my understanding of the system's motion is gone, and once again the shadows are only random and chaotic. Richards is trying to get my attention.

"Hey, Joe? Are you still on earth?"

"Yeah, yeah, I was just...trying to concoct a theorem for defining leaf organization in trees."

No, that wasn't what I wanted to say. It sounds crazy. Is crazy. But when I'm tired, I see patterns in everything and I've slept poorly the last few nights.

Anyway, Richards brushes off my answer as a joke, but I detect a quantum of concern in his laughter.

"Well, at least you still have a bit of humor left. Just remember: You were right when everyone else was wrong. Take some satisfaction in that."

"That's not much, Alex. I mean, I missed out on the fame and, probably, a lot of fortune. Satisfaction doesn't count for much when you're thirty-five and still teaching treadmill courses at a second rate university."

Richards shifts in his chair, clearly uncomfortable with the conversation.

"Hey, listen, you've got to stay off that train. It won't take you any place you'll want to go."

My silence forces him to change the subject.

"So, have you heard the latest on the eclipse?"

"No, what is it now?"

He stands up and walks around to the door behind me. I rise and turn to look. A sheet of computer paper is taped above his class and office-hour schedule. The page is filled with lowercase text, but much of it is obliterated by a large black disk in the center, about three inches in diameter. I lean closer to read a portion of the text still visible:

> stardust plastic bubblegum passion blood needles
> blacklight bikinis starving masses microwave ovens
> nazies marilyn monroe happy days sex bombs fetuses
> antichrist zero generation beauty charms truth
> trees strange love oz dracula lovers batman dali

"Is this supposed to mean something?"

"It represents the world, I think. The black circle is, of course, the eclipse. The Big Blackout. A group of students are saying that the world will end at the moment of total eclipse. They're passing these ads around and trying to get everyone to go outside and join hands when the time comes. Strange, huh? Of course, it's the same typical hysterical behavior with eclipses all through history. None of them have tried to explain why the world will end when the eclipse is here, instead of twenty minutes later when it reaches New York, or earlier, in San Francisco, and so on."

I smile and shake my head.

"Maybe so, but if this is your way of making me feel better, it isn't working. I've got to get ready for class. We must keep up appearances, even if we really are all doomed. Don't you think?"

"Yeah, let's go out like Socrates, teaching till we turn stiff. I'll see you later. If we're still here."

I laugh with him, then turn and walk down to my office. I feel Richards still watching me, speculating on how depressed I actually am. But why shouldn't I be depressed? It is too easy to accept what he said, that I was ahead of my time, and put it all behind me. I quit, simple as that.

At twenty-two I was on fire. An idea that artificial intelligence could finally be achieved with programs based on symbolic geometry. Metageometry. Meta—Latin derivative for "to go beyond." A computer system that could transcend itself, look into a mirror and comprehend its own being. The equations burned so brightly my mind I could see them when I closed my eyes. I spent months writing out calculations, sometimes six hours a day, then programming them during the scant hours of computer time I was allowed. But they were so complex, so intricate...I couldn't make anyone else understand. Just a couple of years and a couple of hundred thousand dollars and I would have proven it to the world. But no one wanted to listen. No university offered research grants. Corporations shut their vaults and labs in my face. So I thought, just teach for a couple of years. Sooner or later, something will break if I keep trying. But one semester went by and my proposals were rejected again. Two semesters went by and my tenure committee said look, we don't want a crackpot reputation here; can't you sit on this for a while? Then three, four and five semesters went by and I stopped talking about my theories in casual conversation, even to Richards, because by then I started to believe that I really was wrong, that I was wasting my time, that...and I gave up.

And now, the lightning has passed to another rod.

As I gather my notes and walk to my basic numbers systems class, my depression gives way to a nagging anxiety. The crazy notion about patterns in the leaves' shadows returns.

Impossible, of course...but something lingers...something that has to do with black disks on white paper.

I imagine myself giving a lecture in a Harvard auditorium packed with glassy-eyed fans of Dr. Conrad, Nobel laureate. An immature fantasy, perhaps, but I need something to vitalize my delivery. A speech professor once admonished me with this wisdom: if you sound bored, your students will petrify with boredom.

Therefore, I have to do something to pump my adrenaline up to speed. Either drugs or an active imagination. I begin:

"Mathematics is the poetry of God...."

A soft groan emanates from someone in the back row, breaking the illusion. I continue to speak, but the students' faces intrude. Their glassy-eyed stares denote only puzzlement and apathy. The room's clock, a large white disk speckled with black, seems to move at an insane speed in the corner of my eye. I glance at it and, of course, its hands move normally. But I look away, and it speeds up again. I resist the temptation to keep looking back. Years of my life subtract away, lost in this very room, lost lecturing to petrified students. Although today's subject is logarithms, my subconscious nags at me to include symbols. I cannot concentrate on bare numbers and formulae because the black disk taunts me, demanding analysis.

Halfway through the hour, I turn on the overhead projector, showering the white screen with complex sets of numbers. Beside the screen on the black chalkboard, I sketch out an abstract geometric shape. My lecture moves back on track now; this is the seed of my own theories.

"Now, class, this is where it all gets interesting. These aren't just numbers anymore. When I assign them the proper isomorphic qualities, they become shapes. Now I'm sure you all remember what an isomorphism is…"

I can see by the faces registered with confusion that many of them don't remember. Oh well.

"For those of you who slept through all your high school math courses, an isomorphism is a similarity between two parts of two different systems. Now take this first set of numbers. The sums of the first three lines equal 90, 45, and 45. Now if we say these numbers can be degrees, then we can say that their counterpart is the right triangle in the sketch over here…."

I'm unable to complete the sentence because a sudden revelation weights my tongue. I see the projected numbers: black shadows on white screen. And then the sketch: white chalk on black board. A system of numbers and a system of lines, opposite but still similar. Chalk and antichalk. And my shadow…my antibody.

I struggle to continue the demonstration, but my mind whirls. I have almost reached the heart of my obsession: something about the isomorphic relationship between shadows and their casters, but the final truth still dances just out of reach.

After rambling through fifteen more minutes of lecture, I dismiss the class early. They are not disappointed. Before anyone can leave, one student raises his hand. "Mr. Conrad, before we go, I'd like to ask…the moment of total eclipse on Wednesday occurs during this class. Can we go outside and watch it?"

The others linger, hoping for an hour of freedom. Seeing that they have noticed my nervousness, I joke: "Okay, sure. Let's meet here first, though. One other condition. I don't want to see you holding hands with any of those doomsayers. This is the age of reason, after all, not the Big Blackout."

Most laugh as they leave. Two or three look offended.

The rest of the day passes without incident and the sense of realization which struck me so violently dissolves, leaving only a core of anxiety. As I walk home in the late evening's light, I watch my lengthening shadow, how it mimics and mirrors my every move. An isomorphism: flesh and empty space. Or am I being emptied as my shadow fills, takes on form of its own? Antibodies? I sleep poorly.

*   *   *

Ten o'clock PM. My Tuesday night class on modular calculus just ended after eons of descriptive equations which are the basis of a new, computerized data assimilation method. Computers, I told the class, will soon make rational decisions like us, only they will think in geometric shapes instead of words. Data fed into these equations will assemble into complex structures in the computer's eye. It will look for the highest peak, say, and the data which created that peak will be the optimum answer to the question asked. I explained how primitive forms of this method have been in use for years now, but soon computer geometry will become a fully functional language, capable of assimilating and evaluating everything from the stock market to the poetry of T.S. Eliot, which is more than can be said of English. The joke drew only a patter of laughter. I chose too esoteric a punch line. It's doubtful any computer/mathematics student has ever attempted to read "The Wasteland."

The shadows cast by the electric lamps along the campus walkways solicit my attention. A thin mist is settling all around me and it affects the shadows with an Xn variable I cannot quite define. I look more intently, trying to identify the optical effect. I sigh as I realize what I'm doing. Once again, my mild obsession to analyze even my most casual sense impressions. But…ahead: three dark shadows hunch down where the sidewalk intersects with the larger, north-south walkway. The flood lamp suspended on a pole ten feet above their heads projects their shadows onto the concrete. The light shines with a daytime intensity, but is faintly orange in color. An anti-moth bulb. Just barely, I can make out their whispered words:

"No, this angle must be obtuse. It's here at the center, you see, where the outer edges begin in the other plane. Think in reverse."

"In reverse? Max, you've been thinking too much on acid. That's your problem. I want to go to bed."

A feminine voice, mirthful: "Yeah, me too. Come on, Max. Let's get back to your apartment. It's cold."

"Wait till I'm finished. I'm trying to demonstrate something here."

I recognize that voice. Max Franklin, one of my brighter students, and certainly my most eccentric, in hyperbolic geometry. Quietly, I step closer.

"Look, Max, talking is one thing; it's a great idea, but get real. You took this whole concept from a science fiction story."

Max grabs the piece of chalk from the unidentified speaker and begins to draw furiously on the concrete, consulting pages of computer paper spread out beside him. After a moment, he speaks, punctuating each word with a short scraping motion on the sidewalk.

"Lovecraft / does / not / write / science / fiction."

"Horror, then. Whatever. That's not the point, for chrissakes. The point is, you're flippin going mental, dude."

"Look, you couldn't find any holes in the theorems. Quote me a single physical or mathematical law that says it can't be done."

The young woman stands and turns in my direction. "I've had enough of this, guys. I'm...hey! Who the hell is this?"

I'm interested now, so instead of excusing myself politely, I step forward and speak.

"Hello, Max. I was just walking home and I thought I'd stop and see what kind of trouble you're making for yourself this time."

I remember the time last semester when he was caught by a security guard painting erratic sine waves on the engineering complex's windows. The dean's office let him off with only a written reprimand, but his occasional displays of erratic behavior aren't going to attract many offers from doctorate programs.

"Oh, hi, Dr. Conrad. This is Sam and Shelley, friends of mine. I just brought them out for a little extracurricular adventure in radical geometry. Do you want to watch?"

"Why not?"

At my acceptance, the other two shy away from the lamp's circle of light; embarrassment blushes across their faces.

"Hey, uh, Max, we'll go over to the Knight Moves for a drink. Come on over when you're done."

"Yeah, don't take too long."

Shelley glances uncertainly from me to Max, then turns to follow Sam, who by now is only a black outline against the faintly lit night mist. Again, I sense that strange optical incongruity haunting the fog.

I look at Max. He smiles and shakes his head.

"They feel like children caught playing with an imaginary friend. They're afraid of being patronized."

"And you?"

His gaze is bright enough to pierce the night and touch my eyes. "I don't care what people think of me. No, that's not true. I want them to think I'm crazy. Then I don't have to prove anything to them."

For a quiet moment, he looks down the path where Sam and Shelley retreated. "Still, I wish they would listen. Or you. I've thought for a long time that you might be the one to understand."

I look at the pattern drawn behind him. At first it seems asymmetrical, chaotic. A spray of lines coming from all directions, but pointing inward. There they collide, merge and interact, creating dozens of angles: right, obtuse, acute. Despite the lines' inward courses, a rough circle of concrete remains unmarked in the center of the structure.

"Okay, I give up. What is it, the shape of the Universe?"

Max grins. "No. It's a doorway. I've read the papers you published, and I could tell you were close to discovering this, too. You started down the right road, but you didn't go far enough. It goes beyond simple metageometry. Transdimensional geometry is the final truth."

I shift my feet restlessly. Not only has my own theoretical work seemed to have contributed to Max's eccentricity, but his statement that I didn't go far enough cracks my self-esteem even more. As I look at him, I realize that in some strange way, Max's inner confusion and his misguided drive to be proven right makes him a shadow of what I used to be.

Max continues: "I think that certain geometric shapes, uh, to simplify: cut through the fabric of our space and time. It's like a piece of paper. A big one, imagine, dividing a room in half. Put the right pressures on it and it splits open and you can step to through to the other side. You know those drawings by M.C. Escher, the ones that look three dimensional? If you calculate it correctly, a two dimensional image could create enough pressure to break into as many dimensions as you want."

I keep my expression neutral because he is confiding in me and I have no idea how damaging my disbelief could be to someone so highly strung. Still, he is clearly a genius and perhaps exercising this fantasy will help him return to reality on his own. Certainly, more brilliant mathematicians than he have embarked on stranger mental journeys and returned with insights no one else ever gained with saner approaches. Then, of course, there is the time I...

"Do you want to see? Watch as I finish it, and you'll understand."

Wary of response, I simply nod. He stoops to consult his printout, then takes the chalk and begins to draw. I can see by the chalk's thick, gummy consistency that it is non-watersoluble. Students are allowed to write on the sidewalks only as long as their messages are inoffensive and wash away in the rain.

"You shouldn't use that here. You could get a pretty steep fine, or a trip to the dean's office."

Nervous from my own warning, I scan the grounds for security guards, but once again the odd, unplacable visual effect of the mist distracts me. Max reads my movements without even looking up. "It's all right. I know their schedules. It'll be another forty minutes before a guard comes in this direction. By then, I'll be done. Watch, now."

Silently, my eyes follow his hands. They move quickly, making precise strokes as effortlessly as a needle etches marks onto a seismograph's paper. Slowly, and a little reluctantly, I see a pattern emerging. The added lines begin to close in around the empty space in the center, scratching a circle into existence with only tangents for its outer rim. It's like the first time I was mesmerized by a firewheel sparkler as a child. Tiny rockets spraying fire from four spokes of a moving axle. It spun faster and faster until the bright points of the rockets' tails blurred with speed and cast the illusion of a solid, white circle of fire, throwing off tangents of fiery tongues. Yes, the pattern now before me has that quality, that mirage, of symmetry and substance.

Max leans back, sits, and breathes the word "finished" with a long sigh. For that instant, a moment short enough for a camera to freeze frame a toy sparkler, I see it all.

I see how the outer angles play off each other, changing the size and shapes of triangles on the opposite side which in turn align the trajectory of a ray which becomes a tangent to the innermost circle, fitting perfectly with two dozen other tangents. And, just for that untraceable second, I see that the pattern is just the surface of a deeper structure, a polyhedron that dives far beneath the concrete. The circle becomes a mouth that opens in numberless directions.

Startled, I step back. As the angle of my vision shifts, the illusion disappears and my mind grasps for that word, illusion, not wanting to let go because it is broad enough and tall enough to hide behind. For now.

"Do you see?" Max asks.

Trembling slightly, I mouth careful words. "Well, at the very least, you may have invented a new twist in geometric imaging or maybe even...what did you call it? Transdimensional geometry. I'm impressed, but," I swallow, "the ground is still there. Isn't it supposed to open up?"

Max considers the small circle of concrete. "Not yet. The final touch comes tomorrow. That's why I used waterproof chalk. It has to last."

"Tomorrow? What happens tomorrow?"

But I know the answer.

"The eclipse. I'm not sure why it's necessary, in terms of logic. I just know somehow the eclipse will make the doorway complete. I do, I really do have the math of everything else worked out, but I have to rely on intuition for this last step. You'll just have to believe me."

I see in his eyes that he truly wants, needs, me to believe. A small twitching in the corner of his eye tells me he has his own uncertainties, and looks to me, the all-knowing professor, for support. But I have my own demons in these matters, so I dodge the issue.

"So, how did you develop this theory? I heard Sam say something about a horror story?"

He laughs, embarrassed. "Well, sort of. I know this sounds a little…whatever, but that's just where I got the idea. There's a story called 'Dreams in the Witch House' about a witch who uses geometric images to travel through other dimensions. But Lovecraft wasn't a mathematician, so it was just an abstract idea at that point. I first began to grasp its possibility when I saw the basic geometric elements in the graffiti on the alley walls downtown…."

"Graffiti?" Only now do I realize how far outside the normal world, outside this dimension, Max has already gone.

"Yeah, I don't know much about how these things work, but I think the people who spray-paint random lines and curves on walls started to develop a sort of collective unconscious image—an archetype, or whatever that German guy calls it—of transdimensional geometry. Of course, they didn't have the intellect to bring it to fruition, but I watched and made notes and eventually it all came clear to me."

I try to decide how to respond, and finally say, "Yes, Max. This is all fascinating, but it's getting late, so…why don't you come by my office soon and we can go over it in more detail."

"Uh, sure, Dr. Conrad. Thanks for listening."

I nod and walk away. He seems slightly hurt by my abrupt departure, but right now, I feel I am the last person who should council the insane. Transdimensional geometry in vandals' graffiti? I recall someone, maybe his advisor, mentioning that Max takes lithium treatments. Or used to, at least. Don't manic depressives tend to see secret patterns and codes in the most random data? I decide to talk to someone about Max tomorrow.

Suddenly, I stop and stare into the surrounding mist. That annoying Xn variable which has been meddling with my vision reveals itself to me with perfect optical clarity. Across the greens, a row of lamps lines another walkway. Between me and them is a row of bare trees that shift and squirm in the breeze. The shadows of the branches cut through the faint white mist and seem to reach toward me. Shadows with arms. A quirk of optics, nothing more. But I can't help comparing them to Max's oddly 3-D drawing. Shadows with substance, not merely cast on the ground or a wall, but extending through space itself, alive and moving.

I lower my eyes and walk on, trying to ignore them, but the shadows still try to embrace me.

*   *   *

In bed that night, I watch the myriad shadows kaleidoscoped on my walls by the pale moonlight seeping through my window. It's the shadows, I think, that have drained me of vitality and substance until I am flat and two-dimensional like them. Unable to sleep, I eventually rise and go to the kitchen, guided by a small night light. I drink some milk, the only thing in the house that is still white at this hour. As I walk back to the bedroom, my shadow looms at the end of the hall, given life by the tiny light. Fear tingles my spine because the shadow seems to be emerging from some deep and terrible land behind the paneled wall. A place of opposites, a place where I'm merely the bright, projected shadow of this dark form. I pause at the end of the hall, marveling at how much it mimics a body of flesh in this dim light. I start to turn into my bedroom, then freeze and slowly look back. My shadow, my antibody, has not moved. It stands in the wall, hands on hips, and laughs soundlessly.

*   *   *

I awake Wednesday morning and the encounter in the hallway during the night seems fuzzy and obscure like a dream. Or like the lights in the mist.

Today is the day of the eclipse. I'm to give a guest lecture on particle physics in the general science core course 2303: The World Inside. Not much different from my basic number systems class, except that it is larger and the students are one or two semesters older. Two hundred students, each sullenly wishing to be somewhere else—the dorms, the campus greens piled high with crackling amber leaves, the bars. Anywhere but sitting around in this windowless, cinderblock classroom because they think my abstract symbols defining the unseeable have no more relevance to their everyday, simple existence than the doctrines of religious mystics 2500 years dead.

Sophomore: Greek derivative of "educated fool." I reflect on this and smile a little as I begin my lecture with an opening carefully chosen to capture what little interest my audience can muster: "Forget everything common sense and high school science classes have led you to believe about the world around you. Nothing, not even this building or the seat you're sitting in or the teeth in your mouth, can be termed as real, as having true substance. For all intents and purposes, everything in our existence is only illusion constructed by the dance of infinitesimal phantoms. Here are their names:

UP	ANTI-UP
DOWN	ANTI-DOWN
STRANGE	ANTI-STRANGE
CHARM	ANTI-CHARM
BEAUTY	ANTI-BEAUTY
TRUTH	ANTI-TRUTH

The class resonates with an impressed murmur as the students read the magical names of the quark pairs, names so unexpected among the dead and dried numerals of science courses.

"Every force, every spark of heat, every gram of matter is nothing more than the interaction of forces, which in turn are interactions of more basic forces. If we break these down as far as they can go, we are left with elementary...'entities' so basic that we can't even observe them directly."

Only now, though I have spoken these words perhaps three dozen times, do I grasp their truth. All this time, never guessing. Shadows. The patterns cast by shadows. They have their own energy....

Automatically, I play out the lecture, but I'm thinking all the time.

"You must understand when we use terms like 'spin' and 'movement' we are only using them symbolically, drawing on concepts from our own frame of reference. In reality, the properties of these particles—and I use that word symbolically, too—are far beyond our comprehension."

Yes, yes, it is possible. Shadows displace heat and visible photons, moving all the time. Pulses of energy channeling in all directions beneath the rustling leaves of a tree, connected. Bound together like computer circuits. Like neural synapses in brain cells.

Somehow, I finish the lecture. Class is not over yet. The host professor thanks me and begins to address the students, but I walk out. In the hall, I meet Richards. He speaks and I struggle to listen.

"Hey, Joe. Are you ready for the Big Blackout?"

I try to convey my excitement, but only succeed in mumbling wildly. "Why couldn't I have seen it before? Patterns, they all make sense now."

"Joe, are you on something?"

I laugh. "No, no, but I wish to God I were. I understand now. I understand!"

I brush past him. The student eclipse sign is still on his office door. I realize it has already begun. Soon, the sun will be totally black. An antisun. That has to be it. And it will shine on the world and for a moment this will be the antiworld. And this time, because of Max, this eclipse will be different from all past eclipses.

"Sorry, I've got to be somewhere," I yell over my shoulder. I missed the boat, the truth, all these years. Could it have been because I was afraid of what I might find? Might unleash? But maybe Max....

Once outside, I stop walking, overwhelmed by the spectacle that I had been blind to for so long. All the shadows, everywhere, cascade in perfect rhythms, at once infinite and minute. The grand pattern, alive and intelligent. Of course. If nerve cells can spring to life from random chemicals, then so can....Is this the forbidden fruit I almost tasted so long ago? And did my antibody—my antilife—conspire to steer me away from it?

I command my lungs to breathe slowly. Calmly, I walk across the greens. Many students are already tempting blindness by staring at the metamorphosing sun. I do not follow their gaze. Instead, I sit in wonder and watch the shadow-dance of life. Antilife. Soon, my own students from basic numbers class emerge from the math building, no doubt confused by my absence. I remember the total eclipse occurs soon after the class begins. I angle across the grass toward the sidewalk intersection where Max drew his doorway. All color now fades as the black disk reduces the sun to a gleaming crescent. Near the intersection, several dozen people link arms. Max joins the chain's end nearest his sketch. He sees me and smiles.

I kneel on the sidewalk and gaze into the sketch's center. The effect I dismissed the night before as an optical illusion returns. The concrete in the center is almost transparent. In the rapidly fading light, I can make out angles below the surface. Angles that lead like a spiraling staircase deep into the anti-world.

I look up at the sun just as it darkens into a black disk, surrounded by the ghostly veil of aurora. And through the doorway at my feet, a portal opens for the first time in all of existence and a fountain erupts. A fountain of almost-light, of evanescence, matching the aurora above. Antilife, made flesh, flows. Shadows brighten as people and trees become dark.

Soon the day returns, but from his point of view a black disk remains, blocking the sun. He realizes the irregular black disk is a head. The head is attached to a form. A figure of flesh. It moves and he moves with it, unable to command his own body. At first, he cries without sound as he mimics its movements. Is this all that remains for him, for all eternity? But soon, his perception strangely turns inward, away from the haloed form of his old body and to the infinite fields of the shadow world. He begins to perceive so many of them, pools and seas of ink, but each unique, full of promise. In these places, he casts and controls his own, more profound, shadow, as if he is his body's ghost and his darker shadow is his ghost, a ghost within a ghost. Time enough later to explore the deep mysteries of these new lands, but for now, it is good to rest, to embrace the languor of being projected and moved by another, lying kinked when strewn across stairs and curbs and flat when cast on the ground.

ESSAYS

ARCHAEOPTERYX

Wes Jackson

THE 3.45 BILLION YEAR-OLD IMPERATIVE AND THE FIVE POOLS

We humans may think of ourselves as more important than other animals. I am certainly not going to take on as a project to reverse that belief. Even so, it is important to recognize the commonalities we share with other creatures since our limits and our fates are tied to so much that is common. We ingest food. We eliminate. We mate. We have young. We grow old. We die. Easy enough to internalize with a little thought, but there is a deeper commonality not widely considered that includes plant life, microbes, and most other living things. For the past 3.45 billion years nearly all life-forms that we have observed have depended on energy-rich carbon as a fuel source. Either cells get this energy-rich carbon or they die. For us aerobic forms, which is to say oxygen-dependent creatures, it is one of the oldest drills. Oxygen travels from the lungs into the blood, enters a cell, comes in contact with an energy-rich carbon molecule (a sugar), and energy is released and made available for work as carbon dioxide and water leave the cell. These wastes go into the bloodstream, then to the lungs, and finally we exhale. The next breath in brings in more oxygen, and so it goes. Fruit flies do it this way. Aerobic bacteria are small enough to avoid the complex mechanics, but they do it, too. Elephants and whales, mice and men, essentially all of us do it. We do it or die. The study of physiology explains all of these goings-on.

This process is similar to the process of ingesting food, but our "hunger" for energy-rich carbon doesn't stop with food. Fossil fuels—products of photosynthesis from ages past—give us synthetic fibers, fertilizer, pesticides, and the ability to make automobiles. Even our nuclear power plants could not have been built without fossil energy. In the interest of what we might call comfort and security, we seem to lack the ability to practice restraint at using whatever energy is available. Why this is so has something to do with our lives shaped during an ancient-beyond-memory past. The outside dimension for humans was modest at first and mostly restricted to clothing and shelter needs. The cotton, wool, and wood we use also grow out of the earth and are held together by the energy in the molecules that make them up. They too are made of stored sunlight collected by green molecular traps called chlorophyll. In our Paleolithic past, we had little need to exercise restraint toward food or firewood, but now we do. Any improvement at getting these carbon-based necessities improves our chance to live. As a psychology teacher of mine once put it, "It is built into our meat." We strive to gain access to energy-rich carbon for our outsides as well as our insides.

THE FIRST POOL

Our very being was shaped by a seamless series of changing ecosystems embedded within an ever-changing ecosphere over hundreds of millions of years. Its ability to support humans into a distant future was not on the line. The context of our livelihood kept our numbers more or less in check. Diseases killed us. Predators ate us. Sometimes we starved. The context that had shaped us was the context within which we lived. Apparently we had been eating grains but not improving them for centuries. But something happened some ten millennia ago called the agricultural revolution. It also became a treadmill. It happened first in one of these ecosystems, most likely in the land to the east of the Mediterranean, but soon spread. Hunter-gatherers initiated what would be recognized later as a break with nature, a split. This new way of being began our escape from gathering and hunting as a way of life. To set the record straight, Eden was no garden and our escape only partial. Where we planted our crops, we reduced the diversity of the biota. The landscape simplified by agriculture locked our ancestors into a life of "thistles, thorns, and sweat of brow." We became a species out of context. It has been said that if we were meant to be agriculturists, we would have had longer arms.

No matter how unpleasant this agricultural work may have been, the food calories increased. Our numbers rose; more mouths needed to be fed. No matter that they disliked thistles and thorns and sweat of brow, our ancestors loved their children and their own lives, and so they kept doing it. They had to eat. Some gave up agriculture when they had the chance. The introduction of the horse by the Spanish allowed some of the Native Americans to return to hunting and gathering, for a short while. Eventually the draft animals, especially the ox and the horse, were domesticated. These creatures used the stored sunlight of a grass, shrub, or tree leaf and transferred it to the muscle to pull a plow or bear a load. They became "beasts of burden."

This step onto the agriculture treadmill was the first toward the current and looming problem of climate change. It was in that time that humans began a way of life that would exploit the first of five relatively nonrenewable pools of energy-rich carbon—soil. Trees, coal, oil, and natural gas would follow as additional pools to rob from. It was here that we began to accelerate the breakdown and waste of what Amory Lovins once called the "young pulverized coal of the soil."

Our crops and we—both of us—were beneficiaries of the energy released as nutrients stored in the carbon compounds in the soil now became available. More will be made of this later, but for now it is enough to say that it was agriculture that featured annuals in monoculture instead of perennials in mixtures where the split with nature began. And so it was at this moment that the carbon compounds of the soil were exposed to more rapid oxidation. Carbon dioxide headed for the atmosphere, and the nutrients formerly bound up in those organic compounds—nutrients such as phosphorus and potassium—were now available for uptake by our annual crop plants. So, this wasn't really a use of the energy-rich carbon in the sense that we were after the energy stored in the carbon molecule. Rather, the breaking of the carbon compound at work in the soil was a consequence of agriculture. With agriculture, the soils that had once safely absorbed the footsteps of the Paleolithic gatherers and hunters and their food supply lay vulnerable. The hoe, along with the power to domesticate plants into crops and wild animals into livestock, turned these people into the most important revolutionaries our species has ever known. They plunged ahead in this new way of life, repeatedly modifying their agrarian technique as they went.

How many were aware they were at the forefront of a way of life dependent on deficit spending of the earth's capital? Certainly long before the advent of writing, humans must have understood that till agriculture not only simplifies the landscape but also compromises soil quality and plant fertility. Even so, the reality informed by the immediate reigned. People needed food. Energy-rich carbon molecules were the workhorses in the soil accommodating a diversity of species. The seeds from annual crop monocultures would feed the tribe. The energy-rich carbon in the grains provided these tribes with a more reliable and abundant food supply and, therefore, made possible the beginning of civilization. Eventually the descendants of these farmers had the tools necessary to expand the scale of shrub and tree harvest. Now the agriculturists could more aggressively exploit the second nonrenewable pool—forests.

THE SECOND POOL

Five thousand or so years passed. It is easy to imagine that as the agriculturists wandered through the forests, their curious minds saw that they could cut down the forests to purify ores. This led to the creation some five thousand years ago of first the Bronze and then the Iron Age and led to a further distancing of nature. But soon this second pool of energy-rich carbon was on its way to being used up beyond local replacement levels. This second use of carbon—deforestation—became, unambiguously, a mining operation. And it came on fast. And so the forests went down as the soils were eroding, first in the Middle East and later in Europe and Asia. And so it went for millennia, relentlessly, until recently.

THE THIRD POOL

Only one-quarter of one millennium ago, the third pool—coal—was opened on a large scale with the launching of the industrial revolution in 1750. But already by 1700, England's forests were mostly gone to heat the pig iron. The Brits then took their ore to Ireland, where forests were still abundant, to purify the metal. The stock of the second pool of energy-rich carbon, the forests, had been so depleted that this third pool must have gladdened the heart of those who would exploit it. Coal reduced the pressure on the forests only slightly, for after the defeat of the Spanish Armada, it cost England its forests to rule the waves for the next three hundred years.

The availability of coal, this third pool, provided a quantum leap in our ability to accomplish more work in a shorter period of time. The density of energy stored in a pound of coal is greater than the density in a pound of wood. The accessibility and breakability of coal sponsored countless hopes, dreams, and aspirations of the British Empire. However, the colonialism those carbon pools made possible also destroyed local cultural and ecological arrangements that will be, at best, slow to replace in a sun-powered world.

It seems inevitable now that Neolithic farmers would move from a Stone Age and on to a Bronze Age and later, an Iron Age. Similarly, given the energy density of coal, it also seems inevitable now that a steam engine would be built to accelerate the industrial revolution.

Without soil carbon, forests, and coal, it seems doubtful that the British Empire would have had the slack in 1831 to send a young Charles Darwin on his famous voyage around the world. And once home, he was given the leisure to investigate his collections, pore over his journals, exchange letters with contemporaries, converse with his scientific peers, and finally, in 1859, have *On the Origin of Species* appear in London bookstores.

THE FOURTH POOL

The year 1859 was an auspicious one, beyond Darwin's publication. It was also the year of the first oil well—Colonel Edwin Drake's oil well in western Pennsylvania—and the opening of the fourth pool of energy-rich carbon, oil. Cut a tree and you have to either chop or saw it into usable chunks. Coal you have to break up. But oil is a portable liquid fuel transferable in a pipe, a perfect product of the Iron Age.

The year 1859 was also when the ardent abolitionist John Brown was hanged at Harpers Ferry, a reality more than coincidental. In some respects, John Brown, beyond believing in the absolute equality of blacks and whites, stands alone in his time. His fervor would have received little traction had not the numbers of abolitionists been growing in the industrial North. The South had coal, of course, but not as much. It was a more agrarian society. Northern supporters, who were more profligate pool-users, could afford to be more self-righteous than the more agrarian, less coal-using, slaveholding South. Leisure often makes virtue easier.

THE FIFTH POOL

Natural gas has been available in some form of use back to the times of the ancient Greeks. But it did not become a manageable pool as a major power source until after coal began to be used. We count it as the fifth pool and likely the last major pool. Other minor pools may follow, such as the lower-quality tar sand and shale oil, both energy- and water-intensive for their extraction, which are in the early stages of being exploited. Over the last half century, we have used natural gas as a feedstock to make nitrogen fertilizer, which we apply to our fields to provide us a bountiful food supply while creating dead zones in our oceans. This process, called the Haber-Bosch process, was developed in the first decade of the twentieth century by two Germans, Fritz Haber and Karl Bosch. Vaclav Smil, a resource scholar at the University of Manitoba, has called it "the most important invention of the twentieth century." Without it, Smil says, 40 percent of humanity would not be here. This is certainly a true enough statement given the reality of our cattle, pig, and chicken welfare programs.

So, in summary, a combination of the 3.45-billion-year imperative and our success in breaking into the storehouse by the discovery and exploitation of these five carbon pools is a central reality behind the "terrible truths" mentioned by Kathleen Raine. When we were gatherers and hunters, the ecosystem kept us in check. But since the advent of agriculture, we have forced the landscape to meet our expectations, and we have been centered on this way of life. We plow. We cut forests. We mine coal. We drill for oil and natural gas. We want the stored sunlight the oxygen helps release. The oxygen that enters our lungs to oxidize energy-rich carbon molecules in our cells is internal combustion—not too dissimilar to the oxygen that enters the air intake of an automobile and, with the aid of a spark, releases the energy to power a bulldozer or to run a car idling in a traffic jam.

We relentlessly rearrange the five carbon pools to get *more* energy or more useful materials. Internal combustion is the name of the game. We reorder our landscapes and industrial machinery to keep our economic enterprises (and ourselves) going, all the while depleting the stocks of non-renewable energy-rich carbon. We are like bacteria on a petri dish with sugar.

So here we are, the first species in this 3.45-billion-year journey that will have to practice restraint after years of reckless use of the five carbon pools. None of our ancestors had to face this reality. We are living in the most important and challenging moment in the history of *Homo sapiens*, more important than any of our wars, more important than our walk out of Africa. More important than any of our conceptual revolutions. We have to consciously practice restraint to end our "use it till it's gone" way of life. We have to stop deficit spending of the ecosphere and reduce our numbers if we hope to prevent widespread sociopolitical upheaval.

Copyright © 2010 by Wes Jackson Reprinted with permission of *Counterpoint*.

Wes Jackson

THE RISE
OF TECHNOLOGICAL
FUNDAMENTALISM

Millions of people go through life without knowing anything about physics. In spite of this ignorance, all the African natives do not starve; nor do all the Eskimos freeze; and the Indians, though they had none of our science, still managed to exist. But these people only exist; they do not really live. They could not live our way, for our world is entirely organized according to the principles of physics. You, yourself, must understand these principles, or you will be more or less like a barbarian in a modern city.

Without knowing physics we might still have some kind of food, shelter, and clothing; but we want a lot more than that. We want a variety of food brought from all parts of the world; we want safe houses, comfortably heated and lighted; we want different kinds of clothing for different uses and seasons. In addition, we have learned to expect quick and easy transportation by rail, airplane, boat, or motor; cheap and ready communication by radio, telephone, or telegraph; and hundreds of other things that increase our comfort, reduce our labors, and meet our demands in the way of sports, hobbies, and amusements. All these science helps us to produce
(Elements of Physics, 1947).

Several thousand years after agriculture began, the ancient Hebrews developed a multilayered, highly sophisticated mythology around the idea that there had been a better time but that we now live in a fallen condition. Whatever myth we assign to our break with nature, our lives in this "fallen world" have led to the exploitation of energy pools beyond the power of the ecosphere and its ecosystems to meet, or for the disturbed ecosystems to be renewed at the rate we destroy them.

Beyond energy-rich carbon pools, we look to nuclear power—ignoring that uranium is a finite fuel and that it is the use of energy that has been the destroyer. If nuclear power becomes a primary energy source, how do we keep it out of trouble? Without regulations imposing restraint, it seems certain we will use the energy to move more aggressively into the wild carbon-based biodiversity of the ecosphere, such as a tropical forest. It will give us access to more carbon-based products and further rearrange the ecosystems of the ecosphere. It is hard to keep high-quality energy out of trouble. This seems worth thinking about, for many of my environmental colleagues see nuclear power as necessary in our time. Environmental historian Angus Wright believes it will become the great divide of the environmental movement. It is one thing to ask what new information has arrived over the last three or four decades that makes it any safer today. The safety-and-storage-of-radioactive-waste problem remains. Yucca Mountain would already be stuffed full if it had been approved. And will we ever have a way of knowing when enough is enough?

We can also go on and address the "one-in-ten-thousand problem." It is generally assumed that the probability of a reactor accident, such as at Chernobyl, to be one in ten thousand years. That might seem safe enough. But with a thousand reactors, we should expect an accident every ten years on average. We currently have around 450 reactors worldwide, which means an accident every twenty-two years on average. Are we not already on schedule?

Now let's assume that we can make them totally safe during their operation and that we can solve the waste problem. Given that we now live in a world in which terrorism is on the increase, what sort of police state tactics must we employ? Such a police state would require stable governments to keep the materials out of terrorists' hands.

Finally, nuclear fusion comes up, the sort of nuclear reaction happening on the sun. Were the horrendous engineering problems ever to be overcome, fusion would be the ultimate simplifier of the ecosphere's creation.

None of these discussions mention the use of energy on a large scale as a simplifier. Agriculture was the first simplifier on the landscape, and with it species extinction and extirpation were huge. Cutting the forests added to the biotic simplification, as did coal and oil and natural gas. This has caused an information crisis: the DNA lost with species extinction is information lost to the ecosystems. The countless skills and cultural know-how for getting along in a sun-powered world that we have lost due to our irresponsibility will be slow in returning. This too is a loss of information. From the use of coal to the present, we have discarded much of the cultural and natural scaffolding for harvesting contemporary sunlight, and in its place we introduced new scaffolding dependent on fossil fuel abundance to keep it maintained. The embodied energy of the new infrastructure, whether it is cars or farm machinery, computers or cell phones, may be so keyed to the world in which they arose that many of these gadgets will become extinct as stocks decline.

THE JEVONS PARADOX

Another unfortunate reality of this age of carbon exploitation is the rise of technological fundamentalism. We have interpreted the Platonic idiom "Necessity is the mother of invention" to mean "technology will bail us out." We hold a widespread belief that we will get more efficient. But this usually means that we will get more efficient technologically and not that we will do with less. (We will come to rely on hybrid cars or no-till farming, not do without.) We also believe that though nature's ecosystems may be destroyed, new energy sources will be found to compensate for our past and future destruction. I know one intellectual who seriously suggested we could invent soil when it is gone.

It should be immediately apparent that the very opposite is true. As the economist Thorstein Veblen said: "Invention is the mother of necessity." Wallace Stegner once wrote about the things once possessed that cannot be done without. Think of how many geegaws in our daily lives we didn't know we needed until we saw them—and then we became dependent on them. As to the fundamentalist tenet, the most widespread at the moment, that technological efficiency will save us, rarely mentioned is the Jevons Paradox, a reference to William Stanley Jevons, a British economist and author of a book published in 1865 entitled *The Coal Question*. Jevons argued that in industrial England greater technological efficiency led to *more* resource consumption, particularly coal and iron. Greater efficiency frees up capital for economic and, therefore, energy expansion. Walmart's truck fleet gets better mileage, but what will keep the owners from building more box stores? Money, like energy, has a hard time staying out of trouble. For example, imagine someone with $25 million derived from a sale of his or her oil wells. Now imagine a Kansas rancher who owns twenty-five thousand acres in the Flint Hills featuring tallgrass prairie. Because the oilman loves to look at beautiful, never plowed, uninterrupted tallgrass prairie, he pays the rancher $1,000 per acre. Compared with most U.S. current agricultural enterprises, the tallgrass prairie ranch uses little fossil carbon, because the cattle harvest contemporary sunlight. For activities such as shipping, processing, and distribution, the fossil energy calories used per pound of red meat gain on the grass-fed beef are lower than a pound gained in the feedlot. Said otherwise, the grass-fed beef uses less fossil energy than the cattle raised in a feed lot. So the new owner's $25 million, derived from oil and spent to buy that Flint Hills ranch, would be a "carbon offset," not a complete offset, but a large one.

But the seller of the ranch will have a hard time keeping his $25 million out of rapid-climate-change trouble. Those dollars will be a magnet to attract other carbon-sponsored activity such as travel, or "stuff" such as a yacht, car, house, welder, lathe, whatever. Suppose he invests in wind machines with electric generators. That would be better, but we need to know how much fossil energy it takes to organize, build, and run that technology. More importantly, how do the investors in wind spend the profits? Not all of the $25 million will turn "green"; in a final accounting it might be very little. One person's attempts to lower carbon use can enable another's increased use.

Without a cap on carbon at the wellhead, the mine, or the point of entry, there is every reason to think that Jevons will be proved right again. Our culture needs to make plans to avoid the paradox. We need to understand, for instance, that in manufacturing, the reasonable consideration is not just the carbon *in* the factory, but also the carbon used to make the factory, to move components in and products out to market, and more.

Since we are already overdrawing the capital of the earth's ecosystems (forests, soils, water), our minds naturally leap to renewable energy sources to be exploited. But given our level of consumption, there are serious problems with renewables. The price for photovoltaics is coming down. Wind-generated electricity gets a favorable rating because electricity is energy of the highest quality. Storage and transmission will be a challenge, but both are being worked on. And so far we have been primarily an oil/natural gas society. As we look to renewable portable liquid fuels, we are now turning to ethanol or biodiesel. Will any of these make us more efficient?

Now to address the belief that we'll forever find new energy sources to compensate for future and past destruction. Sure, there are tar sands and shale and nuclear power, but they aren't nearly as efficient as handling coal, oil, and natural gas. It is worth being reminded again and again that it is not climate change that has destroyed so much of the ecosphere, it is energy. Our use of nonrenewable energy has destroyed rain forests. Our intensive application of nitrogen fertilizer on our farmlands has given us dead zones in our oceans. When we look at the few examples where an energy source has made it possible to restore what we have lost, it resides primarily in the realm of ecological restoration.

What this review reveals is the absolute necessity of conservation, where sufficiency has standing over efficiency, though, of course, we need both. Conservation of scarce materials is our largest source of energy, a source embedded within sufficiency, efficiency, and reduced population.

When my family and I moved back to Kansas from California, it was for the stated, comically expressed purpose of "figuring out a way to stay amused while we live till we die—cheap," meaning inexpensive to the ecosphere. The five of us did a sort of homesteading trip with garden, a milk cow, steer, and pigs. We burned wood for heat. It was somewhat like the farm where I had been born and raised. Yes, we did have a car, a pickup truck, electricity, even a fuel oil furnace, but during that period our ecological footprint must have been the smallest it has ever been. My wife, Dana, was an excellent gardener and beekeeper. The three children were terrific, mostly noncomplaining workers, with their various chores. What did we learn? It was a lot of work, and though we were aware ahead of time, we had the direct experience beyond the abstraction that it is essentially impossible to create an island in the context of our highly extractive culture. Success will require society to commit itself to a resilient future. I am confident there will be an increasing number of creative options ahead for all of us. And we can do it. We can pull away from the damaging shibboleths of the technological fundamentalists. We can begin to move our species into a more sustainable relationship with our natural capital. But first, as a technological species, we must come to terms with the Jevons Paradox and not count on efficiency alone or much from biofuels from the landscape. If we were, as a nation, to put a cap on carbon at the wellhead, the port of entry, and the mine, as well as timber harvest at a renewable level, then we would have the chance to see what technologies emerge from the market forces. Waiting until that energy is allowed to run freely in the culture creates horrendous accounting problems and allows countless bookkeepers of business to cheat even without their knowing it.

Most industrial countries—with more than adequate standards of living—use about half the energy per capita that we Americans do. This includes the sum of energy to households, transportation, manufacturing, and infrastructure. By saying yes to conservation, we are saying yes to efficiency, and have taken the first steps to saying yes to sufficiency. By saying no to our belief in technology as a primary solution, we can involve all sectors of our economy that link us to the terrible truths.

What seems to run ahead of everything else at the moment is that the consequences of increasing technological complexity, spurred by scientific discovery, go unmanaged because society can move only on the available paths, which are limited in number and design. Stated otherwise, the problems generated by the science/technology/economy trinity require solutions that would have to evolve along social/political paths that are too small or not available.

COUNTERINTUITIVE BEHAVIOR

Professor Jay Forrester was a systems theorist and analyst at the Massachusetts Institute of Technology. Four decades ago he trained a group of young scientists who published the famous *Limits to Growth* study in the early 1970s. Donella Meadows, lead author of that important volume, once quoted her mentor:

People know intuitively where leverage points are. Time after time I've done an analysis of a company, and I've figured out a leverage point. Then I've gone to the company and discovered that everyone is pushing it in the wrong direction!

Meadows explained that "the classic example of that backward intuition" was the first model Forrester's group ran. It turns out that the major global problems—environmental destruction, poverty and hunger, unemployment, resource depletion, urban deterioration—are all related. The common culprit was growth, both population and economic growth. "Growth has costs," she wrote, "among which are poverty and hunger, environmental destruction—the whole list of problems we are trying to solve with growth!"

Morris Berman, author of *Dark Ages America: The Final Phase of Empire* (2006), contends that the question before us has to do with how much flexibility we have in making choices and acting on them. Every civilization is a "package deal," he says, and the configuration of that package dictates a trajectory imposed by the constraints of that "deal." Some of those constraints may be positive, others negative, but the important idea is that they crystallize into a specific pattern or direction early. So when economic and population growth has been used to solve problems in the past, has been the "package deal" so to speak, there is little wonder that we might fail to realize that the factors that allowed our civilization to rise to power are the same factors that may do it in. Here is a problem: for our country to get where it is today required that we reject countless alternatives along the way. Berman argues that collapse or decline can only be avoided if the alternatives that have been repressed are incorporated into the dominant way of being. For example, the loss of local dairies, local butcher shops, and local produce through various subsidies, in favor of cheap fossil fuels, now makes us vulnerable.

Forrester once published a paper entitled "The Counterintuitive Behavior of Social Systems." He gave examples in the housing industry and highway building about how deficient housing became more so and how the highways actually led to more congestion. Could it be because our social, economic, and ecological systems are so complex that we have a limited ability to see beyond the complexity to an eventual outcome? For scientists, part of our limitation has to do with our reductive approach to problem solving. Ecologist Stan Rowe said, "Reductionism blunts the higher level search for more inclusive realities." So our very training may stand behind our failure to imagine the consequences of complexity.

I often invite visitors to The Land Institute to take a ride on a merry-go-round I rescued from an abandoned elementary school yard and installed in our yard at home. It stands ready to be ridden at any moment, but it is there for more than fun. I want my grandchildren—and visitors—to experience an illusion. The design features a centerpiece with an offset pivot to which four rods are attached, rods that reach back to handles in front of each of the four seats. A rider, by moving the handle back and forth, can cause all four seats and any rider to move around and around until dizziness (or disinterest) sets in. Anyone riding that plaything and looking to the center where the rods are attached will wrongly perceive that the center and the attached offset pivot part are moving. The perception of movement will be retained in the rider's mind when stepping off. Anyone on the ground staring at the center and pivot will see that neither moves. Anyone sitting on one of those four seats is like a person riding on planet earth who, when looking at the center, perceives that the center is moving.

Four centuries ago Galileo was taken by Copernicus's idea that the sun was at the center of our world. The dominant idea that the earth was at the center and that the sun revolved around it was a derivative of Ptolemy, a geographer and astronomer from Alexandria who lived in the second century AD. After Ptolemy, mathematicians and other thoughtful people elaborated on what seemed obvious to all. They formalized a way of looking at an earth-centered universe. Some mathematicians who built on Ptolemy's ideas predicted the position of the known planets on any particular day of the week in any year. In spite of such powerful prediction, and no matter that Dante had used Ptolemy's cosmology as a map for the paradise section of the *Divine Comedy*, both Copernicus and Galileo believed that the Ptolemaic worldview and the Church were wrong.

Galileo, like Copernicus, was able to mentally step outside the system and expand the boundary of consideration. The power structure of the Church refused to take this courageous mental step. Martin Luther didn't help matters. The Reformation was under way, and the threat to Church leadership was heightened. Some defenders of the Ptolemaic view argued that God would not trick us.

Eventually, of course, others became convinced of the truth of this insight, and a major tenet of science was born—perception is not always reality. This was one of the great moments in the early history of science. Unfortunately, we too often ignore or forget this lesson. It is easy to believe that we are more agriculturally productive than we really are. If we were to step off the merry-go-round and expand our boundaries of consideration, we would immediately see that without fossil fuel and material subsidies from the extractive economy, yields would be seriously lower. We could see that a focus on bushels and acres distorts our view of reality. Were we to eliminate nonrenewable resources from production efforts—stop using natural gas as the feedstock for nitrogen fertilizer, herbicides, insecticides, and more, for example—and force ourselves to rely on the natural fertility of the soil, introducing crop rotations featuring legumes for nitrogen fixation, fertility yields would plummet. High yields dazzle us and give us an illusion that we are sophisticated on the subject of agronomics.

It is only in the last century—the last 1 percent of our history with agriculture—that we have experienced such a major bump in food production. No comparable bump is likely to be attainable again because of the degradation of the natural fertility of our soils, as well as the loss of some of the genetic potential of our major crops. According to devotees of the modern paradigm, it has been a great ride. Social systems, like ecological systems, far more complex than a ride on a merry-go-round, obscure the realities before us.

W. H. Auden's poem "The Age of Anxiety" includes this sentence: "We would rather be ruined than changed."

AGRICULTURE AS ASTEROID SHOWER

A laminated wall hanging in my office, thirty-six inches high and thirty inches wide, is "A Correlated History of Earth." More than four billion years are represented on this convenient chart. Column heads include tectonics, era, period, plants, invertebrates, fishes, reptiles, birds, and mammals. One is labeled "astroblemes" for the asteroids that have smacked the earth and created "blemishes." There have been a few big ones and a lot of little ones. The one that divides the Permian-Triassic was the largest, more than 300 kilometers in diameter. From my reading of the wall hanging, the one that appears to have done the greatest damage was over 200 kilometers across, or 120 miles. That's the one that ended the Cretaceous period sixty-five million years ago. I read once that at the point of impact, the tail of that asteroid would have been as high as Mount Everest. How someone found that out is beyond me. For some time it appeared to many scientists that the asteroid strike alone finished off the dinosaurs, allowing our living supraorganism, the earth, the ecosphere with its embedded ecosystems, to eventually create a diversity of mammal types. As is usually the case in science, tidy stories have a way of becoming more complicated. It now seems volcanic eruptions under way between sixty-three and sixty-seven million years ago created gigantic lava beds called Deccan Traps. Yet even serious blows to the wafer-thin miraculous skin of our planet fail to destroy the power of the ecosphere to create new organisms. The ecosystem processes that are disrupted by the massive extirpations and extinctions will return.

We can see now that agriculture, with its beginning ten thousand to twelve thousand years ago, has been like a shower of small asteroids striking our planet. As the earth was increasingly "peppered" by annual mono-cultures disrupting natural ecosystem processes, we moved on to adjacent landscapes. We are now approaching the end of an agriculture "agrobleme shower." In less than a century, the world's population has tripled, and we could add as many people in the next fifty years as the total population had fifty years ago. Over the past forty years, as we have doubled food production, we have wiped out numerous species, as well as land race crop varieties and local cultures.

If asteroids were known to be approaching earth, ready to deliver an impact, there would be considerable expenditure and heroic maneuvering by the United Nations. All would agree that the earlier we get started to intercept this "agrobleme shower," the better. A nudging at great distance would require a smaller angle of deflection. Economists might even calculate the cost-benefit ratio. The ecosphere as a supraorganism can absorb major blows and continue to create new organisms. The earth's creative capacity will continue. New opportunities for a change in the flora and fauna are always opening up. The asteroids and volcanoes may contribute to the history of this creative endeavor. It should be noted, however,

139

that from a human's time frame, most healing would be observable only in geologic time.

Copyright © 2010 by Wes Jackson from *Consulting the Genius of the Place*. Reprinted with permission of *Counterpoint*.

Merrick Rees Hamer

IN PRAISE OF THE MYSTICAL LIGHT

> *In the beginning God created the heaven and the earth. And the earth was without form, and void; and darkness was upon the face of the deep. And the Spirit of God moved upon the face of the waters. And God said, "Let there be light: and there was light."* (Genesis 1:1-3)

The primeval utterance shook the vaults of heaven, for darkness, which was everywhere was suddenly for naught, and light was in the midst of eternity. These words, commencing the holy writings, speak of the one gift that precedes all other gifts, light. It refers to primal awareness, original instinct and insight, offered by God to the ordained children of His creation who would follow. It is truly the source of the fluidic impulse in man to imitate his divine creator and perpetuate the product of creation. Notwithstanding its august introduction in creation, it is commonly lost to much of humanity, for it is no longer something that appears before humankind without effort on his part to perceive it. He has fallen from the realm in which it was originally conceived. His apprehension of it may indeed be vacuous since his present understanding of light is something of a material order, abundantly fundamental to him from birth. If he is aware of his primal instinct, however, and yearns for what is obscure, his only remedy is to look beyond the common veil of the ages, overshadowing that which has become lost to him.

The seeker must secure the path by which he will make his discovery. Paths, of course, can be traversed to and fro and may be fraught with difficulties; and that which potentially leads humankind to his pristine state has yet to be uncovered. That man has promoted symbols of such discovery means that he may be ready for his return, regardless of what dire consequences may await him. The hermit with the lantern may well greet him upon the path which he has chosen as his destiny. A star may guide the wise to the epiphany of their dreams and a dove may hover above to make more placable the tribulations that lie in wait. An historical tracing of events as they have been told from the Judeo-Christian accounts may illustrate the quest for what has been gifted yet to which the eyes of men remain to be opened.

The excerpt from Genesis implies that darkness was a pre-existent condition, anterior to the inception of light and that it existed only because there was no light.[1] Yet, further penetration of the scripture quoted would reveal that darkness and light coexisted as important counterparts in creation and complemented each other as the creation unfolded. Furthermore, it is clear that among God's most cherished creatures, the children of earth could not have thriven, overwhelmed by the luminous product that might have dispelled the darkness. Wherefore, divine portension and intervention on behalf of the future children must have modified the august command by separating light form darkness; and we learn, as the scriptures continue, of a subsequent action of God to wit:

> *And God made two great lights; the greater light to rule the day, and the lesser light to rule the night: he made the stars also. And God set them in the firmament of the heaven to give light upon the earth, And to rule over the day and over the night, and to divide the light from the darkness.* (Genesis 1:16-18)

The ruling elements would, of course, be meaningless without the ability to discern, and the creation of man as a vehicle for discernment is evidence of God's providence, for He would not suffer His children to live in total darkness; neither would He gift them entirely with light. Yet, what manner of light might the children of earth discern, for it was not until the fourth day of creation that the Sun and Moon and stars came into existence, to give light upon the earth? Furthermore, it might be asked, what was the nature of that light which was of the first order and what became of it when supplanted by something following? There must be taken into account an important contradistinction; and it is made evident by the use of distinguishing scriptural terms. The original dispensation was in the form of something to affect the interior state of awareness, and the scriptural authors called its name *"Aur."*[2] Its meaning could be reasonably compared with the term *"mana,"*[3] used by other primitive religions to represent a spirit-essence that pervaded nature, inexplicable in physical terms. In another usage, the term *Manna,*[4] (with a variant spelling and context) had significance in later Jewish history and will be mentioned later. Since man and beast were not yet formed, the Hebrew expression for light as mentioned above would have had meaning only to the creator Himself and its benefit elsewhere or among creatures would have been deferred. The well-known transgression of the first man and woman might have impaired their ability to discern such a profound property of light and it is reasonable to infer that, until it could be made more palpable in a future age, it would have been abrogated until again called for by divine authority.

The scriptural term for light as manifested in the fourth day of creation was called *"meorah,"* and its exterior value is made evident by the planetary bodies.[5] It is the expression *Aur*, however, that will ultimately be the subject at hand, yet in *meorah* we may find what placates men's search for truth and knowledge since within nature's vast scheme can be detected traces of the most ancient form of light. Man's entire tenure in creative history has been coeval with a mixture of both light and darkness, without one or the other being completely absent or exclusive. *Meorah*, as a separation, depicts simply the difference between day and night, each of which is actually a condition of light, ruled by the "greater" and "lesser" lights respectively; and it should be noted that generally, authorized versions of the Holy Scriptures term it not "dark," but "darkness," signifying a non-absolute condition. Since humankind did not exist in absolute darkness, it must be figured that whether he will ever exist when there is nothing but light is the subject of prophecy and revelation. Yet, it is our present intention to explore how the primeval light, which would necessarily prevail over a condition void of darkness, was communicated to man, that he might become aware of its existence and seek ways to worship its precious and holy presence and preserve its unsullied integrity.

That light found itself in the midst of eternity poses also the aspect of time, as inferred by the expression *"In the beginning,"* and it must be reconciled.[6] Two philosophical problems may present themselves in a paradoxical relationship at such an attempt to reconcile. Firstly, a state of inauguration would necessarily preclude the possibility of the precedence of anything else. Secondly, if darkness is nothing but the absence of light, which is a common assumption, then prior to the manifestation of the latter, there must have been the former. The scriptures certainly support the existence of darkness before the presence of light, yet they do not address whether absolute darkness preceded any act of creation, only that a form of it was present at the initial and subsequent parts of creation.[7] A discounting of it before the divine action would be to assume that eternity perpetuates endlessly but is marked by a definite beginning, thus moving forward only and that God had not sent darkness into an abyss, but regularly devised it to co-exist with light in eternal alternation.

The reconciliation that supports our present endeavors has eternity consisting of the following three aspects: firstly, *absolute darkness*, or nothingness, what a Jewish mystical tradition has called the *Ain Sof*, and it is the eternal beginning; secondly, *time*, which is an admixture of darkness and light and the perfected creation itself; and thirdly, *absolute light*, which is the eternal ending or the dissolution of creation and the final consummation.[8] God, being "the Aged of the Aged," has presided over all of these conditions, whether consummated or yet to manifest. Humankind, in his present estate, however, is subject to that peculiar segment of eternity called time, when light and darkness are ever present; and his involvement in both of which may tend him either backward or forward in the eternal sequence.[9]

> *There are these two ways of light and darkness in passing from this world by which one either doth or doth not return again unto earth.*
> (Bhagavad Gita 8:26)

So it was stated under pen of Brahminical doctrine, which gave birth to dualism. That we must choose between good and evil is an ancient doctrine dating back to Mazdaism, and it stems from a belief that existence is co-governed by the principle of opposites in relative equipoise.[10] As counterparts, these opposites are considered forces of good and evil which find their authorities in principle deities and, respectively, in an hierarchy of angels and daemons. It is obscurely embedded in monotheistic doctrines that allude to the devil as a personified force to contend with or frustrate God the creator. Now, there is no intention here to engage in the contradistinctions between good and evil, notwithstanding the ample traditions that apply light and darkness as their respective symbols. This particular representation will be set aside, in favor of one that acknowledges both light and darkness as vehicles of good. The tradition that symbolizes light as knowledge and darkness as ignorance is nearly apposite, yet it is better to say that the former represents knowledge itself and the latter, the quest for the same. Thirst and satiation are neither evil nor good, but correlative aspects of human nature, affected by a law as inflexible as that which holds the stars in their courses.

Man must interpret the world in which he lives, if he is to realize God's investment in him, and his means to accomplish this is the acquisition of knowledge. In respect to what has been mentioned previously, the original light spoken of in Genesis refers not to the presence of physical light in the world; and it must be further conceptualized that the world itself is not merely a terrestrial situation. Un-tempered light is knowledge and insight into the mind of God. The earth is not only our footage but it contains the very dimensions that conduct us unto higher realms. Light is the primeval gift and it must be received in due course for, like the apple in the palm of a hand, it is truly intended for the worthy and not for the grasping by the unworthy.[11] No teacher would wisely transmit his entire spectrum of knowledge to his student at once, since this would overwhelm the student beyond effective assimilation. Under-nourishment and over-nourishment would lead alike unto a certain and premature death. Judeo-Christian history records instances of seizure and excess and the regret of men for their deeds, as these were allegorically portrayed in the expulsion from Eden, the inundation of the world and the wandering in the wilderness. Postlapsarian man is confined to a world of lights and shadows which, with proper gradations of accomplishment, may result in his seed being returned to the Holy Garden. But until he shall have accomplished his day, guardians are placed there with flaming swords to prevent it.[12]

That divine order is vindicated by the retribution that follows its disruption, was not only played out in man's fall from felicity after he ate of the Tree of Knowledge, for it has been recorded elsewhere in God's chancery. The *Apocalypse of St. John* or *Revelations* refers to the Wars that were in Heaven, in which the Archangel Michael defeated a rebellious host of angels who then fell after their defeat. The expulsion of the heavenly host must not be viewed as entirely a punitive concept. It was in part a reordering of the divine plan, a redistribution of entities that inhabited the cosmos, including the assignment of certain angels to earth, to protect man in his fallen state. The most antediluvian civilizations regarded reverently the luminosity of the stars and saw in them angels and deities. Four of them were believed to protect men from the four corners of the earth and their names were called *Aldebaran, Antares, Foralhaut* and *Regulus* who carefully imparted to men knowledge that exceeded that of which they had been naturally possessed.[13] The early Hebrews later replaced these Sumerian names, derived from a Persian pantheon, with the names of the Archangels *Raphael, Gabriel, Auriel* and *Michael.* Theological assertion in fact poses that originally Satan was thus assigned, not as an apostate angel, but appointed by God Himself as "the adversary" or rather "*ha-satan*."[14] The use of the term Satan as a proper name was a later development, introduced in the New Testament and referred to the enemy of God. Furthermore, an unfortunate misinterpretation of Prophet Isaiah has confused the star of the morning with a dragon expelled from heaven by the Michael.[15] Later scholarly efforts have shown that the haughtiness and rebellion referred to in Isaiah were in the context with the King of Babylon who claimed his equiponderance with God. That the devil acquired the name Lucifer is at the hands of early church fathers who initially made the erroneous comparison.[16] The name Lucifer has been so derogated, that its meaning has been transmuted, from the bearer of light to the bearer of darkness.

True monotheism would not be concerned with enemies of God, for His descendants never were and never can be His equals. Whatsoever is beneath Him is ordained of Him also. Lucifer and Satan respectively regulate the abundance of light and darkness. Whereas the former if the giver of light, he represents fluidity, limitlessness and excess; and whereas the latter is the taker-away of light, he represents rigidity, confinement and want. These entities under whose influence sins are often attributed are a result of one leaning or the other, an imbalanced perception of light and darkness. Initially, after the fall of man, his darkness was great, for even the forbidden fruit of which he had partaken transmuted into the amnesic effects of a stupefying agent after it had been consumed.[17]

Would humankind ever extirpate himself from the darkness of which the Qur'an speaks, darkness so thick that:

Were a man to stretch forth his hand he would not behold it, thus is he by whom the light of God hath not been seen. (Surah 24:40)

Let us suppose that the torpor in which humankind had found itself might be compared with the absolute darkness anterior to creation, a state in which everything was at pre-existence, awaiting only the will of the creator to set it in motion. Figuratively, the birth of the universe sprang out of the womb of absolute blackness. And so came forth man into a world of terrible dichotomies, devouring light and usurping darkness, a world of intense labor and suffering, without memory of the splendor he had prematurely seen, but seeing only glimpses of it in the stars of heaven against a blackened sky, unconsciously yearning to return to his home.

People in historical darkness have required awful revelations or divine and angelic epiphanies to awaken them out of their stupors. Kabbalistic tradition asserts that it was by this means that divine knowledge (which is pure light) was distributed among humanity, emanating from its ancient origin. Accordingly, divine light is said to have been passed on from Adam to Noah and from Noah unto Abraham. It is also said that it was as given unto Moses.[18] It will be the present assertion that, whereas the term Kabbalah means "to receive," the aforementioned lineage might not, in every instance, have been the recipient with conscious awareness.

Primitive men, represented by Adam and Eve received it in the forbidden fruit which they had consumed, but which in them had lain dormant. Yet each night as they glanced at the stars of heaven they might have received measured impulses from the mind of God as these would burn impressions upon their memories in the form an ignes-fatui of thoughts that made no immediate sense, but unconsciously cultivated their souls for perpetuity. Priests of all civilizations, who were their descendants, cultivated the art of the stars and built for themselves observatories and sanctuaries as an appeal to the cosmic entities which they saw in the luminaries. Some of these entities were believed to be among the angels expelled after the heavenly wars; and it is plausible that such as they might have exploited humans due to the fallen state of their species. Furthermore, we may find in these figures an explanation as to how the mysterious knowledge of God would have been transferred from Adam down to Noah.

"The will of God," as an expression constituting Wisdom and Understanding, perhaps denotes our most profound notion of the creator. It distinguishes us among other creatures with an especial affinity for, as the Elohim created man in their own image, there is inferred by this action a divine vestment in humanity. It is symbolized by the presence of light and shadows in the world, detectable to human discernment. It is their combination that makes discernment possible since form is equally invisible in the blinding light as well as in the groping darkness. Sacred history tells us that the light invested in humanity was not always at balance with proportionate darkness, and that entities identifying with one or the other sought to influence that particular condition of the human species by which it was determined men would make choices. Choice did not originally emanate from God since all creation was consequential to a single will. Yet the divine promulgation that forbade the eating of a certain fruit introduced the concept of choice, posterior to the first Sabbath and the completion of creation; for God said:

> But the tree of knowledge of good and evil, thou shalt not eat of it: for in the day thou eatest thereof thou shalt surely die. (Genesis 2:17)

The primal man and woman, having been thus admonished, necessarily perpetuated the concept by recognizing the adversarial actions which followed.

> In the day ye eat thereof, then your eyes shall be opened, and ye shall be as gods, knowing good and evil. (Genesis 3:4-5)

The subtle serpent, upon convincing Eve, initially, to eat of the fruit had prematurely opened the eyes of men. It subsequently established their virtues and proclivities. Courts and congresses, wars and empires are the result of it; for man has been the invariable servant of choice.

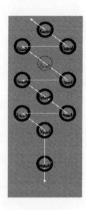

Divine intent crowns the Holy Tree of Life which implants in every existing thing the seed of life, bearing the attributes of God. It is called *Kaether* and, according to doctrine, differentiates into *Chochmah* and *Binah* or Wisdom and Understanding beneath itself, thus collectively forming an upward-pointing, "Supernal Triad." It was not intended that the latter two elements would recombine beneath themselves, forming a downward-pointing triad, but that they would continue to differentiate in deference to the conveyance of an unsullied primal will. Had it been otherwise, the combination would have resulted in Da-at or Knowledge, potentially interfering with the conveyance before completion of the creative glyph called "Otz Chaim" or the Tree of Life. Yet, scripture tells us that within the Holy Garden there were two trees, for it is written:

> *And out of the ground made the Lord God to grow every tree that is*
> *pleasant to the sight, and good for food; the tree of life also in the*
> *midst of the garden, and   the tree of the knowledge of good and*
> *evil.* (Genesis 2:9)

It was the latter that, by His decision, subjected man to a life of choice, outside the paradisiacal realm, a life in which both light and darkness would be comprehended together, but never apart from each other without divine intersession. The angelic detractors who hastened God's knowledge to men, that they might empower the apple within their bellies, in their very act, off-set the perfect balance which God had secretly vested in nature. Knowledge, so gifted sometimes produced dubious consequences, and pseudepigraphical writings tell us that Azazel and other rebellious angels co-habited

149

with the daughters of men and taught men the means of the sword, and caused great consternation and bloodshed upon the earth.[19] From this literary tradition was expounded the story of Henoch (Enoch) who scripture affirms was a "good and righteous man" who walked with God and who for his reward was transformed into an angel.[20]   Henoch had a vision, and from it we learn that God's light for man would have to be deferred, since He did not look propitiously of the human situation. It would occur, after generations and in proper time, at Mount Sinai and after the Nephilim, who were the off-springs of the unholy commerce, had been thoroughly extirpated from the earth.[21]

According to the Qur-an, we also learn that Azazel was rebuked by God for refusing an obeisance to Adam, and Islamic lore credits the fallen angel with the art of fire which he revealed to humanity (Surah 18).[22] It recalls the Hellenic myth of the gifting of fire unto man, to the chagrin of the gods, for which Prometheus had been bound for centuries. Light in the hands of the Nephilim was light beaming out-of-control, like a fire without containment, not tempered with shadows so necessary to mortals in the realm of time. Preceded by implorations from the four Archangels, God would respond, but indeed with vengence and terror, for what but water could extinguish fire in the hands of arsons and amateurs. Anticipating the wrath of God, Noah built his ark, since favored by God for his righteous ways, the patriarch and two of every species would be spared from the coming deluge that would purge the world of its depravities.

The full force of God's will was prosecuted by the turbulence and inundation. The world known to Noah had been washed away and life outside the vessel, by all appearance, had perished utterly. Yet, after the flood had taken its course, Noah seemed to look for a sign from the god of his faith, and this was evidently delivered in the form of a dove and olive branch. Generally, these emblems, the dove and olive branch, are understood to signify a covenant between God and man that no more evil or retribution would follow. Yet, if we accepted this literally, we would incline to the notion that God is a breaker of covenants, for indeed there were instances in which His subsequent anger resulted in such consternating events as the confounding of languages, forty years of misery in the wilderness and the destruction of the temple. Surely the emblems must signify something more discrete.

It may be recalled that, after the flood had abated, Noah sent out both a raven and a dove from the ark. Only the dove returned, and it did so with an olive branch between its beaks (Genesis 8:6-12). The failure of the raven to return may signify the end of eternity when absolute light might at last be perceived by an evolved humanity, when time, requiring both light and darkness, would be no more. It may also typify an omen for man's return to the lofty garden of his former estate, to resume what God had originally ordained, for in the garden, the Tree of Life was an host to doves and the Tree of Knowledge of Good and Evil, to ravens.[23] Furthermore, the dove is typically a messenger and represents the spirit of light. In this wise it may presage the light from God when it quits it flight and perches before the eyes of men. The olive branch signifies in a temporal sense, life and longevity and in a spiritual, light and eternity, for while the olive tree can live for centuries, it seems to transcend time, and while the oil it yields can fuel the lanterns, its flame is seemingly eternal[24] and thus it would burn in the heart of Noah.

If the flood had not thoroughly wiped out a population, it had at least accomplished dispersing it. That people spoke and believed differently was represented allegorically, if not historically, in the story the Tower of Babel and the confounding of human tongues. Most the world worshiped a variety of gods, usually associated with natural forces or phenomena. Gods did not typically interact with humanity and the towering appearance of ziggurats and pyramids used to pay homage to them suggested their remoteness. Yet some of the people evidently began concentrating their worship on particular gods, paving the way for eventual monotheistic practices. It is thought that Abraham's beliefs derived from a Caananitish pantheon headed by the Sky-god, El.[25] In that setting, however, the sky-god was not prone to condescend. If divine action was required on earth, lesser gods were usually sent on his behalf; and in such instances, interaction was with other deities, rather than with men. If the god of Abraham had descended from the sky-god, then the transition of understanding would have been from a god in his most remote aspects to a god of the people.[26]

The calling of Abraham depicts such a god, for in anthro-pomorphic form, between two angels, God appeared before the patriarch (Genesis 18:1-8). His mission was two-fold: to carry out the purging of an unholy remnant that perhaps the flood had not efficaciously accomplished, and to bear a message unto Abraham whom He had chosen to be the progenitor of a blessed nation. It was the third of four epiphanies before Abraham; and there can be observed in its arrangement a hint toward the classical notion of divine appearance.[27] The future Ark of the Covenant would depict God at the mercy seat betwixt two angels which Kabbalistic tradition calls "God in exile," and it marked a new concept in the relationship between God and man. It is not merely that doves were sent from the Holy Tree of Life, but, indeed, that God Himself had condescended. At first, Abraham did not recognize the significance but looked upon the occurrence as three travelers whom he would greet and treat with the fairest amenities. It was in this correspondence that God revealed Himself to his chosen one and proclaimed His name *"El Shaddai,"* meaning God Almighty, or God of the Mountain.[28] The message that God had communed, with its accompanying instructions, eventually came into fruition, and the future Israel had been born. Within the bosom of Abraham would be the Light of God.

All were harbingers of what might come. Still, darkness would cover the earth and gross darkness, the people. In contrast to the luciferous excesses that might have prompted the flood, the toppling of the Babylonian edifice and the destruction of Sodom and Gomorra, now the effects of Satan weighed heavily upon the people when they could at best see only the faintest traces of light through their melancholic dispositions. Pestilence and ignorance, famine and abject conditions would continue to plague humanity. Spiritually, the people were truly inert. When would the Light of God, as related in the vision of Henoch, visit Mount Sinai? After years of enslavement of his people in Egypt we learn that Moshe (Moses) led his flock to the backside of the desert and came to the mountain of God, even unto Horeb, for it has been written:

> *And the angel of the Lord appeared unto him in a flame of fire out of the midst of a bush: and he looked, and, behold, the bush burned with fire, and the bush was not consumed.* (Exodus 3:2)

Moses questioned what he had seen, for what he beheld was quite beyond what the ordinary senses would have dictated to human consciousness. Here he was temporarily displaced from the outer world of awareness into an interior state in which what he saw was akin to the Tree of Knowledge with its light bearing fruit. This flame would burn eternally and would require no fuel; and Moses was worthily the recipient of such an extraordinary gift from God. The expulsion of their primitive parents from Eden had taught men the consequences of defiance and indifference, yet even still God had reinforced the idea of proper preparation when he admonished Moses to put off his shoes from off his feet, for the ground on which he stood was holy. The future law giver had seen a fragment of the light that would rescue his people from the darkness of bondage. The tireless flames were evidence of a covenant and it would require leadership thus to emancipate the people, for they themselves had not seen the burning bush. Indeed, theirs was a darkness that could not comprehend the light. They would understand drought, pestilence and separation. They would undergo an initiation of wandering forty years in the wilderness before the eyes of their anointed ones would unseal before the light of God. Like the original parents who had been separated from the land of splendor, the followers of Moses remained ignorant of the light, yet were linked to a dormant form of it by what they had ingested during their lengthy sojourn. Regarding the former activity in Eden, it is conceivable that God understood human weakness when He proscribed the eating of the designated apple and perhaps even anticipated the subsequent transgression.

Although the expulsion was without doubt, the separation was not so thorough as would prohibit an eventual return of man to the garden, for a link had been sealed; and within the veins of Adam and Eve, flowed blood that had been nourished by fruit from the supernal place. The children of Israel were weary from an exhausting peregrination of forty years in the wilderness, far from the holy place at the nucleus of creation. Yet, to perpetuate the linkage with Eden, something descended from that realm into the land of barren desert below, like apples falling from a tree. The children had discovered the mysterious *manna*, the radiant food of angels, upon the ground and partook thereof.[29] Theories abound over the origin and composition of this miraculous food that sustained them, yet its identity has never been confirmed. Their contact with it was serendipitous and there was no proscription against its consumption. It would remain entirely symbolical, however, since in thus, the filling of their hungry bellies with a satiating fruit, there lay hidden within them, that which might fuel the kindling of a future age.[30]

Until such a time that the common people would evolve to achieve greater epiphany, they relied on the strengths of the few who were more perceptive than they. To that end the priesthood had also evolved. Theretofore, it was a role naturally attributed to the father, the head of an household or community, in which the priest would offer leadership and blessings, moral guidance or pay homage. By the time of Moses, no doubt influenced by his vision of the burning bush and by his association with Egyptian nobility and priestly customs, it became the vehicle to interpret the will of God. The Hebrew term for priest, *"kohen,"* became essential. It has no traceable etymology, yet, when paralleled with an Arabic root it reveals the meaning "to draw neigh," for such as the priest only could approach the divine.[31] Since the common people were incapable of discerning anything other than ordinary light, the priests had to be invested with the attributes of wisdom, understanding, knowledge and truth, of which the light they might see was symbolical; and to formalize their standing, Moses, by divine command, erected a tabernacle in which Aaron and his seed would form a lasting priesthood. As the High Priest, Aaron and his successors engaged the *Aurim* and *Thummim,* which were certain stones mounted to the breastplate of the ranking priest and in thus, the manipulating of the two stones, and possibly a third which had no name, the ancient officiators began the oracular tradition of sacerdotal Judaism. Specifically, the appellations of the stones referred to "the lights" and "the perfections," respectively. Collectively, they equated light with truth, which would suggest that the phenomenon of light had greater meanings in the things it symbolized than in its own physical nature.

The ancient Aryans equated light with wisdom and paid homage to it in the form of fire. Other cults would see in it symbols of purification and consecration.[32] The more it became associated with worship, the more guarded it became and greater was the sanctimony. The first, second, and third tabernacles of nomadic Israel became progressively associated with exhausting and stringent rituals, in hopes that the light of God would once again be seen by mortals who had earned it. Once Israel had become settled, however, and the people feared God, temples replaced the tabernacles, and the Holy of Holies within them, were duly consecrated as receptacles for divine presence. Solomon had spent more than seven years in the construction of the first temple and it was built with such perfection and richness that surely God would descend into His earthly habitat and proclaim His presence and approval from the Seat of Mercy. Yet, no man would behold His Countenance, save him who had been properly prepared, save him only who would approach from the outer world into the court of the tabernacle or temple, where he would purify himself at the Lavre of Water and make sacrifices at the burnt altar of offering. This they did before even the highest priest could hope to enter the Sanctum Sanctorum; for woe unto the man would look upon the face of God who had not been thus prepared; for in the day when the work on the temple was completed, and all Israel had congregated for its consecration, it was said of them who had gathered:

> *And the priests could not enter the house of the LORD, because the glory of the LORD had filled the LORD'S house. When all the children of Israel saw how the fire came down, and the glory of the LORD on the temple, they bowed their faces to the ground on the pavement, and worshiped and praised the LORD, saying: "For He is good, for His mercy endures forever."* (2 Chronicles 7:2-3)

It can be assumed that those present at the consecration had indeed seen the light; and it must have instilled their minds with a concept of God's mercy and goodness and that He would truly dwell among them. Israel was a pragmatic people, and faith, which was a remarkable feature in their religious setting, was developed upon the knowledge that God had done something on behalf of His children.[33] The promise to Abraham that he would father a great nation under extraordinary circumstances and the commitment to Moses that his people would be freed having both been consummated, are examples to explain the pragmatism. This particular identity was further sealed by the arduous work that the children had performed on behalf of their God, resulting in His approval of their accomplishment. All humanity longed for light, yet arduous was the quest for it, as the lives of the patriarchs have already attested. Many would hear the call, but few would be chosen. *"Procul, O Procul, Este Profani,"*[34] "for come not nigh, if ye are not worthy," uttered the Hierophants who presided over the mysteries of the ancient world. Some traditions would claim these promulgations to be as archaic as the submersion of Atlantis and that they were heard long before Israel had named her tribes. The ritualistic fabric of both the priesthood and the initiatory schools gave them something in common, and it is likely that one evolved out of the other. The distinction that is to be considered between them, however, is primarily the object of their rituals, and to a lesser degree, the nature of them. The priesthood, once it became formalized, was the representation of God (or gods) to the commons. In this wise, it was the vehicle to bring God and all influential concepts of God to worshipers of a congregation. Never was a worshiper exalted higher than the priest whose work, although revered, was perfunctory in nature. The schools, by contrast served as means to bring the laity at one with God. It accomplished this by allegory, in which the individual was symbolically endowed with the attributes of an hero, blessed by God. Officiators subordinated themselves to the ultimate objective of transforming the individual into all aspects of an heroic life. So far as they were worthy, they were called to the test. Those who were fortunate enough to be considered were subjected to the most terrifying feats and horripilating adventures, ere they could prove their worth. No less than a convincingly simulated death would open the eyes of Epoptae to the mysterious light that was so carefully entrusted. They secreted themselves beyond detection and they were utterly exclusive.[35] The rites heralded by these primitive calls influenced the Egyptian and Greek schools of initiation. They handed down to us the mystery tradition of death and rebirth, light growing out darkness, the resurrection of life, and the seed and flower of return. The profundity of their doctrine and the secrecy they maintained must have influenced developments in the Judeo-Christian world as the securely situated priest-craft had illustrated. But as God's munificence became more widely appreciated it was believed that His luminous gift would be withheld from none of His likeness, for if He truly loved all and would disinherit none of His children, His Countenance would then shine. Would not, after all, the divine Shekhinah who suffered Herself to descend into the dark realms of earth embrace all? Would not She tender unto them, touch their eyes and smile upon them opened? Would not She visit them remotely from Her Mercy Seat, whithersoever dispersed might be the lost among them? [36]

Far across the desert, by the strains of a river's current, was heard the voice of an Essenian preacher crying:

"…in the wilderness, Prepare ye the way of the Lord." (Mark 1:2) [37]

It is not known whether the Baptist had yet seen a manifestation of light, but he believed in its imminent arrival; and thousands flocked unto him in anticipation of what they must do to prepare for it. He purified with water but spoke of another after him who would consecrate by fire, who would manifest in his mission the Light of the World!

It is written:

> *Whosoever Exalteth Himself Shall Be Abased; and He That Humbleth Himself Shall Be Exalted.* (Matthew 23:12)

Behold the remnant had been opened! The poor and the lowly hearted could at last see the light of God if they would but open their eyes, for the King of Glory had humbled Himself before men. At the feet of the Baptist knelt the Son of Man to accept purification by submersion, at which the former knew that his mission was about to be accomplished and that thus a new one would begin; and as the latter departed from the waters of the Jordan and set straightway upon his journey of initiation, it was said of him:

> *I saw the Spirit descending from heaven like a dove, and it abode upon him.* (John 1:32)

Wherefore, another glimpse had occasioned itself. The light of God in the form of the dove that had visited Noah returned again to earth to bless generations, the high and the low, the rich and the poor, the respected and the rejected, for His Light would not be occluded but would permeate the hearts of men.

> *In him was life; and the life was the light of men. And the light shineth in the darkness; and the darkness comprehended it not.* (John 1: 4-5)

Once entered into the heart it could not be extinguished, for therein lie the remnants of the original light, passed down through the ages by divine right; the Aur of God which existed before the stars and to which no opened eyelid would ever again close.

"Blessed are the pure in heart: for they shall see God."
(Matthew 5: 8)

Alas, the Judeo-Christian world had received the rite of passage, the roots of which were paralleled in the Greek and Egyptian schools, as portrayed in the Eleusinian mysteries and the Book of the Dead. The cult of Osiris had established a belief in death and rebirth, and the mission and resurrection of our Lord would transfer that belief to the non-pagan world. Indeed the torch by which the earlier teachings were lighted; by which the subjects of Plato's cave might have emerged enlightened and not darkened, would be carried under a new standard, under the shadow of the Almighty with the Christian dispensation.

The trials and tribulations that characterized the epic lives of patriarchs, martyrs and prophets marked the origin of initiation. Indeed, humiliation truly is the indicator of exaltation. As the Nazarene preacher left the baptismal waters of the desert, he ascended the slopes where he would encounter the dazzling effects of the tempter who would sway him into actions against his will. Regardless of the denomination quoted by scripture suggesting it was Satan who thus tempted him, it is more likely that the encounter was between Lucifer and Christ. Although the emulation of the forty years wandering of the children of Israel by forty days fasting by Christ must have been innervating, it was an initiatory process that was motivationally driven by the fear of God and His commandments in the one case and the love of God in the other. Christ was purified in the chilly waters of the river and consecrated under the scorching heat of the sun. The body might have suffered exhaustion, yet the spirit was robust! The mission had just begun and presently there was an attempt to manipulate the will and incite it into diversion. This could hardly be viewed as the inertia that Satan would have exploited. That attempt would be reserved to the final stage of tribulation when Christ on the cross quoth: *"Eli, Eli, lama sabachthani?"* meaning, "My God, My God, why hast Thou forsaken Me?"[38]

Both the events instigating temptation and doubt were clearly aborted, however, by an unshakable faith in God and retention of the irreversible light, for it came to pass that the mission was fulfilled and that life held victory over death.

Now we see in the stars what were seen by our primal parents, luminous fragments of the divine, but against a blackened sky, reminding us that we are but mortals working in the center of eternity. As such, we encounter struggles and dichotomies as consistent patterns of living and, according to our dispositions treat them either as challenges or modes of depression. Upon them we erect creeds and philosophies that will either prop us up or cast us down. The checkered designs with which we pave our temple floors teach us how arduous are the tasks of assimilating the lights and shadows of our souls, of arriving at that light which has no contour and needs no contrast, of intuiting our way to the mind of God. When we have leaned overly one way or the other and have found ourselves either divorced from or embroiled in our environment, we have given up hope for what lies beyond us, because we have set aside the tools of discovery. If our negligence has been in favor of the material, then we are only temporarily satiated, routinely grasping for more than we have previous acquired. If our departure has been too ascetic, then we have voided the secrets that the physical world can yield to us. From our earth we draw forth materials with which to build cities and civilizations. These may or may not include temples as conduits for the light of God to make them thrive perpetually, or to decay with the sands of time. It is not necessarily true that most men live lives of quiet desperation since most know not what they lack.[39] Most humans are too preoccupied with the small things in life to be turning their eyes toward the skies, thus losing sight of where they fit in the eternal plan. They see not the great secrets hidden in nature, and tread ignorantly over the manna which covers their paths. They observe the great luminary setting and rising, but know not the immortality it signifies. The loftier skies are dark and cloudy unto them and their eyes incline no higher than the horizons. They behold the radiant lilies of the field, but consider not the seed of life that gives them effortless glory. The deeper earth is dank and sable unto them and they penetrate no further that the surface.

As descendants of the mystery schools, our assiduity would be purification, receptivity for the wonderful works of God, concealed within nature, awaiting the birth of discovery. As inheritors of luminous blood, latent within our veins, our endeavors must be to make the blood reach our hearts, to revive them from their inertia, to clear the portals to the temple. That we shall bring the *Aur* of God, as seen in the heavens, into our beings, means that we shall pass the trials and afflictions and discover the holy radiant angels within us. Yet, as human beings under a common parent, our duties never end with ourselves. Much consternation exists in the world and the great mystery of light and darkness is not understood. What will bring our fellow beings out of their spiritual inertia would be the leadership of those who have prayed, and have seen signs as a result of their supplications; who have read the characters of light and life, seen in the skies above them and in the pages of nature around them, traced by the very finger of God. As inheritors, ours is the inspiration to lead, to "lead the blind by a way they know not, to lead them in paths that they have not known, to make darkness light before them and crooked things straight. These things we shall to do unto them and not forsake them".[40] In the manner of those faithful ones of God, who courageously carried out their mission of light and life, and who supplicated with atonement before Him, let it be so with us!

"Hail, Holy Light!"[41] Perfected and unchanged, Thou were born of a single thought. Radiant and unsullied, Thou didst dispel the clouds of doubt and didst draw aside the sable curtain of obscurity. Unseal Thy children's eyes; that we may look upon Thy beautiful feet; that we may be purified by Thy radiance and sustain us in our earthly endeavors! Oh Light of God, which did visit our fathers Noah, Abraham and Moses, which appeared unto Ezekiel in the heavens as a chariot of splendor, and at the pinnacle of the ladder before Jacob in his dream, and in the dream states of Sarah and Miriam. Thou who didst hover over the Holy City and beam Thy light into the cradle of a manger, who didst minister unto hungry and oppressed everywhere, and Who didst cast asunder the seal of a tomb and resuscitate all mourners from their darkness; send forth a single ray of Thy holy essence, that it may reach even unto us! Expand our hearts which we offer as vessels to receive more abundantly the fiery waters with which to fill our veins. Make us initiators of hearts and make us whole! Harken our ears unto the voices of Thine angels who breathe forth Thy will; and incline our eyes unto the beacons of Thy messengers. May we bask in the scintillating effects of Thy glory and wash away the tears of pallidness. If we have passed the trials and tribulations of life and are found worthy, lift us upon Thy radiant wings unto Thine heavenly abode, where time shall end and all else be consumed and become infinite and holy. Notwithstanding our present duties here below, tender unto us the mercy to which Thine ancient light hath aspired. With it, may we disentomb Thy forgotten teachings and heal the sick among us. With it may error be no more and prejudice and superstition cease! With it may truth prevail! And now, O Radiant One, between this our present bidding and the day of our final supplication, let there be peace between us; and though our earthy lights may evanesce, yet Thy Holy Light shall never fail.

NOTES

[1] "The face of the deep" is interpreted to mean the face of chaos; and darkness upon which was dispelled by light, a generative principle resulting in order. Unger, Merrill F.: Unger's Bible Dictionary; Chicago, Moody Press; C1957, 1961, 1966 by The Moody Bible Institute Of Chicago; P241.

[2] "*Aur*"; AUR (א ו ר): Gen 1:3

[3] *Mana* is a term presumed to be of Melanesian or Polynesian origin. Some lexicons apparently narrow its meaning to "power of the elemental forces of nature embodied in an object or person" [i.e. Merriam-Webster; Webster's ninth new collegiate dictionary; Springfield, c1991], yet original sources refer to "supernatural" powers thus invested [i.e. Webster's unabridged dictionary; New York, Random House Reference, c2001 and Oxford English Dictionary, 2d ed., Oxford, Clarendon Pr. 1989]. The above definitions infer magical ideas which may have been prevalent in pagan culture. Karen Armstrong has related that the spirits of Marduk and Baal were experienced through ritual and myth [See: Armstrong, Karen, A history of God, New York, Alfred A Knopf, Inc., 1993, p13]. Such thinking appeared in early Judaism when the sacrificing of the eldest son was made to appease the God [Armstrong, Karen, Opt. Cit. p18]. Yet the term has been applied to later development in biblical culture, in which case it is seen as a spiritual force that less theurgical and arises directly from deity such as in the events of Abrahams first epiphany and Jacob's confrontation with the angel [Armstrong, Karen, Opt. Cit. p16, 17].

[4] Exodus 16:14 renders: "And when the dew that lay was gone up, behold, upon the face of the wilderness there lay a small round thing, as small as the hoar frost on the ground." The similarity between *mana* as presented above and *manna* as associated with a miraculous food from heaven is striking, although no parallel etymology has been seen. A Hebrew translation of the word *manna* is exclamatory "What is this ('Man-hu')?" or perhaps it was the result of an early encounter with an exclusively Egyptian food called *mannu*.

5 *"Meorah"*; MAUR (מ ו א ר): Gen 1:16

6 Time is viewed in this reference as following the Leibnizian position, that is time is viewed as the succession of events. Since the present writing deals with the succession of light as it has been transmitted and transformed in an historical and spiritual sequence, its relationship exclusive of events is out of scope. For a correlation between this view and Kant's view that the world would have had a previous beginning, consult Bochert, Donald M.; Encyclopedia of Philosophy (2nd ed.); Detroit, Macmillan Reference USA, c2006; v9, p467.

7 Kant presented two antithetical arguments in which infinity is incompatible with beginning and end, as might be illustrated in numerical sequences: 0, 1, 2…and -2, -1, 0. In one argument he postulated that if the world had begun at a certain time, the all previous time would have been a "blank" [void], constituting no reason that the world should have begun at the time it did rather than at some other time. Conceivably, the original darkness as described in the present writing could be equated with the Kantian "blank." See: Bochert, Donald M.; Encyclopedia of Philosophy (2nd ed.); Detroit, Macmillan Reference USA, c2006; v9, p467.

8 Kabbalistic doctrine is a product of Mediaeval Jewish mysticism that attempting to explain the nature of man, God, and the universe. It addresses ontological questions and theorizes Creation. Although it is not itself a religion, it often accompanies Jewish thought and heavily reflects the Jewish cannon. It parallels many Neo-platonic ideas and has influence modern philosophers such as Leibniz. *Ain Sof* is a term used by kabbalists to express God in His pre-manifested state. Its components are *Ain*, meaning "nothing" and *Sof*, meaning "limitation," hence, limitlessness. It is the condition that gave birth to Aur Ain Sof, or limitless light (to wit, the addition of the component *Aur*, meaning "light").

9 The expression *"The Aged of the Aged"* is a Kabbalistic appellation for *Ain Sof* or the pre-manifested state of creation. For this and several other appellations, consult Ginsburg, Christian D, LL.D.; The Essenses, Their History and Doctrines; The Kabbalah, Its Doctrines, Development

and Literature; London, Routledge & Kegan Paul LTD, 1955; p89.

[10] Brahminical doctrine, of which Mazdaism is a derivative, teaches the continual struggle between good and evil forces, ever tempting humankind to follow one force or the other. Mazdaism, or Zoroastrianism, was the result of a reformation of the old Persian religion in which many of the old gods were reduced to spirit beings serving one of the other of the forces. "The old Persian religion was like that of the Aryan Indians, as seen in the Rig Veda, and much of this reappeared after Zoroaster, whe the old gods became different classes of spiritual beings" [Parrinder, E. Geoffrey; A Dictionary of Non-Christian Religions; Philadelphia, The Westminster Pr., 1971; p 316]. Brahminical doctrine also speaks to a psychological dualism, thusly: "The Hindu god-creator is a personification of the dual tendency that inhabits all living things, everywhere. A timorous shrinking from possible dissolution, with, at the same time, the valiant impulse to increase, to multiply indefinitely and thus become a complete universe through progeny, are the two complementary aspects of the one fundamental impulse to keep going on and on." [Zimmer, Heinrich; Philosophies of India; ed. By Joseph Campbell, Bollingen Series XXVI; New York, Pantheon Books, Inc., 1951; p. 300-1]

[11] This is a reference to the traditional story, shared among teachers of Kabbalah, of the student being offered an apple by his mentor. Thrice, he tries to take the apple, but his fellow students beckon him against it until, at last the student realizes he must cup his hands in order to "receive" the apple.

[12] Taken from Genesis 3:22-24: [22]And the LORD God said, Behold, the man is become as one of us, to know good and evil: and now, lest he put forth his hand, and take also of the tree of life, and eat, and live for ever: [23]Therefore the LORD God sent him forth from the garden of Eden, to till the ground from whence he was taken. [24]So he drove out the man; and he placed at the east of the garden of Eden Cherubims, and a flaming sword which turned every way, to keep the way of the tree of life. [KJV]

[^13] *Aldebaran* is a double star in the constellation Taurus, 68 light-years from Earth, and one of the brightest stars in the sky; *Antares* is a giant red, binary star, the brightest in the constellation Scorpio, about 424 light-years from Earth; *Fomalhaut* is the brightest star in the constellation Piscis Austrinus, 24 light-years from Earth; and *Regulus* is a bright double star in the constellation Leo [from American Heritage Dictionary]. In their original Persian nomenclatures, *Aldebaran, Antares, Foralhaut* and *Regulus* were known as *Tascheter* (in connexion with the vernal equinox), *Satevis* (in connexion with the autumnal equinox), *Haftorang* (in connexion with the winter solstice) and *Venant* (in connexion with the summer solstice) respectively. "The process begun in Daniel, and continued in the entire apocalyptic literature, finally led to the assumption of a heavenly hierarchy of stupendous proportions.

The mystic lore, intended only for the initiated few, dwelt on the prophetic theophanies (Ma'aseh Merkabah, "the heavenly throne chariot," Ezek. i.-iii., viii., x.; Isa. vi. 1-3; see □ag. ii. 7); turning the imagery of the seer into gross realities, and greatly amplifying it in accordance with an expanded view of the universe and of its cosmic forces. Yet this angelic lore, the knowledge of which was the special property of the Essenes or □asidim (Josephus, "B. J." ii. 8, § 7), while the Sadducees rejected it (Acts, xxiii. 8), was not merely a theoretical speculation, but was also practical in so far as it enabled its possessor to control the spiritual forces by use of the specific names of the angels in incantations and conjurations. It was the application of this principle, derived from the Babylonian magi and Mazdaism, that brought about a well-developed system of Angelology such as is found already in the writings preserved under the name of Enoch. The strange story of the "sons of God" (in Gen. vi. 1-4), which, combined with Isa. xiv. 12-15, gave rise to the story of the fall of the angels, offered the means of establishing a relationship between the good and the bad angels and, through that, between legitimate and illegitimate magic. These two ideas then—the celestial throne with its ministering angels, and the cosmos with its evil forces to be subdued by superior angelic forces—are the determining factors of Angelology. According to Enoch, xxi., as the text has now been critically fixed (see Charles, "Book of Enoch," p. 357), there are seven archangels ('irin we-□addishin, "holy ones who watch"): (1) Uriel ["God is Light"; compare II Esd. iv. 1], set over the world's luminaries and over Sheol [compare Enoch, xxi. 5, xxvii. 2, xxxiii. 3, 4]; (2) Raphael, set over the spirits of men [compare Enoch, x. 4, where he is told to bind Azazel and to heal the earth with Tobit—iii. 17]; (3) Raguel [Ra'uel, "the terrifier"], who chastiseth the world of the luminaries; (4) Michael, set over the best part of mankind, over the people of Israel; (5) Sariel [Æth., Sarakiel, Suriel, "God turneth"?], set over the spirits who seduce the spirits to sin; (6) Gabriel, set over paradise, the serpents [seraphim?], and the cherubim; (7) Jerahmeel ["God is merciful"], whom God set over the resurrection [compare II Esd. iv. 36; Syriac Apoc. Baruch, lv. 3; Steindorf, "Elias Apoc." p. 152]. Whether corresponding with the seven amshaspands of Persia or with the seven planetary spirits of Babylonia (see Herzfeld, Kohut, and Beer in Kautzsch's "Apokryphen u. Pseudepig. d. A. T." p. 251), these seven archangels recur in Enoch, xc. 21-22 (compare Pir□e R. El. iv. and Hekalot, iv.; the Revelation of John, v. 6, and Hermas Sim. ix. 31; 6, 2; Vis. iii. 4, 1; see Spitta, "Zur Gesch. u. Lit. d. Urchristenthums," ii. 361). Michael, named as the fourth, is probably meant to stand in the middle as chief (Luecken, "Michael," p. 37). He is the leader of the seven (Enoch, xc. 21, 22)." [From Jewish encyclopedia, 1906—Angelology]. "With this arrangement, it is reasonable to figure angelic beings in the place of former deities who might have occupied the Ziggurats of another culture. It has to remain unsettled, regardless of how plausible it may seem, whether this aspect of angelic lore has descended from a previous mythology or whether it has emerged in its own right but with notable parallels." [Hamer, Merrick Rees; The Watchtowers]

[14] Davidson, Gustav: Dictionary of Angeles, A, including the fallen angels. New York, The Free Press; c1967; p261

[15] Isa. 14:12; Rev. 12:7-12

16 Eusebius Sophronius Hieronymus, commonly known as Saint Jerome, was the chief architect in the composition of the Romish Vulgate. His translation was taken from Hebrew in which the reference was rendered "Helel" (meaning "Shining One"), rather than from the Greek Septuagint in which case the reference was rendered "Heosphoros" (meaning "Dawn-bringer" or the morning star). Latin for the "Shining One" would clearly be rendered as "Lucifer," and thus the confusion is explained [Davidson, Gustav: Dictionary of Angeles, A, including the fallen angels. New York, The Free Press; c1967; see: "Lucifer"]. Although scholarly trends seem to favour the original attribution as a reference to a haughty king of Babylon, evangelical trends seem to hold fast to a double metaphorical meaning which includes both the ancient king and the fallen angel. [Archer, Gleason L.; Encyclopedia of Bible Difficulties; Grand Rapids, Zondervan Publishing House, 1982; p. 268]

17 Manly P. Hall had aptly stated the idea thus: "If Satan were to go out of the scheme, man would be burned up by the fiery passions of Mars and the angels of Lucifer. Without the chill, caution, and curbing of Saturn, his soul would speedily be lost in utter debauchery and licentiousness. If on the other hand, Lucifer should withdraw, man would soon be a stone again, incapable of incentive, of motion or emotion, and chained, like the sufferers of Dante's Inferno, by the icy fingers of death." [Hall, Manly Palmer; Magic: A Treatise on Esoteric Ethics, Los Angeles, Philosophical Research Society, 1978].

18 Ginsburg, Christian D, LL.D. [Opt. cit., p84]

19 It has been put in this wise in the Book of Enoch: "And Azazel taught men to make swords, and daggers, and shields, and breastplates. And he showed them the things after these, and the art of making them; bracelets, and ornaments, and the art of making up the eyes, and of beautifying the eyelids, and the most precious stones, and all kinds of coloured dyes. And the world was changed" (8.1); and further in this wise: "And there was great impiety, and much fornication, and they went astray, and all their ways became corrupt. (8.2) [McCracken, Andy; The Book of Enoch, A Modern English Translation of the Ethiopian Book of Enoch; Tr. By by M.

Knibb; S.O.A.S. Library at the University of London., Ch 3, Rebels Among the Watchers, p 16]

[20] The patriarch Enoch, on his translation to Heaven (Genesis 5:24), became Metatron, one of the greatest of the hierarchs, "king over all the angels." [Davidson, Gustav: Dictionary of Angeles, A, including the fallen angels. New York, The Free Press; c1967; p106]

[21] The visions of Enoch are two, with the first giving weight to the world depravities and the extirpation of evil (the Deluge), Chapters LXXXIII-LXXXIV, and the latter, having to do with the History of the World to the Founding of the Messianic Kingdom, Chapters LXXXV-XC. [McCracken, Andy; The Book of Enoch, A Modern English Translation of the Ethiopian Book of Enoch; Tr. By by M. Knibb; S.O.A.S. Library at the University of London., Ch 3, Rebels Among the Watchers, p 16]

[22] The Qur'an: Surah 18:50 states it thus: "Behold! We said To the angels, 'Bow down To Adam": they bowed down Except Iblis. He was one of the Jinns, and he Broke the Command of his Lord...[The Holy Qur'an; Tr. A. Yusuf Ali; US, American Trust Publications, 1977; p744].

[23] Cooper, J. C. (Jean C.): Illustrated Encyclopaedia of Traditional Symbols, An; New York, Thames and Hudson, 1987; c1978 By Thames And Hudson, Ltd, London.; p54, 137

[24] Gibson, Clare: Signs And Symbols, An Illustrated Guide To Their Meaning and Origins; New York, Barnes and Noble, 1996; C1996 Saraband Inc.; p118

[25] "...it is highly likely that Abrahams God was El, the High God of Caanan [Armstrong, Karen, Opt. Cit. p14].

[26] Abraham (originally Abram) may have been a tribal name denoting "God on High."   Later, when the individual member of the tribe became progenitor of a people and h was added and, when vocalized, implied an additional vowel. Thence, the name acquired an associated meaning of "father of the faithful and fried of God". [Gehman, Henry Snyder; The New Westminster dictionary of the Bible; Philadelphia, the Westminster Pr., 1970; P8].

[27] Epiphanies can be described as Theophanies if they constitute visible appearances of God before the eyes of men. Abrahamn had four communications which are generally regarded as divine in nature: firstly, Gen. 12:7, the Calling, which states: "And the LORD appeared unto Abram, and said, Unto thy seed will I give this land: and there builded he an altar unto the LORD, who appeared unto him."; secondly, Gen14:10, the Blessing, which states: "Also, Melchizedek king of Salem (Jerusalem), a priest of God Most High, brought out bread and wine and blessed Abram and God. Abram then gave Melchizedek a tenth of everything."; thirdly, Gen. 17:1, the Covenant, which states: "And when Abram was ninety years old and nine, the LORD appeared to Abram, and said unto him, I am the Almighty God; walk before me, and be thou perfect."; and fourthly, Gen. 18:1, the Revelation, which states: "And the LORD appeared unto him in the plains of Mamre: and he sat in the tent door in the heat of the day." Some theorist stray from the view that belief that the Blessing of Abraham by Melchizedek were divine and not humanly ordained, yet it is in this case regarded as epiphanic. The Zohar (redacted by Moses de León c.1290s) finds in "Melchizedek king of Salem" a reference to "the King Who rules with complete sovereignty," or according to another explanation, that "Melchizedek" alludes to the lower world and "king of Salem" to the upper world (Zohar 1:86b-87a). The Zohar's commentary on Genesis 14 cites a Rabbi Yitzchak as saying that it was God who gave tithe to Abram in the form of removing the Hebrew letter He from his throne of glory and presenting it to the soul of Abram for his benefit.[citation needed] The letter he is the letter God added to Abram's name to become "Abra-ha-m" in Genesis.

[28] "El Shaddai": Gen. 17:1. One of the traditional titles applied to the Caananitish most high god [Armstrong, Karen, Opt. Cit. p14].

[29] "Manna", a miraculous food, regarded as unnatural and gifted directly from God, mentioned in the following scripture: Exod. 16:14-36; Num. 11: 7-9; Deut. 8:3, 16; Josh. 5:12; Psa. 78:24, 25; Wisd. 16:20, 21. "According to the Slavonic Book of Enoch...the bodies of angels are radiant, their faces

like lightning, their eyes as flaming torches (Prayer of
Aseneth, xiv.; compare Pesi☐. I. 3a; Cant. R. iii. 11; Matt.
xxviii. 3; Luke, ii. 9; Acts, xii. 7). The food of angels is
manna, of which Adam and Eve ate before they sinned (Vita
Adæ et Evæ, 4; compare Akiba, Yoma, 75b on Ps. lxxviii. 25,
and Yoma, 4b with regard to Moses)." [From Jewish
encyclopedia, 1906—Angelology]

[30] Vita Adæ et Evæ, 4-5, states: "and he hath sent me to bring
you out of the water and give you the nourishment which
you had in paradise, and for which you are crying out (4).
'Now come out of the water and I will conduct you to the
place where your victual hath been made ready' (5)" [From
"The Apocrypha and Pseudepigrapha of the Old Testament"
R.H. Charles Oxford: Clarendon Press, 1913 Dracones
Alchymical Omnibus, *Vita Adæ et Evæ*, 4-5]. Symbolically,
therefore, the forbidden fruit, previously consumed by Adam
and Eve, often called an apple, is equivalent to light,
particularly Aur. A correlation can said to be established
since, dating back to the ancient Aryan culture, light and
knowledge and been considered synonymous. The previous
attribution of manna as food of angles is consistent with the
role that angels have played in disseminating knowledge to
men.

[31] A supposition of Baehr (Symbolik, ii, 15) makes a connexion
between an Arabic root and the Hebrew term qarab,
meaning to draw near: Unger's Bible Dictionary; Chicago,
Moody Press; c1957, 1961, 1966 by The Moody Bible
Institute of Chicago; P882.

[32] The Zend-Avesta appropriately relates the higher spiritual and
intellectual attributes of fire as taken from the Yasnas, thus:
"To Ahura and the Fire: 1. We would approach You two, O
(Ye) primeval ones in the house[2] of this Thy holy Fire, O
Ahura Mazda, Thou most bounteous Spirit! Who brings
pollutions to this (Thy flame) him wilt Thou cover with
pollutions (in his turn). 2. But as the most friendly do Thou
give us zeal, O Fire of the Lord! And approach us[3], and with
the loving blessing of the most friendly, with the praise of
the most adored. Yea, may'st thou approach to aid us in this
our greatest (undertaking) amon the efforts of our zeal. 3.

The Fire of Ahura Mazda art thou veily'; yea, the most bounteous one of His Spirit, wherefore Thine is the most potent of all names (for frace), O Fire of the Lord! 4. And therefore we would approach Thee (O Ahura!) with the help of Thy Good Mind (which Thou dost implant within us), with Thy (good) Righteousness, and with the actions and the words inculcated by Thy good wisdom! 5. We therefore bow before Thee, and we direct our prayer to Thee with confessions of our guilt, O Ahura Mazda! With all the good thoughts (which Thou dost inspire), with all the words well said, and the deeds well done, with these would we approach Thee. 6. And to Thy most beauteous body[2] do we make our deep acknowledgments, O Ahura Mazda! To those stars (which are Thy body); and to that one, the highest of the high. [such as the san was called]!" (YASNA XXVI) [The Zend Avesta Part III: The Sacred Books of the East Part Thirty-One; Ed. by F. Max Müller; Tr. by L.H. Mills; Oxford, Clarendon Pr., 1887; p284-5]

[33] Armstrong describes the pragmatism of the Iraelites throughout her work. For example when relating the controversial appellations of God between sources J and P, she states: "Israelite religion was pragmatic and less concerned with the kind of speculative detail that would worry us" [Armstrong, Karen, Opt. Cit. p14].[34] Virgil, in The Aeneid, wrote: "Procul, O Procul, Este Profani," which in English is rendered: "Keep away, oh keep far away, ye profane ones!" [Virgil; Aeneid, Books I-VI; ed. By T.L. Papillon, M.A. and A.E. Haigh, M.A.; Oxford, Clarendon Pr., 1890; Liber VI, 258]

[35] The former citation from Virgil is actually a derivative of an idea that flourished from antiquity considerably anterior to the Roman poet (70 BC –19 BC). Such expressions as "Apo Pantos Kakodaimonos" and "Hekas Hekas Este Bebeloi," are attributions to the old mystery schools of which, perhaps the Eleusinian was the oldest. The concept have been interwoven in literature as may be in Aristophanes:

All must now observe the sacred silence: we ban from

337

our choruses any
whose brain cannot fathom the gist of our wit: whose

171

hearts and feelings are dirty;
who never has witnessed and never partaken in genuine
cult of the Muses,
who knows not the speech of bullgobble Kratinos, who
knows not the Bacchic fraternity,...
...Such men I forbid, and again I forbid, and again I

368

Forbid them a third time,
Let them get up and go from our choral mysteries.
[Aristophanes; Four Plays by Aristophanes; Tr. By William
Arrowsmith, Richmond Lattivore, and Douglass Parker;
New York, New American Library (div. of Penguin Books
USA Inc., 1984; *The Frogs*; p 509-10]

[36] Shekhinah (הניכש) is Hebrew for "dwelling." The noun is
grammatically feminine, hence the use of the feminine
pronouns; and some theorist believe it refers to the feminine
aspects of deity. The customs acknowledging it avoid
anthropomorphic tendencies, in deference to Maimonodes
philosophy of "Divine Incorporality." Furthermore, it
reflects Jewish exilic history, as may be exemplified in
Talmudic literature thus: "Wheresoever they were exiled, the
Shekhinah went with them." Megillah 29a).

[37] With three principle Jewish sects of the time, the Pharisees,
the Sadducees and the Essenes, the latter was latter was most
aligned with narratives depicting the Baptist, hence there has
been wide speculation the preacher in the wilderness was
either orphaned at an early age by, or later a member of, the
acetic sect as characterized in the Dead Sea Scrolls and other
literary instruments.

[38] The expression in the New Testament is rendered in Aramaic
(Matt. 27:45-46), and it is believed that Jesus was quoting
older scripture when repeating it: עֲזַבְתָּנִי לָמָה ,אֵלִי אֵלִי (Ps.
22:1.).

[39] "The mass of men lead lives of quiet desperation." [Thoreau,
Henry David; Walden, or Life in the Woods; Boston,
Ticknor and Fields, 1854]

[40] An allusion to Isaiah 42:16, which states: "And I will bring the
blind by a way that they knew not; I will lead them in paths
that they have not known: I will make darkness light before

them, and crooked things straight. These things will I do unto them, and not forsake them."

[41] "Hail, Holy Light!" Milton, John: Paradise Lost; Book III, Line 1. [Milton, john; Paradise Lost; ed. By William Kerrigan, John Rumich, and Stephen M. Fallon; New York, Random House (Modern Library PP ed.) 2007; p93]

Albert Wendland

LOVE IS A PLACE: LANDSCAPE AND DESIRE IN MICHAEL ONDAATJE'S *THE ENGLISH PATIENT* AND PEETERS' AND SCHUITEN'S *THE INVISIBLE FRONTIER*

At first, a comparison seems unlikely between a realistic if poetic World War II love story and a graphic novel in a science-fiction series called "Cities of the Fantastic." But given the flexible nature of both "the fantastic" and "the poetic," or the elasticity of surrealism as well as metaphor, a thematic tie should not be too surprising. Both works share an interest in *boundaries*, perhaps obvious in the graphic book's title, *The Invisible Frontier*, and in the realization from the novel that the "English patient" is not really English. The common element in these two works is the arbitrary nature of a frontier, the notion that an apparently precise border is modified by the impositions of politics or psychology, and that this Indeterminacy Principle can be found in the boundaries between people, between individuals and nations, and between ourselves and the landscape. Matters of place, of where and how we locate ourselves, share a concern with loyalty to the abstraction of a country as well as to desire for a tangible person. Thus, whether we confuse the map of a landscape with *being* the landscape, or whether producing a map is a free intellectual exercise or an act of political and personal possession, depends, in the end, on where cartographers, and lovers, draw the line.

Though both works depict frustrated attempts to stabilize a fluid reality—as attempted by dictators, generals of war, possessive husbands, and makers of maps—they also involve love stories that are caught up in and blocked by affairs of state. So within these similarities, the main difference between the stories is found in the male leads. Both fail in their romance and attempts to escape or change politics, but while one is overwhelmed by history, the other contributes to his own fall. And a second obvious distinction is that, though both of the female lovers at the ends of the stories are absorbed into landscape, this is achieved in one work metaphorically through words, and in the other through the graphic medium of pictures.

The two-volume graphic novel by the Belgian artist Francois Schuitten and writer Benoit Peeters is an installment in their famous series about a strange and surreal desert planet containing isolated and peculiar cities.[1] In the story, Roland de Cremer is a new and upcoming map-maker who arrives at a cartography center to be caught up in a political struggle. He at first is instructed by an older man, Mr. Paul, who enlists him in traditional views toward maps. But the old man's ideas are threatened by new forces, from both the younger cartographers and the ruling marshal of the country.

The young cartographers want to dominate the world intellectually by reducing it to a model, a set of hand-made miniature landscapes with little artificial trees and pre-cut blocks of mountains. But they're so involved with their model that paying attention to any real world becomes irrelevant. The cartography center where the mapmakers work is an enclosed globe the size of a town, that in many ways *becomes* a world globe, whose immediate and physical surroundings are ignored and thus fall into a desert waste. The look inside the globe is solely inward. The "stars" in its interior sky are just windows in the roof.

The marshal or leader of the country wants to use the cartographers to prove the extent, and thus the glory, of his nation.[2] If the map can show its dominance through size then the world must conform to its rule. As he says to the map-makers, "I'm expecting you to provide me with irrefutable justifications for my struggle for a greater Sodrovny" (I 60). The marshal uses cartography to justify his ideas of manifest destiny or a Hitleresque lebensraum. He says, "As every living being, nations have their needs...The genius of our people is to spread out...to regain the territory to which their glorious history entitles them. It's the responsibility of our time to make manifest the true frontiers of our greater Sodrovny" (II 20). These boundaries defined by the human-made maps will be used as locations for monstrous stone barriers, that will be built and imposed on the outside world—and if a wall goes straight through a city or someone's home, that's no concern of either the cartographers or the bureaucrats. This is not just the imposition of foreign and unrelated names on a landscape through maps (which, as we'll see, bothers the English patient also), but the use of fiction to support fictional claims. Maps are granted as subjective creations but then subsumed by a *1984* mentality, a Ministry of Truth's declaration of lies.

Such acts are repellent to the old Mr. Paul who feels that the current map-makers have lost the "feeling for landscape...everything that makes a map a condensation of events and drama" (I 40). He grumbles that broad and thoughtless compilation of data is now more important than analysis, that "It's not geography that interests them, but politics" (I 18). Yet the younger cartographers welcome this activity—they want to eliminate maps as interpretations and become wholly objective, to have machines draw the maps and not people (though the machines seldom work). As Mr. Paul laments, "Farewell to maps showing rainfall, game, and cultures! Farewell to maps showing rumors and beliefs! Make way for material data, for [only] the most visible elements!" (I 39). In a similar way, Marlene Goldman, in an article appropriately discussing *The English Patient*, describes the difference between map-makers who "orient themselves toward the future" in an "imperious assertion of the...knowing subject over the object to be known," like the marshal, and other map-makers like Mr. Paul, who "dialogue with the past," who prefer maps that are transmissions of communal and generational knowledge, that are offered "out of respect and love for the dead" (910-11).

Roland de Cremer, the protagonists of the books, has a certain charm in his innocence (though a cartographer, he gets lost on his way to the cartography center and can't find an open door to enter it), in his stand against the growing militarism, and in his emotional involvement with a woman named Shkodra. Shkodra is the least promiscuous of the prostitutes at the center (they're "perks" for the all-male cartographers and an unquestioned part of this sexist culture), and she prefers to stay dressed during love-making because of strange markings on her back. Annoyed that cartography at the center is becoming more a "branch of military art," de Cremer becomes fascinated by these lines on her body. It's "like a secret" (I 45), he says, similar to what Mr. Paul calls a "map of beliefs"—a specific and ancient map called "Msyterium Magnum" that shows the original boundaries of the country (I 60-61)—and he copies the markings as much as he makes love to her.[3] The map, he believes, "has a meaning, a link with the frontier. It's the negation of everything the marshal's been trying to prove" (II 25). He feels that "Her body is like the memory of our territory" (II 66), and that she satisfies the lyrics of an old national song, making her a near prophecy-fulfillment:

> *Like the lines on a hand,*
> *As the wrinkles in a stone,*
> *All the frontiers of the land*
> *On her body shall be shown.* (II 31)

Significantly, a woman and her sensual body counters the male-imposed abstract imperialism. But that doesn't mean she's free of being exploited. De Cremer feels she's in danger because of the map on her body and he has her hidden away. She accuses him of possessive jealousy, and though this is inaccurate, he's not very thoughtful when he hides her in a place of big sinister skulls and mutated creatures in glass cases (they're never explained), with the old Mr. Paul who once used her as a prostitute and who, when left alone with her by de Cremer, tries to do so again.

In the same way that frontiers in the Schuiten work are shown to be subjective, to be outcomes of both history and story, boundaries in *The English Patient* are demolished, the differences between place and self-erased. Four people, all withdrawing from their pasts and identities, or "shedding skins" (117), come together briefly in a World War II setting that itself is transitory and undefined. The house where the characters stay, an abandoned villa in Italy after the departure of the Germans, has its walls in ruins and thus lies open to the outside: "There seemed little demarcation between house and landscape," and the wild gardens are like further rooms (43). Hana, the nurse who cares for the patient, has left her unit. Because of recent emotional trauma (she's lost her father and her unborn child), she is trying to reject her own identity—she has all mirrors removed from the villa. Caravaggio, an old friend of Hana, is a thief and a spy, an "evasive man" (27) who feels safest when "Revealing nothing" (27); he claims that in war all is lies, that he once created fictitious agents or "phantoms" (117) to fool the enemy. And Kip, the Indian Sikh, "accustomed to his invisibility" (196) and "being able to hide in silent places" (201), is an "international bastard," like the English patient himself, "born in one place and choosing to live elsewhere," both of them fighting "to get back to or get away from" their homelands all their lives (176).[4]

The Hungarian Almasy, the so-called "English" patient, is dying and only slowly reveals his secret past. In a plane accident, his body was burned, and so now he is a "man with no face ...all identification consumed in a fire" (48). Though learning his identity is a main focus for the reader, only one person at the villa, Caravaggio, is concerned about it; at first he's obsessed with discovering if the patient were a spy for the Germans (through whose betrayal Caravaggio was tortured). But after hearing the patient's story, Caravaggio concludes that he can't find in him an enemy (265), and that "it no longer matters which side [the patient] was on" (251).[5]

All these experiences support Almasy's disgust with boundaries and imposed definitions. He claims to hate "ownership," and in his chosen landscape, the desert, he says he can temporarily escape the concept. Though his European home is a "fully named world" (21) where all is labeled and compartmentalized, "In the desert, it is easy to lose a sense of demarcation" (18). He loves the desert because there he can become "nationless." He says he "came to hate nations," that he and his companion explorers in the desert can't help being "deformed by nation-states," but that the "desert could not be claimed or owned—it was a piece of cloth carried by winds...given a hundred shifting names" (138). Outside the desert are only sterilizing "trade and power, money and war" (250). Almasy describes himself and his fellow archaeologists and cartographers as wishing "to remove the clothing of our countries" in this "place of faith. We disappeared into landscape...I wanted to erase my name and the place I had come from...not to belong to anyone" (139). Opposed to people who look at mirrors and want their names to last and extend into the future, as in the labels for locations on maps, he and his companions see themselves as sailing into the past: "We knew power and great finance were temporary things. We all slept with Herodotus" (142). As in *The Invisible Frontier*, a distinction is made between maps produced to dictate and control a future, and maps that respect a subjective past. In the same way that Hana's childhood "seemed a place rather than a time" (90), Almasy wants to join and be a part of such a timeless space—where all is flux, where "nuance took you a hundred miles" (231), where dunes shift, where oases disappear and reappear, where cultures impermanent come and go, and where nothing is owned, where one can walk with "legends and rumors through history" (140-1).[6]

As with de Cremer, Almasy's ideal is complicated by both war in that desert (between the English and the Germans), and by his own love for Katherine Clifton, the wife, ironically and tragically, of an English spy, which makes their affair politically as well as emotionally suspicious. Being married to a jealous husband she is thus owned and bounded. But this love story, as does one other in the book (between Hana and Kip), is shown to dissolve the boundaries. A wide gap of racial, historical, and cultural differences separate the Canadian Hana from Kip, the Indian sapper: "between them lay a treacherous and complex journey," where the distance across even just the opposite sides of the room makes for "a very wide world" (113). But Almasy and Katherine are more intense in overstepping barriers. He admits his greatest hatred is ownership, and she adds that what she hates most is a lie (152); she says that, if confronted, she will not keep the affair a secret, and thus Almasy concludes, "There would be no compartments in her world" (171). He too speaks of destroying rules and restrictions. He claims that the heart is an organ of fire, and that a "love story is...a consuming of oneself and the past" (97), that it is primal, beyond artificial constraints, that he has been "disassembled by her" (155), that his "hunger wishes to burn down all social rules, all courtesy," that what ultimately counts in an illicit relationship "isn't the morality, it's how much you can bear" (154). In the same way that the novel's fragmentary structure breaks linear expectations,[7] its poetic metaphors also cross boundaries, yoke unlike things together. Significantly, he first falls in love with Katherine when she's reading a poem aloud.

But the two lovers cannot disassemble or ignore the history they are part of.[8] The relationship fails, not through rejection but through Almasy's inability to save the life of his Katherine. In a plane crash, a combination suicide/murder by her jealous husband, she is fatally injured. Almasy, leaving her in the desert and going for help, is delayed by the British who are suspicious of him for the disappearance of their spy. Finally, in order to return to her body (long after the time has passed in which he could have saved her), he has to give secret maps to the Germans who are planning to invade the desert—the reason why he was seen as a traitor by Caravaggio. He recovers her body and, in a state of near madness, paints her with ancient cave-art pigments to "make her eternal" (261).[9] The cave they are in is decorated with such primeval art. And, in a memorable and poetic passage that can relate as much to *The Invisible Frontier*, he carries her body into the desert while contemplating:

> *And all the names of the tribes, the nomads of faith who walked in the monotone of the desert and saw brightness and faith and colour. The way a stone or found metal box or bone can become loved and turn eternal in a prayer. Such glory of this country she enters now and becomes part of. We die containing a richness of lovers and tribes, tastes we have swallowed, bodies we have plunged into and swum up as if rivers of wisdom, characters we have climbed into as if trees, fears we have hidden in as if caves. I wish for all this to be marked on my body when I am dead. I believe in such cartography--to be marked by nature, not just to label ourselves on a map like the names of rich men and women on buildings. We are communal histories, communal books. We are not owned or monogamous in our taste or experience. All I desired was to walk upon such an earth that had no maps. I carried Katharine Clifton into the desert, where there is the communal book of moonlight. We were among the rumour of wells. In the palace of winds.* (261)

For Almasy, we are not separate selves. We are communal histories. We dissolve boundaries by absorbing, and being entered by, tastes, lovers, and tribes. We swim in other people, climb into characters, hide within feelings. Metaphors transform bodies into landscapes, people into trees, fears into caves. Even if labeled, both places and persons cannot be owned. Katherine's body, "pressed against sacred colour" (261), becomes a sacred map. Faith results when our cartography makes our frontiers vague, or invisible.

Roland de Cremer also encounters a body on which a liberating cartography is marked. But he too fails his love, and in a more insidious way. The military takes command of the map center and he and Skhodra are forced to leave. The landscapes they walk through are increasingly surreal, an exaggeration of war's effects: huge fields of artillery shell casings, vast ruins, endless cemeteries, and the people they meet are untalkative because terrorized by the events of the wars. The splash-page openers to each chapter are bizarre fantasies where all things meld, where the landscapes are maps (II 51), where the cartography of the body and the past are both threatened by the shadows of fascism (II 62), where the mapmakers' center transforms into a skull (II 19) and the machineries of war like rivers fill canyons (II 57). Schuitten's images work like Ondaatje's metaphors to blur distinctions. The army finally captures the two lovers and the bureaucrat-tyrant marshal comes to judge them in a huge air machine that dominates the sky like a vast lid.

Though ostensibly working against political ownership, de Cremer then compromises himself by humiliating his lover further (she's already been humiliated and made into an object by the fascists who named her after the town where she was "picked up"—the town was then destroyed—and forced into prostitution). When captured by the marshal's forces, he strips Shkodra, not obeying her plea for him to stop, so that all the soldiers (all of them men) can view the marks on her body. Though he does in self-defense to prove his claims about the map, he foolishly encourages them to "study things even closer," for then "other secrets would surely be revealed" (II 66). The marshal reprimands him maliciously: "So that's your matter of state security! A wretched girl, a foreigner with a birthmark on her ass" (II 67). Though the marshal's arrogance, imperialism and sexism are obvious, de Cremer thus reveals that he himself is not free of making exploitable objects out of people. He didn't forsake all nature of frontiers and ownership by joining with either his lover or the landscape. He got lost in maps instead, in his own fantasy prophesy of them, the dreaded "cartographer's phantasm," as he calls it, the bane of his profession where "all contact with life" is lost and one is left with only "points, lines, mileposts, traces of frontiers" (II 70-71).

After Shkodra abandon him, fed up with his use and thus abuse of her, and after rejected by the marshal who claims to have expected so much of him, he wanders through barren landscapes alone, "unable to orient himself" (II 71), which perhaps for him is progress. His words are especially ironic then, for having lost everything, his job, his love, his assumed purpose no matter how noble it might have begun, he realizes his errors, and he is determined to be more open. He says to himself that he has "to learn everything anew. Learn anew how to see. Learn anew how to observe" (II 71). But he perhaps is still lost in only abstract representations of the world, in his own internal thoughts, for he's too preoccupied (with his own need to see) to *actually* see that the surrealistic shape or memory of his Skhodra has entered the landscape, has become a part of it in perhaps the same way that Almasy wanted Katherine Clifton to become—or it perhaps even symbolizes his own transformation of her from person into thing, having lost her living body his unconscious transforms it into topography. As he walks on, not looking beyond him, in the final and full-page image of the story, the shape of his lover's body materializes out of the landforms, but it remains by him unseen and is noticed by only the reader.

Both women ultimately enter the landscape, metaphorically or surrealistically, through words or pictures. "It is important to die in holy places," says Almasy (260), and though Skhodra is not dead, the love between her and de Cremer, and her body, for Roland are. Do the two women then enter the "sacred," since such words as "faith," "holy" and "prayer" were used by Ondaatje to describe the experience, and Schuitten's work argued for maps to be filled with "story," "drama," "rumors," and "beliefs"? Is the sacred whatever transcends boundaries, rejects definition, like the desert, or surrealism, or metaphor? Is poetry holy? Is the fantastic?

Such vanishing of frontiers demonstrated by Ondaatje in ownership, monogamy, and country, are similarly suggested by the "invisible" frontiers of Peeters and Schuiten. But in both cases the vanishing is more hoped for than true, a matter of faith. Katherine Clifton dies, and perhaps can join the communal and map-less desert only in poetry and death. The absorption of Shkodra's body into the country is more a thematic image, whether a suggestion of the abuse and exploitation shared by both women and landscapes or an ironic comment on de Cremer's self-absorption—and demonstrating a clear use and advantage of the graphic medium. Though unions occur—as in those final pictures, or in the final shifting lines of the novel where Hana dislodges and drops a drinking-glass in Canada and in the same sentence a falling fork is caught by Kip in India—these are mere consolations, symbols. Ultimately, if we do connect, we do so through only metaphor, or on bridges of the fantastic.

NOTES

1 A useful survey in English of the volumes in this series, called "Les Cites Obscures" and translated as "Cities of the Fantastic," and a glossary of places and characters referred to in the stories (up to 1998), can be found on Sylvain St.-Pierre's and Jim Harrison's website, "The Obscure Cities." A later summary of Schuitten's work can be found in *The Book of Schuiten* (2004).

2 The review in *Publishers Weekly* states that the graphic novel is a "satire of political unrest in the former Yugoslavia." The book thus is not as surreal as what it first might seem.

3 In a similar way, the irreverent suggestion from the prostitutes—now working for the new cartographers—that they should make a "pink map" which would show the "frontiers of pleasure" duly rejects the enforcement of material and political analysis.

4 In arguing for Ondaatje's "cubist objective" in the novel, of "viewing the same object from multiple perspectives simultaneously," Kristina Kyser says that the result is a "zone of limbo in which categories and demarcation erode" (894). And Amy Novak points out that Kip "penetrates the fixed boundaries of colonial identification [and] moves silently between radically different, but overlapping, cultures" (221).

5 Susan Hawkins and Susan Danielson, in discussing Anthony Minghella's 1996 film version of the book, which in this case is similar to the text, show how Almasy's burnt body and "amnesia" resist the attempts to "read him, to contain him within an identifiable European discourse with an identifiable role in the European war" (143).

6 Both Kyser and Novak analyze fully the book's treatment of the past. Kyser argues how Ondaatje counters an official collective history by bringing to light individual stories or "what has remained unofficial" (892). Novak describes how the work emphasizes the "dead-ends of history": "These accounts of the past do not provide an alternative linear narrative of the past, but rather, offer a supplement, which interrupts the movement of historical progression by introducing discontinuous moments into the narrative

progression," making history in the book "multiple, fragmented, and haunted" (212).

[7] Kyser describes the style of the novel, quoting Ondaatje's own description of how he writes, as "a 'cubist or mural voice' that draws on 'little bits of mosaic'" (894). She also points out, again quoting him, that he prefers "nuance" to the "steamroller of plot" (892). Goldman too says that the story is in "non-sequential fragments" instead of an "organic, chronological account," much like Almasy's much added-to and clipped-in copy of Herodotus (904).

[8] Hawkins and Danielson state that a main distinction between the film and the book is that the film substitutes "passion for history" and prefers "dramatizing doomed love" while the book does not (142). I add that neither does The Invisible Frontier.

[9] Goldman calls this act a "melancholy and sadistic translation of the body into an allegorical emblem...an artifact" (917).

WORKS CITED

"Cities of the Fantastic: *The Invisible Frontier*, Vol. 2" (Book Review). *Publishers Weekly*. 251:43 (Oct. 25, 2004), 30.

Goldman, Marlene, "'Powerful Joy': Michael Ondaaje's *The English Patient* and Walter Benjamin's Allegorical Way of Seeing." *University of Toronto Quarterly*. 70:4 (Fall 2001), 902-922.

Hawkins, Susan and Susan Danielson. "The Patients of Empire." *Literature Interpretation Theory*. 13 (2002), 139-153.

Kyser, Kristina. "Seeing Everything in a Different Light: Vision and Revelation in Michael Ondaatje's *The English Patient*." *University of Toronto Quarterly*. 70:4 (Fall 2001), 889-901.

Novak, Amy. "Textual Hauntings: Narrating History, Memory, and Silence in *The English Patient*." *Studies in the Novel*. 36:2 (Summer 2004), 206-231.

Ondaatje, Michael. *The English Patient*. 1992. New York: Vintage International, 1993.

Peeters, Benoit. *The Book of Schuiten*. New York: NBM, 2004.

St.Pierre, Sylvain and Jim Harrison. "The Obscure Cities." *Web Archive—IKON Press*. 1998. Web.

Schuiten, Francois and Benoit Peeters. *The Invisible Frontier*. Vol. I. Joe Johnson, trans. New York: NBM Publishing, 2002.

-----. *The Invisible Frontier*. Vol. II. Joe Johnson, trans. New York: NBM Publishing, 2004.

C. Jason Smith

VIRTUAL MINDS

I: VIRTUAL LIVES

In 2001 I came across an article in *Texas Monthly* about an apartment complex in Houston named W@lden that was designed for the high-tech employees of the computer industry. It had, at the time, what was purported to be the fastest domestic internet connection in the world (a T-3) which the residents lovingly called "The Big-Fat Pipe." The main focus of the article was the soap-opera ups and downs, friendships and betrayals, hopes, dreams, and nightmares of this growing class of white-collar geeks living on the tension of the dot-com bubble (and well before the first hints the burst). Overall, the piece was a localized version of the now infamous stories of The WELL, and countless other online communities like it; but one minor detail of the story of the residents of W@lden stuck with me, and I could not shake the feeling that it said something very important about human nature and how and why we interact with technology.

One of the residents of the complex told the story of "The Dude," or what I have come think of since as "The Stain." The Stain was a largish young man who showed up at the apartment complex one day to stay with a friend and proceeded to sit in front of a large computer screen he set up on the floor in the living room and play the massively multiplayer online role-playing game (MMORPG) *EverQuest* for days on end. As days stretched into weeks, he sat in the same spot, moving away from the screen only long enough to answer the door for pizza delivery, grab something to drink, and go to the bathroom. If he slept, which no one ever saw, he slept in the same spot. Trash piled up around him. I found it difficult not to imagine the detritus of weeks of Pizza Hut deliveries, Big Gulp cups, potato chip bags, and so on. The Stain played *EverQuest* religiously until the friend finally kicked him out and cleaned up the trash, only to find that a dark circular stain had permanently formed in the carpet around the spot where the unwelcome visitor had sat, staring into the flickering light of the computer screen, lost in another world.

Something about that image—the screen, the human body, the virtual world, and the circular stain in the carpet, grabbed hold of me and would not let go. In fact, I thought about it for several years while I co-wrote a book on the *Alien* film series with my partner, Ximena Gallardo C., published several articles on various topics including gender representation in online gaming, and ultimately moved from West Virginia to a new life in New York City. Through it all, there was image of The Stain.

I have been a fan of online games, and specifically MMOs, since around 1996 when I started playing an early 3-D online Robo-tech style game whose exact name I can no longer recall. About that time *Ultima Online*, launched in 1997 by Origin Systems, was hitting the major publications. After reading an article in the 11 March 1999 issue of *Newsweek* about the kid who sold his *Ultima* account for $1500, I charged $9.95 a month to an already over-stressed credit card and gave *Ultima Online* a try. Five minutes of wandering about the virtual town of Delucia and I was hooked on killing (and being killed by) rabbits and chickens and stuffing loot in the bank. I played *Ultima Online* for years afterwards and subsequently had my turn at *EverQuest*, and pretty much every other MMO that came out, and I eventually became a beta-tester (one of the people who play a game for free while in production so the designers can work out problems) on quite a few games. So, certainly, something about the story of The Stain struck home. I too had sat for hours on end at the computer screen lost in the "other world" of light and magic, hacking away at the keys and holding my bladder until the right moment when nothing bad would happen to my online character (there are no "pause" buttons for live games). But my reaction to The Stain seemed broader than mere self-reflection: it seemed somehow more meaningful.

The image I could not get out of my head, the notion that bothered me deeply, was that The Stain was like some sort of religious ascetic engaged in a spiritual quest. I remembered a scene from the *Ramayana* where the hero Rama encounters sages meditating in the forest. They are so deeply in a meditative trance that ants have built swarming hills about their bodies and only their ant-covered heads can be seen. I found that image deeply moving when I read the

Ramayana. The more I thought about it, and the more I connected The Stain with those ascetics, the more interested I became.

At the time, I considered online gaming, when I thought seriously about it at all, as an extension of table-top role-playing games (RPGs). In the past I had played pen and paper RPGs such and *Dungeons & Dragons*, participated in the maddeningly slow email version of the game at one point, read the "choose your own adventure" books, played solo role-playing video games (RPVGs), and logged-in to early multi-user dimension (MUD) role-playing sites to interact with others in real-time in text-based worlds. *Ultima Online* simply seemed a more visual version of the same thing and the natural progression of the RPG genre. My college buddies and I, now spread out over several states and countries, could log-in at the same time and play together for hours like we used to in college. When I finally started to think about it, however, I wondered if online RPGs were just a natural progression from the paper and pencil version, why then did I keep thinking about The Stain? After all, gamers are often obsessive, which is why you will find many current and former gamers in academe. We are an obsessive lot by nature and training as it takes a certain amount of intensive focus to conduct research at the needed level and sustain it over a long period of time just as it does to actually master the basic three volumes of *Advanced Dungeons & Dragons* in order to run a game.

My own work at the time focused on how notions of gender are expressed and transmitted through technology. My background, however, was in mythology, world literature, and cultural theory, and my graduate training included a heavy dose of psychoanalytic theory and criticism, including the usual suspects of Sigmund Freud, Carl Gustav Jung, and the more esoteric Jacques Lacan and Slovoj □ i□ ek. Of the lot, Jung had a particular attraction for me. I have read his collected works several times, though I was often warned in graduate school that Jung, and his literary descendent Joseph Campbell (author of the best-selling *The Hero with a Thousand Faces*) were "out of favor" in academic circles, and that my time working on publications would be better spent elsewhere. I turned to French philosopher Michele Foucault and the American gender theorist Judith Butler and found myself happily working with sex and gender construction in literature and film. But, I did not give up my affinity with Jung's work and something about the story of The Stain seemed distinctly

Jungian. I could use other words, of course, such as "mythic," "epic," "religious," or any other number of terms to indicate a sense of transcendence, of something bigger than our selves, but the sense is the same. The Stain was not simply playing *EverQuest* (albeit obsessively), he was, like the ascetics and mystics, travelling to a magical Somewhere Else and leaving his mortal flesh behind.

And there we come to the point: where the residents of the apartment complex saw The Stain as an obsessive, out of control, weirdo, loser (a shocking mirror of themselves in many aspects), I began to see him as the contemporary embodiment of the ancient archetypal story of a certain type of religious figure. Fat, slovenly, unwashed, and reeking, The Stain was having what amounts to a religious experience, travelling in other plains of existence, virtually disembodied in his rejection of all but the most essential needs of physical survival. He wasn't exactly living on bread and water, of course, but the general principle was the same. What was distinctly different from his religious predecessors was the means of transcendence. Rather than mantras or koans, the *Analects* of Confucius, or the *Tao Te Tching* of Lao Tzu; rather than the stories of Rama or Krishna or the Buddha, or the poetry of the "Song of Songs" from the Torah and Old Testament, The Stain had *EverQuest*: a computer mediated virtual environment, more specifically termed a persistent state world (PSW), massively multi-player online role-playing game (again MMORPG, which is oddly pronounced "morgue").

This was several years before a young South Korean man, Seungseob Lee, died after playing *StarCraft* for 50 hours straight in an internet café in 2005, and not long before the short film "The Kid" from *The Animatrix* (released in 2003) implied suicide can set you free from the world we know to the "real world". William Gibson, of course, set the tone for this level of immersion in his inimitable *Neuromancer* (1984) where we see two variations on the same theme: the immersive entertainment console and the hacker lost in cyberspace who leaves his "meat body" behind. But what Gibson saw and what he described in the video arcade that served as the basis for his idea of cyberspace was for him something new and potentially, for all of us, horrifying. When I read *Neuromancer* as a teenager I had the same sense: we were in the process of something new, a "terrible beauty," as Yeats might have described it; though it was sometimes difficult to see the future Gibson described in a game of *Space Invaders, Centipede,* or *Ms. Pac Man.*

After reading the story of The Stain, however, I suddenly had the opposite sense: I was not seeing something new, but seeing something deeply psychological and monstrously ancient, what Jung would have called "archetypal," and it was on those terms that it interested me. At the time, I had trouble putting a name to it. Was what I was seeing a symbol or symbolic action? Was it a story being enacted? Was it the horror of the unruly, filthy body and the stain it left behind? Or was it, on the other hand, the pristine virtual landscapes and the sleek virtual bodies that occupied it: bodies of light that do not sweat, defecate, or urinate? In fact, I had no idea what the "something" I was seeing was nor what it meant.

Essentially I was asking what the pieces of the puzzle were that made up this act embodied in The Stain. Most obviously we have a human body interacting with a technology—a moment in time—so I started there, with The Stain and worked my way back along the path of bodies and technologies that led up to the moment represented by The Stain. It was not a straight path. If you can imagine looking at one bud on one tiny twig on one branch of an enormous ancient oak tree and then tracing back down to the root that was the experience that opened up for me as I worked my way back through the innumerable technologies and psychological structured that added up to that one moment of that one body sitting before that one screen and interacting with thousands of other bodies sitting in front of thousands of computer screens. I set out purposefully to track the origin of the moment I labeled "The Stain," and, as a writer, to write about it if I could: what follows is the story of that quest.

I realized that I needed to have to get a handle on the language of my investigation, and the first term that needed to be addressed was "virtual reality." Having been trained in English, Spanish, and Arabic, I knew my way around a dictionary and own a couple of dozen myself, but in this case I planned to hit the Oxford English Dictionary—first the multi-volume print version then, later, online (they both have distinct advantages)—to find the origins of the term. I knew that origins can tell us a lot about the hidden meanings of a word or phrase and what they mean historically. But first, I sat down and wrote out what I thought "virtual reality" meant so that I would have a record of my perceptions before they were changed by the formal definitions (the denotations), cultural references (or connotation), and history of the word (the etymology).

What I knew was that virtual reality (VR for short hereafter) was hot in popular culture and promised to remain so for quite some time. Films such as *Total Recall* (1990), *The Lawnmower Man* (1992), and later *The Matrix* film series, and *Eternal Sunshine of the Spotless Mind* (2004), to name a few, draw on the enduring popularity of computer games which has elevated a technical computer concept to the level of cultural phenomenon. Even more, these films seemed to be rooted in serious philosophical issues that invoked potential long-lasting cultural implications. The most popular of these films *The Matrix*, *The Matrix: Reloaded* and *The Matrix: Revolutions* (1999, 2003, and 2003 respectively) each explores the age-old fear of technology replacing humans in the world's hierarchy and invokes the very essence of philosophy by asking "What is real?"

In the popular media, parents and politicians obsess about violence in video games. Around the world millions of people log into virtual environments to interact with people they have never met in real life (or RL in the lingo) and more and more often these interactions involve virtual bodies (called "avatars") inhabiting virtual spaces. Games like *The Sims Online* (now defunct), *EverQuest, World of Warcraft*, and the first really popular of these massively multiplayer online role-playing games *Ultima Online*, take video games to a new level that moves beyond simple one on one action into a fully designed world where hundreds and even thousands of players can engage together in long drawn out narratives in worlds that never (or *almost* never) "turn off." Like real-life (RL), this VR continues with or without you. Virtual Reality—the very mention of the term invokes images of computer generated fantasy worlds.

The general denotation of the term from a standard dictionary, however, turned out to be quite mundane: a construction that expresses or manifests the virtues of human experience. But what did the *Oxford English Dictionary* have to say about it? I decided to first have a go at the 20 volume library print edition that contains the etymology (or history) of virtually every word in the English language. Though obviously the online version is more up to date, I felt that looking for my terms in the more traditional format would give me some grounding in traditional research before I hit the web. When I began reading the entry, I was actually quite surprised at how much information there was on "virtual reality". The phrase "virtual reality" was first used in computer science to describe a computer generated environment in the late 1980's by Jaron Lanier, who claims to have coined the term. However, the origin of the term is actually a bit more convoluted. For example, Myron Kruger coined the term "artificial reality" in the 1970's; The French poet, playwright, and actor Antonin Artaud used the term "*la réalite virtuelle*" in his 1938 book *The Theater and Its Double*; and science fiction author Damien Broderick used the term "virtual reality" in a related sense in his 1982 novel *The Judas Mandala*. But it was Lanier who invested himself in the term and popularized it.

It certainly felt to me like it had been around much longer than that, but then I remembered that William Gibson used the conflated term "cyberspace" and not "virtual reality." But, we should remember that even scientists and engineers tend to choose terms for the potential "buzz" they might start. Like the coining of the term "Chaos Theory" for popular descriptions of the theories arising from the field of "complex dynamics" caused great furor due to its philosophical and religious connotations, "virtual reality" is a term composed of not one historically loaded term, or even two, but three interrelated terms. "Virtual reality" is based on the complex philosophical concepts of "virtual," and "reality," obviously, but also "virtue" (the root of "virtual") which is a close conceptual corollary to "reality." In fact, "virtual" is an adjective that already implies a "reality" being emulated, therefore saying "virtual reality" is rather like saying, as second-rate Tex-Mex restaurants are wont to do, "*chili con queso* with cheese." Of the long and complicated history of the three interrelated terms, I would like to draw attention to several factors which will have a direct impact on this history of the idea.

First, the word "virtue," the noun form of "virtual," is strongly associated through much of the development of the English language with the power or powers of the divine; thus, to "have virtue" was to exhibit or embody some quality of the divine power. The important point here is that to "have virtue" meant to *embody* the divine, to open oneself up to an external power and let it in. Thus, Christ embodied all virtues because he was God embodied—what may be called an "avatar" from the Sanskrit "*avatara*": a term that will have relevance to our later discussion. Likewise, the hero and heroine of the Ramayana, Rama and Sita, and have both been described as avatars of the Hindu god Vishnu (the 7th and 8th, respectively). But, we will come back to avatars later.

Second, the word "virtue" is historically tied to gender. "Virtue" is from the latin *virtus* meaning "excellence, potency, efficacy" but more literally "manliness," the root *vir* indicating "man" as in "human and male." Thus, virtue is a quality, power, or essence that has its roots in the male body and is, therefore, no doubt tied to the most obvious symbol of male power, the phallus, as both the male sexual organ and the symbol of masculine strength. For if "vir" indicates the male then it must originally refer to that obvious indicator of sex from birth.

Through time, the virtues expanded in scope and divided into "active" and "passive" virtues. Predictably, those qualities not considered "masculine," albeit still associated with the divine, came to be associated with women. These "civilizing virtues" of faith, hope, and charity, and so on, contrasted and complimented the more masculine virtues such as justice and the all-encompassing honor. These virtues were also associated with women in form if not in actuality. Justice, like Liberty, is portrayed most often as a woman, and women become "the keeper" of male honor, and thereby the family honor as well, though they do not "defend it" or "wield it." Therefore, the term "virtual", tied up as it is in the complex web of signification surrounding "virtue", is a term heavily imbued through time with gender issues and gendered meanings.

Third, "the virtual" is part and parcel of an ancient philosophical and theological discourses on representation, imitation, and simulation, including Plato and Aristotle's classical discourses on *mimesis*, the Buddha's meditations on the nature of lived reality as illusion, the Christian notion of Heaven (all from around 500 B.C.), and in contemporary discourse, Jean Baudrillard's critique of simulacra in *Simulacra and Simulation*. The term, therefore, invokes a long history of discourse on the nature or reality: what the philosophers call "ontology."

In general, then, the "virtual" is something that has the qualities of something else without actually, or literally, being that thing. However, just to confuse matters further, it could effectively be that thing at which point the line between the "real" and the "simulacrum" would blur. A woman named "Faith" for example could also embody the virtue of her name and, therefore, "be Faith [by name]" and "have faith" and "act out of faith" where the inscribing of the name to the child was in hope of enacting that virtue within her body and life. This was, perhaps, more true in an earlier era but we still understand this naming business when we name our children. Few people would want to name their children names such like "Satan", "Adolf", or even "Loser" as we would fear the social repercussions as well as the possibility of invoking the traits of the namesake.

What we term "the virtual" is, in philosopher Jean Baudrillard's terms, a "simulacrum"—the virtual simulates something else that approaches reality, though it never quite attains it. Though we have given the term "virtual" a new shine with computer technology, the concept itself (and even the word in one form or another) is very, very old; and I believe, and will attempt to demonstrate, that is cuts to the core of what it means to be human. By my way of thinking, to be human is to be self-reflexive, to wonder about ourselves, our origins, our place in the universe, our destiny. Thus, "virtue" and its adjectival form "virtual" is a core concept of the human experience.

Our fourth concern is that the term "reality" is one of those terms like "god" and "virginity" that everyone assumes they understand when they do not and assumes everyone else knows when they cannot. We are all supposedly somehow in silent agreement. If we start to talk about it, however, we quickly recognize that while everyone seems to "know" it, no one seems to agree what "it" is. For example, I teach a course on sexuality in literature and every single semester I ask my student-learners to raise their hands if they know what a "virgin" is. They all seem to. I then ask each student the following: "Please write a definition of 'virgin,' limiting it only to the human female to avoid confusion." They think. They write. They all smile happily when done, comfortable in the knowledge that they all have "the right answer." (It is, after all, very early in the semester yet). "So," I ask, "what is a 'virgin'?" "A person who has not had sex!" exclaims one young woman. "Everyone agree? OK, then, all we have to do is define 'sex' and we'll be done and can move on to the poetry for the day! So, what is sex?"

Imagine a well-trained choir all secretly handed a different song, singing the first note in what they assume will be unison only to produce an ear-splitting cacophony of disagreement followed by nervous confusion. Is it "penis and vagina?" "Intercourse?" "Breaking of the hymen?" "Oral sex?" "Any sexual contact?" What is "sexual contact"? Do you have to "fall in love to really lose your virginity?" I have heard all of these and the tendency to over-share is strong in this situation—one young woman claimed to be a virgin because she's never been "on bottom." Another a few years ago asserted in all seriousness to the class that, even though she had given birth to a child, she was still a virgin. I thought it improper at that juncture to pursue that particular line of reasoning any further, but I think the point has been made.

You might be surprised at the sheer number of responses to what seems like a simple question, and a question that seems so fundamental to the sexual mores of a society. They invariably laugh and call each other "liars" and "idiots" in an attempt to force the individual reality onto the collective whole. Rather than admit the subjective (and political) nature of an apparently essential term like "virginity" or "sex," each of my students would rather suppress all of those "other" voices. But, by the end of the class, the point is clear—"virginity" is not a natural state but a socially constructed and culturally invested phenomenon used to define and, thereby control, bodies through cultural created mores and laws.

"Reality" may not be quite as contentious as the nature of virginity, but it operates much to the same effect. As far as the dictionary definition, or denotation, goes, "reality" is historically tied to "property" or "land" (therefore "*real*-estate", or actual property, as opposed to money or investments) and the root of "real" specifically refers to the fixed nature of land or property—that which is immovable and unchangeable. As they say in my home state of Texas, "Land is everything. It's the only thing that is real."

The "real" refers directly to a particular *virtue* of things which makes them exactly what they seem or purport to be, so that "a real wrestler" embodies the traits of the wrestler in a way which posits the person as defining the term itself (a measure by which to test other wrestler's skill) while at the same time acknowledging that simulation is possible and denying the simulation in this particular manifestation: if Joe is a "real wrestler" then others who purport to be "real wrestlers" must really be just playing the part (pretenders or mere simulations). To say something is "real," therefore, is to admit the possibility of mistaking it for the simulation (a simulacrum) as when an advertisement on a juice carton reads "real juice" or as I ran into recently while shopping for milk, "real milk from real cows"—a phrase designed to call into question the "reality" of the other brands of milk on the shelf.

In common speech there are three major schools of thought on reality that have been succinctly summarized in baseball metaphor as the three different varieties of baseball umpires. Reality 1: "Some are balls and some are strikes, and I call them as they are." Reality 2: "Some are balls and some are strikes, and I call them as I see them." Reality 3: "Some are balls and some are strikes, but they ain't nothing until I call them". The first group—"Hey! A strike is a strike!"— espouses the objective view of reality which essentially argues that reality exists and reasonable humans have access to that reality through observation and the application of formal logic. Anyone who does not agree has not properly applied their observation and logic to the event. Most scientists would fall into this category, though certainly not all (some of the quantum mechanics physicists among them).

The second group—"I'm a trained umpire doing the best I can under the circumstances"—believes that reality is a bit more difficult to get at primarily due to the slippery nature of language, in this case the "rules" of the game, and our inability to describe what we perceive to others. This ambiguity is compounded with our cultural prejudices to "see" what we have been taught to see or, worse, want to see. Thus, an umpire born and raised and trained in Texas might be accused of favoritism when calling balls in Queens, particularly if the Rangers are playing. If he also ascribes to this view of reality, he knows he could be prejudiced but does his best to exceed his upbringing and follow his training.

The final category of umpire knows that he is the first and last authority on balls and strikes (at least in this game) and that is because the rules of the game give him the power to decide reality within the context of the game: "What I say goes!" And because the rules of the game and the authority are behind him, the record books will thereafter record a strike regardless of those yahoos who (operating in Reality 2) argue about it for years. This view holds that authority, derived from law or other source of power, sets the nature of reality. Umpires collectively define what a strike is or is not in general, and specific umpires decide in every specific case, and each umpire has the power, as defined by rule, to decide what is or is not a strike in the reality of that game. This view of reality we might term observer dependent (from physics) or informatics (the science of information): essentially we might say that those who control the rules (information) define what the rest of us—including the players and the fans—experience as reality.

Since receiving my Ph.D. some years ago, my father takes great pleasure in annoying me with the old question "If a tree falls in the woods and there is no one there to hear it, does it make a sound?" The range of answers includes "Yes, of course," "No, because 'sound' is a function of 'hearing'," and "How would I know if I wasn't there?" to "How do you know it fell if you weren't there?" My favorite answer for him, though I change it up to keep him entertained, is "Well, it depends on whether it is a real tree and a real sound or a hypothetical tree and a hypothetical sound." I tend to be a bit of a smart-ass with my father. Regardless, though the above is an extreme oversimplification of the variety and depth of ontology, it should suffice for the moment for our inquiry into the nature of "virtual reality" to proceed.

Let us finish, then with the assertion that "virtual reality" means literally "something that exhibits the virtues of reality to some degree." Thus, a virtual room would have a doorway and walls and a floor and a ceiling and any of the other "virtues" that imply a room. What makes this room a "virtual room" as opposed to a "real room"? The one trait that the real room has that the virtual does not is that the real room does not require a technical mediator in order for me to experience it, whereas the virtual room requires that the senses of my body be in some way augmented and/or modified for the duration of the experience. I go into a room, but the virtual room has to come to me by fooling my senses in some way. For example, we have early examples of virtual art in rooms that were painted to simulate forests. The paint and painter's technique, then, is a technology that interacts with the senses in an attempt to fool them. Burning pine incense in the room would further the illusion and so on. The virtual room may seem, then, more interactive than a real room because of our awareness of its artificiality and our desire to interact with it and "test it out", so to speak, by touching the walls and looking for the source of the smell. We wonder at the illusion of the created "virtual reality" and enjoy it but this also may lead to our questioning the nature of "reality" as well. After all, why else would we enjoy a room of fake trees if it did not make us see real trees in new ways, and if we can see the real in new ways then how real is it?

Which is to say, for good or ill the virtual pushes us towards Reality 3: "they ain't nothing until I call them" while at the same time hiding the means of production of the simulation: we do not see the process of the painting of the trees on the wall. This concept is just one step away from games like *World of Warcraft*. Virtual spaces are created for the players who have no access to the means of their creation (the rules and coding that are the real game).

All of which led me to some very interesting and uncomfortable ideas on which to base my investigation. I started to think that the notion of "virtual reality" is based upon three central concerns of the human experience. First, it depends on the experience or belief that the human body is a "made" thing. This is not a particularly novel idea. After all, most mythology systems include a creation story where humans are created from mud or ash or ribs or some such. Humans are embodied beings; therefore, part of the "illusion" of this world is that very embodiment. No wonder we imagine a part of the body that is eternal, can escape and travel around without the body, can go to heaven, or can be born again. Like virtue, the notion of a soul or spirit, of an eternal part that survives our death is so prevalent that "virtue" and "soul" seem to operate as mutually supporting metaphors. As we shall see, however, virtue arises from the primal body and gives birth to such notions as the soul and eternity.

Second, reality—our experience in the world—seems to many of us to be not only subjective (meaning prone to distortion by the individual senses and mind) but also very limited. Throughout recorded history humans have been convinced that there was more to the universe than meets the eye and that "reality" was not the whole story. As Calderon de la Barca wrote more than 300 years ago, "*La vida es sueno*," or "Life is a dream." Life is a dream of our own making—or even more terrifying, life is a dream made for us by others as in Plato's "Allegory of the Cave". This is the fear expressed in a broad range of literary works: even those written for children. For example, in Lewis Carroll's *Alice in Wonderland* Tweedle Dee suggests to Alice that "If that there King (who dreams the world into existence) was to wake, you'd go out 'Bang!' just like a candle!"

For Plato in classical Greece, Buddha in India, and Jesus in the Middle East, and many others who believed variations on the theme that the "world is a dream," all the common man calls "reality", what we experience through our senses every single day, *is* virtual, exhibiting the qualities (the virtues) of reality but hiding the *real reality* behind it (heaven, nirvana, the Real). This notion is the basis for all religion and theology and much philosophy. Our inescapably human feeling that this can't be all there is leads us to the belief that all this is somehow not real and is therefore a copy of what is real that has somehow been lost. Thus we come to the postmodern pop-psych mantra that "I just don't feel like myself anymore."

Freudian psychoanalytic theorist Jacques Lacan describes this sense of loss as the very basis for the establishment of the ego. In effect it is the pain of losing the Real (or uninhibited participation with the world) that makes us individuated persons. Or at least makes us believe we are individuated persons. And what causes this primary trauma? Language. Once I say "I" there has to be a "you" and we are lonely and misunderstood ever after, trapped in a world that is not quite as it should be, not quite *real*, trapped as it were in a virtual world. And, according to Lacan, thank heaven for orgasms because that is the closest you'll ever get again to feeling "at one with the universe" again.

Orgasms aside, I believe now, at the end of the long journey that culminated in this book, that the virtual is our Alpha and Omega, our beginning and end, and that it ties together the great web of what we call "being human". So, let's start at the beginning, at the root of the tree, and see how far up the branches we can go. To do that, however, we will need some sense of the layout of the branches of knowledge that we will be delving into. Starting from an online game like *EverQuest* or *World of Warcraft* what groups of technologies or techniques are necessary for the event of engaging in that online space to happen at all?

Working from the image of the virtual environment on the computer screen I can begin my list by saying the existence of that moment requires the ability to represent bodies and to recognize those representations (or what we might call representational art or technology). I can see a body on the screen, what is called my "avatar" for reasons we will get into later. It was designed by an artist and I can recognize it for what it is supposed to be (a body) and what it actually is (a simulated body). That body occupies a space in the screen, and that space too was created, and I can recognize this created, virtual space as being like the space I occupy. For those spaces to be created and for me to understand them (to see what they are or are supposed to be) requires a basic understanding of geography (negotiating spaces) and cartography (visualizing spaces) and cartography also requires an understanding of artificially rendered perspective (imagining spaces from positions other than standing in them).

To understand the unfolding of the online game, I must have some grasp of narrative structures to be able to follow the "story" (the story of my character and/or the unfolding story of the virtual world as a whole) from point to point, and that story has to be conveyed to me. This technique is based in our human ability to tell stories, to make narratives, and transmit stories through time and space as in mythology and history. Narratives themselves include the ability to imagine bodies moving through space and time as we have to "imagine" the events of the story as we hear them. Though I do not need to be aware of it to play an online game, the online environment requires the additional understanding of the actual rules of movement in spaces through time and the ability to formulate new rules of bodies and spaces and times (logistics) as movement in simulated environments is based on our movement but is not the same. Movement is, however, based on rules, which is part of what makes it a "game."

But what is a "game?" We might think of the difference between throwing dirt in the air (play), to stacking blocks in a pattern (an individual game), to a game with more formal rules such as Hide and Seek, or even more complex, *Dungeons and Dragons*. *EverQuest* is certainly more complex than hide and seek, but the same basic principles are there. Speaking of *Dungeons & Dragons*, our MMO is also a Role-Playing Game (or RPG), making it an MMORPG and all RPG's are based in *Dungeons & Dragons* (actually its predecessor *Chainmail*) which are in turn rooted in the rules (logistics again) of miniature war gaming.

And then, of course, we have the computer itself. For all of the above to happen, the PC must bring together a long history of technologies that include the ability to record and transmit sound and/or data, record and transmit images, record and transmit moving images, produce computing power, design and encode computer games, design and encode computer text-based role-playing games, design and encode video games then multi-player video games, connect computers together into a network to form the Internet, and then combine elements to produce multiplayer internet text-based environments followed by the addition of video-game technology to produce massively multi-player online role-playing games like *World of Warcraft*. That is a lot of technologies and techniques.

Stripping out all of the potential sub-categories for the moment a short list of the broad clusters of technologies and techniques needed for me to log in to an online game like *World of Warcraft* might break down into a list like this:

- Representation of bodies (representational art)
- Representation of spaces (cartography and representational art)
- Telling stories or creating and conveying narratives of events (narrative)
- Describing how bodies move in space and time (logistics)
- Inventing rules that simulate reality (role-play and formal games)
- Information recording technologies (such as writing, music records, DVDs, or hard-drives)
- Information transmission and reception technologies (such as books, radio, television, the Internet, and WiFi)
- Computing power (mainframes and personal computers)

This list is, of course, only one way to think of some of the different technologies that support a virtual environment, and any list is, by its very nature, exclusive. However, what I like about this list as a starting point is that it clearly demonstrates the process of producing virtual environments as a historically rooted progression and compiling of technologies and techniques. The representation of bodies, for example, historically precedes the representation of space, which necessarily must come before narrative as "stories" involve bodies moving in space and time (for example, "He went to the store.") which in turn precedes the invention of rules that simulate bodies moving in space and time (such as in a chess game where the figures represent individuals or armies and the board a country or collection of countries). Still, we have an imposing list to say the least, but if we want to come to some sort of understanding of the story of The Stain, then I will need to start somewhere on that list. One of my professors, James A. Grimshaw Jr., was fond of asking students a question about tackling a large research project. "How do you eat and elephant?" he would ask, one eyebrow rising slightly up his pale forehead. We would all wait for the answer in mute silence, though many of us had been in his classes before and already knew the answer. He would smile slightly, lean in to the class confidentially, "How do you eat an elephant?" he would ask again, and deliver his line: "One bite at a time, people. One...bite...at a time." Taking that to heart, then, I will begin at what seems to be the first bite: the emergence of representational art and the simulation of bodies.

II: MAKING BODIES

In the late 1990's the sexy female video game hero Lady Lara Croft was kicking-ass across the pages of American magazines and fighting her way into the hearts of game players worldwide. Across the globe millions of teen boys (and some girls) were playing a female action adventure hero and loving it. With her impossible body and equally impossible acrobatics, Lara Croft sashayed her way through castles run by evil overlords, monster infested tunnels, and underwater rivers. Lady Croft, an Indiana Jones style archaeologist from a British noble family, fought them all with her ubiquitous twin pistols and sometimes—if the player was skilled enough or lucky enough—she triumphed. More often Lara died. As was the case with my feeble attempts at the game, she died, and she died, and she died some more. She fell off cliffs onto spikes, drowned, smashed into walls, was bludgeoned to death by falling traps and generally had a miserably bloody time of it all around, but she always came back as good as new, ready to swing her long braid towards adventure and imminent death once again.

Now a popular film series starring Angelina Jolie as Lara Croft, the sheer popularity of the franchise was both overwhelming and unexpected. It may seem normal now for both men and women to play games with protagonists of varying genders, or even no gender at all, but at the time of its release Lara Croft was really something new. For several years I read magazine articles, and listened to myriad academic papers, about exploring the perils of this latest expression of violence towards women, Lara Croft as an expression of female power, Lara Croft as a role model for young women, Lara Croft as the expression of rampant imperialism, Lara Croft as the expression of post-colonial angst, the psychological benefits of cross-gender identification, the psychological risks of cross-gender identification, and on and on. What I found fascinating as I sat reading the newest article or listening to the latest neo-Marxist reading of Lady Croft's adventures was that so many people from so many different walks of life were playing and writing about a video game. A video game? Seriously? As I listened to bright-eyed graduate students justify the hours and hours spent playing *Tomb Raider* instead of studying for comprehensives or working on theses and dissertations by applying whatever critical approach was at hand or hot at the moment (at that time Michel Foucault and Judith Butler) I began to see that all this theorizing was a well-researched smokescreen subconsciously constructed and executed by the critic-fan community to hide one fact: Lara Croft was not real. Yes, she was beautiful and sexy, and we enjoyed playing her and guiding her to her win and lose and live and die, but what really mattered was that Lara was a created woman who was intentionally designed to "turn us on" on many different psychological levels. There is something deeply imbedded in us that responds to the artifice of the female form.

Even more: making representations of human form, and particularly the female form, is one of the oldest art forms we know, and some argue it is the oldest. Thus body representation serves as the first evidence for, and perhaps the jumping off point or "alpha incident", for everything we now consider "human culture". Any art history book will tell you that the oldest pieces of representational art, those that depict bodies, were called the "Venus figurines". Though, being more than 35,000 years old, they are obviously not part of the myth of the Greco-Roman goddess Aphrodite/Venus, the assumption was that these figurines were the earliest ancestors of statues like the famous Venus de Milo. We have some indications of decorative arts previous to these figures, but the symmetrical scratchings on the surfaces of simple bone tools are not representational in the sense that they do not try to represent physical forms but, rather, patterns that may have been the product of the attempt to reproduce the patters of visual illusions such as those caused by staring into the sun or the result of early trance states. To understand how this might come about, all you have to do is look at a smooth surface such as a piece of blank paper, then look into a bright light for a few moments, then look back at the paper and new shapes will magically appear. Try to trace those shapes on the paper while you still "see" them and you have pretty much discovered the "meaning" behind the earliest human attempts at representation.

The most famous of the bunch of small figurines is the so-called Woman of Willendorf (or "Venus of Willendorf"). I first learned about this figurine in a class on sex and gender taught by Dr. Lisa Stark, then at what is now Texas A&M University-Commerce (formerly East Texas State University). Dr. Stark was a spunky, newly minted Ph.D. with research interests in sex and gender, Shakespeare, the silent film star Louise Brooks (who she bore more than a passing resemblance to), and the pop-singer Madonna. In her class we covered the gamut of sex and gender theory in art, history, psychology, literature (the supposed subject of the class), television, film, and print media, including a healthy dose of pornography. It was a truly exciting course that felt, somehow, dangerous. After all, who knew our library carried subscriptions to both *Playboy* and *Penthouse* at the request of the Psychology Department? As graduate students at a rural university that had traditionally been a teacher's college (what had been called in an earlier era a "normal college" which I still find amusing) we were thrilled by the contemporary piratical feel to the class, and I developed an obsession with psychology and critical theory that obviously continues unabated.

We started the class with a slide and video presentation that began with the Woman of Willendorf and ran through, as I recall, a visual history of the female body in art culminating with Madonna performing as Marilyn Monroe in "Material Girl" and as a private dancer in "Open Your Heart". Having been a Political Science undergraduate with very little exposure to the then burgeoning field of Cultural Studies, it took years before many of the ideas presented in the class began to sink in and make sense. I still find new ideas and discover new meanings in all the texts we read and interacted with in the class, and the Woman of Willendorf was no exception. Therefore, it seems entirely appropriate to return to her now in this discussion of virtual culture.

The Woman of Willendorf (unearthed in 1908 near Willendorf, Austria) is a little sculpture with a length of 11.1 centimeters (or 4 ¼ inches) which fits snugly in the palm of the hand. The simplest way to describe the Woman of Willendorf is that she (for it is clearly a female) is all breasts, belly, buttocks, and vagina. There is a head without a face—she is either wearing a woven mask or looking down and showing only her plaited hair—diminutive arms, and plump thighs leading to footless calves, but little else. Though she was originally dubbed the "Venus of Willendorf" because of a visual similarity in the minds of the archaeologists to the Venus de Milo and the early presumption that the figurine represented a fertility goddess, there is some disagreement as to whether she is merely corpulent, a fat body being a symbol of wealth and prosperity to hunters and gatherers, or pregnant, making her more likely to be a fertility symbol. My impressions were, and still are, that the enlarged vaginal area and large breasts as well as the vestigial arms resting protectively on the breasts would seem to indicate pregnancy and an impending birth, while the buttocks and thighs look simply fat as from a diet made up of large amounts of fatty foods. Therefore, I have no problem seeing her as both a symbol of wealth and prosperity and female fecundity. But, that is just me using what I know about gender and culture to make an intelligent guess. What she meant to her creator and to her viewers—what her purpose was in their culture—is another matter altogether. What we do know is that more than 12,000 years before man was painting animals on cave walls he was walking the ancient plains with sex in his hand.

It is odd considering the size that most photographs of the figurine make it look enormous. No doubt this occurs through a desire to show the details of the work. The effect, however, is to give the figurine a sense of massive historical importance in direct opposition to its physical size and I have come to think that these images are telling: whatever she might have represented then, she is now our Eve. She is the first "woman" made by or out of "man" by which I mean this is the first indication we have that humans had become conscious of the fact that "woman" was a different thing from "man," conscious enough to be self-conscious about it and carve a figure representing that difference. We really don't need to know what it was *used for* after it was made, the fact that it exists at all tells us what we need to know: the sexed body had come into existence as something to think about. Humans were no longer just "having sex" as all animals do; they had begun to make sex. This little stubby piece of rock may seem a far cry from Lara Croft, but the essential elements are all there—both Lara and the Woman of Willendorf are *made girls*: fantasies from an individual human mind made manifest for all to see.

In *The Mind in the Cave* (2004), Anthropologist David Lewis-Williams convincingly argues that early art, and in particular cave drawings, are not simply crude artistic representation of "a day in the life" of early humans. Rather, examples of cave art, such as the famous images of Lascaux, are the result of dream states (self-induced or otherwise) where the artist was essentially "seeing" the images in the shapes of the rock and believed they were looking "through" the rock into another world. What they drew, according to Lewis-Williams, was an attempt to release from the stone the beings on the "other side", as it were, in the spirit realm.

After reading *The Mind in the Cave*, I imagined our figurine artist using a rib-bone tool to carve the figure, to set his little Eve free, to release her from the rock so she could bring her magic of birth and rebirth, of the change of seasons and the phases of the moon into the world. Though the rib-bone tool is a complete fantasy based on my own desire to make some poetic reference to the *Book of Genesis*, Lewis-Williams' notion of seeing figures in surfaces and trying to release them rings true in the case of the Woman of Willendorf. I think the artist saw the woman in the rock—saw his own desire for a woman and all she represents including sex, offspring, bountiful food, a warm partner at night, her cycles and the associated magic of the cycles of the seasons and the moon, and etc.—and set about to free her from the rock so she could be his and he could share in that magic.

This is what C.G. Jung meant by the archetype he termed the "Anima": the idea of Woman with a capital "W" as viewed through the male psyche. But while archetypes may have universal characteristics across human cultures they are not static; rather, they are dynamic. Which mean that they move forward through time and, doing so, they proliferate and change, but the root still remains. From the Woman of Willendorf we may trace forward a history of sex and gender culminating in our own manifestations of the Anima in supermodels and Hollywood stars. The Woman of Willendorf is, as it were, a virtual "woman"—or the first "woman"—representing the properties of "woman" as understood by an individual within a defined cultural framework. She is the first notion, the first expression, the first definition of "woman."

We see in the Woman of Willendorf the act of making bodies, making images of bodies, and thereby imagining sex and bringing it into being as a cultural trope (or idea) as an essential human activity in the most basic way. And the mind that made the Woman of Willendorf is essentially that same mind that designs avatars for *EverQuest* and *World of Warcraft*. Which is why, though separated by millennia, we can immediately recognize the Woman of Willendorf as human and understand that it is a human female.

Once our ancestors began to see three dimensional shapes in rocks such as the bodies of people and animals, it was a short step to seeing three dimensional images in increasingly "flat" surfaces such as rock faces and cave walls. The rock faces operated as a concealing screen between this world and the other realm of spirit. For the cave artist the paintings had a three-dimensional quality as they reached into that "other world" and at least some of the images incorporate features of the surface of the rock into the image, further indicating the three-dimensional quality of the works. But we were well on our way to being able to understand two dimensional images as simulations of three-dimensional space. It is not that far at all from the Woman of Willendorf, the cave walls of Lascaux, and the screen of my Alienware computer. Once we could imagine bodies and manifest them for view, it was perhaps inevitable to begin representing spaces for those bodies to occupy.

III: MAKING SPACE

I am an explorer. Or, at least I am a *virtual* explorer. The minute I log-in to a new virtual environment such as *Guild Wars* or *Second Life* the first thing I want to do is try to run through walls, fall off cliffs, and reach the edge of the world. I may stop to fight an orc, an alien, or a killer rabbit here and there, but that is just a pit-stop on the road to see everything and go everywhere possible. If I can do all that without dying—a task much easier in an environment like *Second Life* where one does not "die" and have to "back up" than in a game like *World of Warcraft*—the more is the better; but in all honesty, I die a lot. That is to say my virtual characters die a lot and that probably explains why I am a virtual explorer but a real world professor. There's a lot less dying in the professor business, and I am rather fond of breathing and eating and drinking red wine. Movies are nice too, but they don't come up until a later chapter. What I want to discuss now is that joy of discovery that fuels exploration and how we imagine spaces.

In his novella *Heart of Darkness*, Joseph Conrad has his narrator Marlow describe how he felt about maps. "Now", he says, "when I was a little chap I had a passion for maps. I would look for hours at South America, or Africa, or Australia, and lose myself in all the glories of exploration. At that time there were many blank spaces on the earth, and when I saw one that looked particularly inviting on a map (but they all look that) I would put my finger on it and say, 'When I grow up I will go there.'" This desire to know eventually leads Marlow to Africa and to the heart of the white space on the map along the coiling snake of the Congo River: a heart that he finds is full of the animal darkness of the human spirit. All of which is a poetic way of saying that Marlow, like his creator Joseph Conrad, made a habit of getting quite lost and then finding himself again—just for the hell of it.

Why do we do it? Why do humans go places, then make some record of that place, and then use that record to later describe and imagine what it must be (or have been) like? Even more bizarre is the fact that we make up places that no one has ever physically been. There are archives upon archives of maps of The Happy Hunting Grounds, Heaven, Hell, Purgatory, Narnia, Middle Earth, Xanth (which looks amazingly like Florida), and any other number of imaginary landscapes. In their *The History of Cartography Vol. I: Cartography in Prehistoric, Ancient, and Medieval Europe and the Mediterranean*, J.B. Harley and David Woodward describe this interest in representing space this way: "Curiosity about space—no less than about the dimension of time—has reached from the familiar immediate surroundings to the wider space of the earth and its celestial context. On another plane, men and women have explored with the inward eye the shape of sacred space and the realms of fantasy and myth. As visual embodiments of these various conceptions of space, maps have deepened and expanded the consciousness of many societies" (xv). This is to say maps not only describe or render spaces in virtual form, but they also create spaces in the imaginary landscape of a society. Maps help us understand who we are as a people and as individuals. Maps serve as the space for the cultural imagination to work and grow as they not only represent spaces but define what spaces may exist.

Take Marlow's concern with the blank spots on the map of Africa. What exists there within those borders put down with ink by Europeans from their ships sailing along the coasts? I believe the whole point of Marlow's story is that the making of the map, the act of exploring and filling in of the names and courses of the rivers, the charting of hills and mountains, and the dots with names that indicate villages and cities and points of interest, creates something as much as it describes something and in creating something new, such as the European capitalist version of African reality, something else is destroyed or diminished, such as a native populations' understanding of their territory as a spiritual space.

I have no desire to head into political territory here and enter into a digression on evils of colonialism or post-colonial angst; rather, the point I am trying to make is that maps are not simply powerful tools for exploration that describe our world, they also make the world of our understanding. Americans grow up seeing American maps and Russians are educated on very different maps, and this greatly affects our view of the world (in philosophical terms, our "weltanschauung"). Take me, for example. I consider myself an educated person with a quite broad base of knowledge. In college I studied political science, world literature, philosophy, and several foreign languages. Many of these studies included heavy doses of geography for which I was sometimes tested on. I distinctly remember filling in the countries of South America on more than one test. I have also travelled the world some and learned many interesting things about the prejudices of everyday life. Yet, I once vehemently asserted to my partner that my home state of Texas was approximately the size of Brazil. I was, of course, completely wrong. Brazil, the fifth largest country in the world, is 8,511,965 square kilometers (5,289,090 square miles) in size to Texas' relatively tiny 696,200 square kilometers (or 268,820 square miles). How could I have made such a mistake? Is it true that Texans have an inflated view of themselves and their state?

Well, yes, actually. For a moment my internalized cultural geography as a Texan superseded my internalized cultural geography as a world citizen. I felt silly, of course, confronted as I was by a group of very amused international friends, but I also felt intrigued. Of course I knew Brazil is larger than Texas in actual square miles. How could I not? I knew it and yet I also knew something else— Texas is, partly by self-acclaim, "larger than life", particularly to those raised in the Texas educational system where state history is a strong part of the public education curriculum throughout. I had certainly seen massive images of Texas in textbooks and on walls and in films. Brazil was just a tiny country in a black and white map on my Spanish test. I was certainly factually wrong (and, under the circumstances, very badly wrong) but I was also culturally correct: for many Texans, Texas is bigger than just about anything.

Maps are fascinating; at least to me, because they are not just an extension of the body (strictly speaking, a tool like a hammer or pickaxe) but also an extension of self-perception, point-of-view, and imagination. The map extends the eyes by extending vision, but it not only allows the viewer to see a distant place and/or from a different angle, but to see that place *as* imagined or remembered and from a disembodied perspective.

Tool-making extends the body out into the world. Visual art places the human body within the realm of tools. Cartography then frees the body from the constraints of time and place: cartography is the first disembodied art form. That may not sound like much, but I will attempt to explain why this technology is so terribly important for our psychology and our history.

Imagine: we are a band of hunters stands on a plain. We have traveled this way many times and know the layout of the land. Ahead is a small hill. To the left a creek bed that is dry because it has not rained in a long time. To the right stands a clump of trees. Our prey—a small band of ibex none the worse for wear in the drought—wanders from the trees towards the hill chomping at small dried blades of grass. They are eating. We need to eat. But we know that if we get too close to them they will see us and smell us and run away. How do we sneak up on them? Or, how do we trap them so that one of us might get in a good shot? We only need one of the ibex after all, though several would certainly be better. Our stomachs are growling and there are babies crying back at the huts.

I look forward and point, finger extended towards the left of the hill indicating "We should go that way, around the hill." You know what I mean because my hand indicates the direction. I might even twiddle my fingers back and forth like little legs to give you more of a clue as to what I mean. This behavior is not particularly sophisticated, but it gets the job done. I could even split the group up in the same manner: "You three go that way, the rest of us this way. We will catch them in a crossfire in the middle."

All this is easy enough as we know the lay of the land and what lies beyond the hill. Even more importantly we remember (from the Latin *rememor□ r□* composed of the prefix "to go back" (re-) and "memory" or "mind" (*memor*), essentially mental time travel) what the terrain is like and can imagine (from Latin *im□ go* meaning "imitation") being there again. The terrain we remember is not actual terrain but an internal representation of it. The terrain has been internalized. As complex as all that might sound, however, even tiny white mice can be taught to memorize a maze for food and the situation we now find ourselves in is just a larger more complicated, less defined sort of maze. I have been this way before. I know what I should do. I can see myself, remember, doing it and can follow that memory. I can fashion myself in that place through a purely mental act by recreating the space and place and my physical presence solely in my mind: I remember the image and thereby recreate it, fashion it anew.

Back at the huts: I cannot go hunting today because I injured my foot on a sharp rock, so I have decided to stay home from the hunt and try to make something that will protect me from the burning pain every time I take a step. Not having any antiseptic, I will probably die from infection in the wound in any case, but I don't know that yet, so I am sitting around playing with pieces of hide and trying to lash them to my foot. I want to send you hunting instead as a runner has just returned and informed me that ibex are munching their happy way along towards the hill.

I describe the hill to you, the creek bed, the trees and my plan to capture the ibex in a crossfire. Even though I am not going with you, I can see how it should work because I have been there before. You don't seem to understand me. It is very hot today and you are obviously sleepy. You need a strong cup of coffee, but that hasn't been invented yet either. So, frustrated, I decide to draw you a simple picture in the dirt as I remember the terrain. Hill. Creek bed. Trees. Ibex. "Ah," you say, "right." What I have done is to remember my own body in a particular space and then externalize or represent that space with a crude drawing to help you remember the terrain. If you happen to have never been there before then it will be my drawing you remember as you try to match it to an external reality somewhere vaguely "that way."

If I am a terrible artist, I should try for a distinguishing feature: for example the hill is shaped like a woman's breast (and thus an epic poem is born). In any case, you might get lost if I do not communicate properly. This is what Swiss linguist Ferdinand de Saussure (1857-1913) was trying to explain with his famous triangle. In brief, communication has three parts: 1) transmitter, 2) the message, and 3) the receiver. For example, spoken communication has 1) a speaker, 2) the words combined into sentences, and 3) the listener. The speaker has an intention to communicate, frames the words and speaks them, and the listener then interprets or decodes the message. Things can go wrong at any stage in the process—I might not have a clear thought, choose vague words, and the listener might speak another language all together, and so on. For effective communication to take place, all three of these stages must be working in concert, and even then there are invariable misunderstandings and miscommunications. So amazingly difficult is communication, in fact, especially considering the great proliferation of languages, that the philosopher Baruch Spinoza (1632-1677) asserted that no one really communicates anything at all. However, we are going to be a bit more optimistic and hope that I can devise a map (my "text" for communicating) that will get the hunters to where they need to go.

As a form of communication, my representation of the hill attempts to visually express the location as I remember it from my own bodily experience of being there. Though it demonstrates a passing similarity to cave paintings (which have been considered as simple maps by some scholars) the main difference is in intent. Maps may describe spaces for a variety of reasons, but all maps imply a verb tense in the sense that they mark what was (past), what is (present), or what may be (future). If cave painting is history, then we might consider it a type of map. If it is predictive, we also might consider it a type of map, but if, as Davis Lewis Williams has argued, it is descriptive then it is visual art and not a type of cartography. The space exists, the wall itself is the space, and the artist is merely "highlighting" what is "already there"—at least to his or her eyes. There is for example, a significant difference between cave painting and one of what is arguably the earliest known maps, that of Çatalhöyük in Turkey (circa 6200 BCE). If the image truly is a map, and there is some significant argument that it is not a town plan but a leopard or leopard-skin costume, then the image demonstrates a clear shift from first-person perspective and this is one of the defining characteristic of what most people would agree is a "map" rather than a "drawing" or "painting." The image seems to be, particularly in artist enhancements, a town plan seen from above including the image of a nearby volcano. Likewise, in the caves at Lascaux, there are spots that have been identified as stars. If they are stars, then they would arguably be maps, though with a shift in location only (from the sky to a cave ceiling) and not one in perspective—I look up and see the stars then, later, look up and draw what I remember. Much more likely, I believe, is the Lewis-Williams' argument that the "stars" in cave paintings are the result of optical illusions caused by heightened states of awareness (i.e. a trance). Regardless of which contestant for the first map wins out in the professional literature (if one ever does), by the time we clearly are dealing with what we can all agree is a "map" we are dealing with the demonstrated ability to imagine disembodied perspectives. Humans have learned, or acquired, or discovered, or wandered blindly into the ability to disembody the imagination. Rather than seeing a woman in a rock or seeing animals in stone shapes, rather than projecting ones' imagination onto something, cartography indicates the ability to imagine being someplace you currently are not or have never been.

Even fairly simple perspective maps have a change in perspective. If I draw a map with me standing on a hill waiting for ibex to pass, my imagined body will not be in proper proportion to the hill nor to the trees nor ibex. (Vanishing point perspective was still thousands of years away.) In fact, if I were actually seeing what I have drawn—an image of the plain from above—"I" would be floating in the air. There is a simple answer for this—I am not able to draw perspective properly. The same is true of this map of Çatalhöyük. This is, as it were, an impossible viewpoint for a human being short of having some sort of flying machine (which may be partially responsible for all the arguments for an alien intelligence having visited Earth in the past). The map is two-dimensional showing a flattened mountain and the street plan from above, what we now call "bird's eye view", but it is lacking in any depth.

But where is the "viewer", the person who sees the city from above? Where is the body that holds the eye as they look down on the hill? Looking at the map, if this were what I was actually seeing I would be floating in space somewhere: an impossible place where only birds can go and not be burned by the sun. The map maker has imagined himself outside of his usual bodily experience and range of vision. It seems quite possible that bad art (what I should, rather, call the use of symbol rather than representation) has led the map maker to create an impossible bodily position. He has gone, in his mind, where no man can go. He have become, He has made himself, disembodied…and more. This is how the gods must see! Even the most simple of modern maps now require that incredible bird's-eye view perspective. We might think of the common football (of the American variety) playbook with the Xs and Os and lines indicating the direction the players should run. Which brings us to another interesting point because once we are able to imagine the 3rd person perspective; we have the ability to represent the passage of time with successive maps.

Maps may not have always been around, but cartography is certainly a very old human technology and it operates as the marker for the ability of humans to use imagination to attain a disembodied perspective and to transmit and receive that perspective via symbolic images. Thus, whatever else the map may be, we may assert that the map is a tool that represents the conjunction of observation, perception, memory, representation, imagination, and communication. Obviously, maps are based in some sort of observation, and what we call perception is the act of understanding what one has observed. We might describe this act as the difference between "looking" and "seeing"; to look is to observe, to see is to perceive or to look closely by which we mean to observe and think critically. The map further relates to memory because we either must recall what has been seen or sketch what is being seen. In the latter case the map functions as a primary memory translatable to other viewers. But even in this case, the image must first pass through the map maker's mind and be translated to the page. In both cases, the map is a recorded observation of some sort, even if, as we shall see, the observation originates in imagination.

The map is, of course, also a form of representation. Like the Woman of Willendorf, the map is an externalization of an internalized vision or truth. Just as the carver of the Venus knew about (saw in the flesh) real women, the map maker also sees real hills and dales and bushes and ibex and bison. But the map, like the carving, is not a realistic, or photographic, image but an expressive

214

image that both reduces the detail and increases the symbolism, however unintentionally; though there is little doubt that the impulse behind the creation of images is itself symbolic. The map is not intended to be the thing but to represent the essence of the thing: to embody its virtues. The importance of this step should not be misunderstood. As Harley writes, "The development of the map, whether it occurred in one place or at a number of independent hearths, was clearly a conceptual advance—an important increment to the technology of the intellect—that in some respects may be compared to the emergence of literacy or numeracy."

Imagination is that individual inexplicable leap that makes all the others possible. Imagination lifts the body above the plain, makes the eye fly even into the heavens, gives the artist the "God's eye view" and makes them able to see beyond what mortal eyes can see. To imagine is to see more clearly, but also to see what cannot usually be seen. Imagination is the "divine spark" of creation. As Arthur H. Robinson phrases it, "The use of a reduced, substitute space for that of reality, even when both can be seen, is an impressive act in itself; but the really awesome event was the similar representation of distant, out of sight, features. The combination of the reduction of reality and the construction of an analogical space is an attainment in abstract thinking of a very high order indeed, for it enables one to discover structures that would remain unknown if not mapped."

Sigmund Freud, a pessimistic psychologist at the best of times, believed that all creation comes from dissatisfaction, or the experience of pain and suffering, and on this point I am inclined to agree as I can imagine what it must have felt like to want that illusive ibex for dinner, to see how it should be done, and to have a bunch of yahoos with me who just can't seem to do their parts right. I imagine this experience being rather like suddenly finding your arms and legs are no longer working. Certainly there are lots of animals that get by with a minimum of communication and everyone still flocks as they should (or almost everyone). That is what we call instinct: hardwired behavior that can lead to groups working together as a unit. But as instinct started to wane in the human animal, for whatever reason— dissatisfaction seems the likely culprit—communication became increasingly important to keep the rabble on the same page.

Ants work together, not by what we would call "choice" or even a perceived "necessity", but because that is what ants do. Humans work together because they have to by which I mean that we have feelings that drive us towards behaviors that are counter-productive to individual, or even collective, survival (what Freud called Thanatos or "the death drive"). Ironically, according to Freud, this very dissatisfaction, the ability to feel dissatisfied due to a perceived future pleasure, is the basis for what we call "civilization".

We see this same idea in evolutionary theory: the grumpier and more prone to dissatisfaction a species is, the more highly evolved, more complex, it is likely to be or become. We call this tendency towards bitchiness, and note the word we use from the female canine who grumbles and growls and howls, "striving". We might say that ants are always trying and that humans are always striving. In any case, this talent to be unhappy, which, of course, also brings "happiness" into being as its dialectical opposite, is at the core of our psyche and the driving force of the human animal. We try to communicate because we are in general unhappy with what others are doing. We want to tell them to do something else: we want to say "No". When that does not seem possible our lives become more complex and we have to ask them what they are doing and why: "What the heck are you doing?" Then, if we pass that hurdle we have to explain what we want: "Stop waving your arms like an idiot and sneak up the creek bed, you dufus."

Essentially, we must draw others into our pain; and, as they say, pain is a matter of perspective, so we must draw others into our perspective so they can feel our pain and see the problem. Enter the map: "This is you, and this is the creek bed. Crawl. Kill ibex. Get it?" Thus, we cross the boundary of primary first-hand experience restricted to a particular time and place and enter into the realm of recorded experience that may be remembered and forecasted.

Thus, the map also operates as a tool of time, though it does not demonstrate the movement of time itself as does narrative to be discussed later. The map may represent what was, is, or what will be. In this function it serves both a practical function as recorded experience and a mystical function as the act of map making itself becomes an act of perceiving the past and the future of ownership through the ability to render. As if from a tall tower, the owner of the map can see the world and lay claim to all the eye beholds. Thus, the map becomes a commodity and a tool of conquest.

If one can represent something, one can seem to own it rather like one owns the car by having the keys. If we can represent heaven, then we can own that too, because we will be the ones who know, and can show, the way. There is with maps, as Harley writes, "an immediacy about the message in a map that makes it more readily perceived than knowledge encoded in other ways...It has been said that maps have an 'extraordinary authority' even when they are in error, that may be lacking in other forms of images." It allows us to imagine fantastic places that have never been, or at least have never been anywhere outside the map itself and the minds of those who gaze upon it. One of my favorite authors, J.R.R. Tolkien was, by his own admission, fascinated with maps from the time he was a boy, and from this fascination he created worlds and histories and peoples to live in them and languages for them to speak. Now we can see Middle Earth on the big screen and on the computer screen in the MMO game version and, even if it looks strikingly like New Zealand, it is indeed a whole other world made by us and for us.

Indeed, I probably have a better working knowledge of the geography of Middle Earth than I do of the United States. Some might think that is pathetic, irreverent, irreligious, or just plain geeky, but I think this is an essential trait of the human condition. After imagining and making bodies, we imagine the spaces for them to occupy. Some of these spaces are practical, some mythological or mystical or magical, still others fantastical, but we imagine them nevertheless and physically and mentally occupy them. In fact what we commonly call "culture" is based in our interactions with mapped cognitive terrains. We all have maps in our heads that chart the spaces in our lives. This is part of who we are as human beings. The power of the map is not simply the power of representation, but the power to create a cognitive social space for a culture to occupy and express itself. The map speaks of bodies and spaces at a particular time. It may even speak, as does Dante's map of Hell in *The Inferno* or Tolkien's Middle Earth, of places imagined. But what the map cannot do on its own is tell the story—as much, as it might imply it, the map is locked in time. Which brings us to the third virtual discipline: after bodies and spaces comes the narrative. After all, once we find and kill that ibex we have to tell the tale.

IV: INVENTING TIME

Gilgamesh was a terrible and mighty king who ruled over the land of Uruk (in what is now modern day Iraq) sometime around 2700 BCE. We know of Gilgamesh in part because his name is listed in the Sumerian kings list. Even more importantly, however, his story is told in what is one of the oldest known recorded narratives: *The Epic of Gilgamesh*. The most complete version of the tale was discovered by the British archeologist Austen Henry Layard in 1849 and has been dated to around the 7th century BCE, but other pieces of the epic discovered at various locations in a variety of languages and dialects, date from 2150-2000 BCE. By comparison, the oldest recorded samples of the Iliad date from 200 BCE and are believed to be from texts dating as early as 800 BCE; and the earliest existing versions of the Old Testament or Torah date from around 200 BCE and are believed to derive from texts estimated to originate as early as 1000 BCE. There may be disputes about the origin dates of our oldest stories, but *The Gilgamesh* is demonstrably amongst the oldest written narratives and arguably contains pieces of the oldest mythological stories ever told.

Like many epic heroes, Gilgamesh is at least half-god, and this status sets him apart from the common people. Even the aristocracy that serves him directly fear him. Unfortunately, as the story goes, Gilgamesh is so isolated from others that he becomes dangerously bored, and a bored god-king is never a good thing. As the story goes, "the men of Uruk muttered in their houses, 'Gilgamesh sounds the tocsin for his amusement, his arrogance has no bounds day or night. No son is left with his father, for Gilgamesh takes them all, even the children; yet the king should be a shepherd to his people. His lust leaves no virgin to her lover, neither the warrior's daughter nor the wife of the noble". The people can do little but pray to the gods that Gilgamesh will once again behave like their true King and shepherd. So, hearing their lament, Aruru, the goddess of creation, made an equal for Gilgamesh out of the earth and named him Enkidu. Enkidu, who is covered all over his body with matted hair and has long hair like a woman's, knows nothing of civilization and runs wild with the animals. Perhaps the first eco-terrorist, Enkidu destroys the hunters' traps, but they devise a plan the catch him. "Go to Uruk, find Gilgamesh, extol the strength of this wild man. Ask him to give you a harlot, a wonton from the temple of love; return with her, and let her woman's power overpower this man. When he next comes down to drink at the wells she will be there, stripped naked; and when he sees her beckoning he will embrace her, and then the wild beasts will reject him."

As plans go to catch a wild man, I must admit that sending for a harlot would probably not be the first thing that would come to my mind. I certainly cannot see hunting for Bigfoot with a prostitute outside the framework of a really bad horror flick. However, I have to admire the Adam and Eve simplicity of the idea: if you want to civilize a man, to bring him from the state of nature into the society of work and responsibility, what you need is a woman. And here we find ourselves staring back through time to the Woman of Willendorf for the unnamed prostitute, the "child of pleasure" as Gilgamesh calls her, does appear to Enkidu naked and she is the symbol of sexual pleasure and fecundity. They make love for six days and seven nights. Afterwards, the animals do, in fact, reject him and he returns to the woman who prepares him to be a man. She shaves his body and teaches him to eat bread and drink wine. Enkidu helps the shepherds by killing lions and is generally happy being a man until one day a man shows up with the news that Gilgamesh has claimed the kingly right to have sex with all new wives before their husbands. Angered, Enkidu declares that he will go and challenge Gilgamesh and change the old order.

After a fierce battle, Gilgamesh and Enkidu become friends and adventure together until, one day, Enkidu is injured by the forest demon Humbaba and, eventually, dies. Gilgamesh is inconsolable and wanders the desert in search of the power to bring Enkidu back to life and along the way learns the lesson that lead him to become a wise and fair ruler for his people. We do not have the space to cover the whole tale here, of course, but it is a fascinating tale full of events that resonate throughout the history of world mythology and literature which is part of the reason it endures beyond the first 40 pages or so of World Literature textbooks. Though it spoiled the ending for me, I was pleasantly surprised, for example, to find that the *Star Trek: The Next Generation* episode "Darmock" (aired 30 Sept. 1991) retells the tale of Enkidu, Gilgamesh, and Humbaba as the encounter between Captain Picard and an alien whose language is constructed solely from mythico-historical analogies. Thus something like "Gilgamesh and Enkidu at the Forest against Humbaba" would mean in English "Two friends who stand together against a common enemy even unto death".

My point here is that even our earliest recorded narratives still have the power to enthrall us in their worlds whether they be fiction, mythology, or history or a combination of all three; and what we find enthralling about these tales are bodies moving through spaces over time. Thus, *The Gilgamesh* not only names, but physically describes, sometimes in minute detail, the people, animals, monsters, and gods who populate the tale. Like the Woman of Willendorf externalizes the thought of "Woman", so the *Epic of Gilgamesh* transmits the image of "Gilgamesh," and "Enkidu," and "the Harlot" who is also called "the Woman." I may not see the exact same Humbaba as you see, but we both see Humbaba nonetheless. This ability to transmit the image from one mind to another (albeit in altered form) is an evolved form of the artistry needed to make the Woman of Willendorf, but it is rooted in the same impulse and aims at a similar result.

Likewise, *The Epic of Gilgamesh* is a geography. It describes actual landscapes, mythological landscapes, and the socio-political terrain. Uruk was an actual place: a city-state with massive walls, a palace, and a marriage house, all as described. Just like the Woman of Willendorf evolves into the unnamed prostitute, so the map evolves into the narrative terrain where we can imagine the spaces and their relative locations without an actual map before us or an actual person standing there telling us the way and pointing. Though narratives are not maps per se, they do not require the technique of representing and understanding representations, or renderings, of various points of view. In the case of *The Epic of Gilgamesh*, in order to read and understand the tale I must know who "I" am in relation to the "teller." In this case I am a "listener" hearing the recorded (written) voice of a "speaker." Though as a linguist could explain more fully, there are elements of *The Gilgamesh* that have moved beyond the strictly verbal, the recording of spoken sounds, into what is often called "the literary," or the use of written language to its own ends.

The mythical spaces in *The Gilgamesh* seem to adjoin the real spaces or to overlay them. "Heaven," for example, is not so much a place as is Mt. Olympus to the Ancient Greeks, but an overlaying space with access points (including dreams) through which the gods and their servants can pass. Likewise, the riverfront where Gilgamesh stays with a woman and almost gives up his quest seems more a state of mind than an actual place. Like the cave paintings at Lascaux, these "other worlds" seem to show through the walls of the mundane world. And, of course, the socio-political spaces cover all as the "terrain" of the tale exists in order to describe a society and its people and, thereby, to help create and maintain it. *The Gilgamesh* was, for its people, a nationalizing literature that helped create a mental terrain of connections between people (bodies) and places (or spaces). Which brings me to the point that *The Gilgamesh* does something more than simply put a bodies in spaces and describe them, it engenders time for with the invention of narrative (with the evidence that narrative had been invented) comes the invention of time as we know it.

Humans are the only animal that experiences the world almost entirely through memory. Narrative engendered time as an asynchronous concept through the invention of past-tense where one can describe, through the act of speaking, actions which have already happened: in other words, narrative is a form of disembodied memory. Again, like the Venus of Willendorf and the map, narrative is essentially perspective sharing. Like the map, narrative allows a speaker to recreate in words events of the past or even to give verbal form to events that transpire solely in the mind that originate in dreams or imagination. Thus narrative incorporates both the functions of the made body by describing the actions of bodies not currently seen and the function of the map by creating (again in words) spaces not currently accessible. Body, space, and time meet in the narrative.

Returning to our ibex episode from the previous chapter, we might recall that we left the hunters heading out to find dinner. Upon their return I notice, however, that they have no ibex and I am clearly distraught. After all, my stomach is rumbling. The hunters see my reaction and interpret my body language correctly as frustration. They have a desire to explain what happened. One hunter points at the map still lingering in the dirt then uses his fingers on the sides of his head to mimic an ibex and another plays himself as a hunter. The hunter follows the ibex unaware, closes on it and prepares to leap. However, a third hunter leaps out from imaginary bushes and growls fiercely—a lion! And the hunter feigns running away.

This acting out of a past event is just a short step from telling the tale in words, but the effect is the same: for narrative to operate we must have the capacity to "make" bodies (either graphic, emulated, or described verbally) imagine and share spaces, and have a clear enough concept of time to understand that "before" can be drawn into the "now." Thus, in demonstrating their story to me the hunters have "explained" what happened using virtual bodies, spaces, and times. Considering the centrality of our own bodies in the making of tools, art, and maps it should not be surprising that our bodies also serve as the basis for narrative.

We see in *The Gilgamesh*, then, the basic technologies needed for all human endeavor—the ability to describe a body moving through space and time. This is the basis for all of what we now call "the disciplines" from physics to psychology to neurology to theology, and on and on. From quantum mechanics to Harley mechanics, we all use the same basic building blocks to describe and teach and learn what we do: bodies moving through space and time.

But why did we start to tell tales in the first place? No one knows when or why humans began to tell stories, but it is safe to say that what we think of as "humans" have always told stories because we are, as fantasy author and satirist Terry Pratchett writes, *homo narens*, the ones who tell tales. This is to say that humans have been making up reality since they first invented a rudimentary language. What we do not know will be answered; the wide gaps in knowledge will be filled with, as we say in Texas, bullshit. Why? Because in spite of what some say, as long as humans are thinking self-reflexive beings, what we do not know can hurt us. Therefore, we come up with tools to explain how things work and predict what will happen around the next bend—make some sense of the world that is so earnestly trying to kill us off one by miserable one. It is certainly to our evolutionary advantage to use ever tool (which quickly becomes most of everything in the world) at our disposal to prolong our lives and reduce suffering and most suffering comes from unfulfilled desire, which is perhaps the one thing that Jesus, Buddha, Marx, Freud, Jung, Lacan and all the rest all agreed upon. And, weaving verbal sense out of it all—creating a verbal virtual reality—eases the pain of living a brute life. Stories (narratives) ease the physical pain of life by predicting future events and outcomes based upon past experience. Something happens to me, I tell you about it, you tell Fred and then Fred one day finds himself in a similar situation and he does what I did, improves upon it, and (if he lives to tell the tale) an action evolves into a Neat Idea.

This sense of increased security, the ability of the narrative to increase our chances for survival, makes us feel more secure and less afraid. We believe in the power of narrative and, therefore, feel better because we worry less about the millions of things there are to worry about when one is a self-reflexive mammal. Eventually, this belief in the power of the narrative is confused with belief in the subject of the narrative and a fetish object is born. For example, the short narrative "I put my doohickey down here over his erect thingamajig, we bounced around a bit, and then my tummy grew and nine months you came out" is a useful narrative for explaining a person's origin (what is called an "etiology" meaning "where things came from") and for teaching the basics of procreation. Not to mention that it is a fairly complex observation on cause and effect that is considerably far along from the instinct to copulate. But, by associated logic and human's need to explain what they do not know (filling in those "why" gaps again), this short narrative can quickly morph into a phallus cult or cult of the woman where the instructional power of the narrative form is hidden and supplanted by the subject of the narrative. If anything is magical it is the power of story and not the run-of-the mill penis and vagina and (sorry kid!) all too mundane human baby. Let's face it, the so-called miracle of birth is not the real miracle because every living thing on the planet does that including worms, and they would be doing it even if we weren't around to call it miraculous. I daresay worms do not find worm sex "miraculous." What the real miracle is, the origin of the "miracle" itself, is that we can tell the tale.

NOTES

1 Katy Vine, "Love and War in Cyberspace," *Texas Monthly* (Feb. 2001 [29.2]) 80-85, 126-133.

2 "WELL" is short for Whole Earth 'Lectronic Link. For more about The WELL see, for example, John Seabrook, *Deeper: My Two-Year Odyssey in Cyberspace* (Simon & Schuster , 1997), Katie Hafner's *The WELL: A Story of Love, Death and Real Life in the Seminal Online Community* (Carroll & Graf Publishers , 2001), and Fred Turner, *From Counterculture to Cyberculture: Stewart Brand, the Whole Earth Network, and the Rise of Digital Utopianism* (University of Chicago Press , 2006), to name a few.

3 See, for example, David Lewis-Williams' *The Mind in the Cave: Consciousness and the Origins of Art* (London: Thames & Hudson, 2004).

4 Actually, Marlowe narrates his own tale within the larger narrative told by an unnamed first-person ("I") speaker. A similar device is employed in Mary Shelly's *Frankenstein*, though in that case we know the speaker's name (who is actually writing letters to his sister).

5 "As images they [maps] evoke complex meanings and responses and thus record more than factual information on particular events and places." J.B. Harley and David Woodward, "Preface," in *The History of Cartography Vol. I: Cartography in Prehistoric, Ancient, and Medieval Europe and the Mediterranean*, ed. J.B. Harley and David Woodward (Chicago: University of Chicago Press, 1987. xv-xxi) xv.

6 J.B. Harley "The Map and the Development of the History of Cartography" in *The History of Cartography Vol. I: Cartography in Prehistoric, Ancient, and Medieval Europe and the Mediterranean*, ed. J.B. Harley and David Woodward (Chicago: University of Chicago Press, 1987. 1-12) 4-5.

7 Arthur H. Robinson, *Early Thematic Mapping in the History of Cartography* (Chicago: University of Chicago Press, 1982) 1.

8 J.B. Harley "The Map and the Development of the History of Cartography" in *The History of Cartography Vol. I: Cartography in Prehistoric, Ancient, and Medieval Europe and the Mediterranean*, ed. J.B. Harley and David Woodward (Chicago: University of

Chicago Press, 1987. 1-12) 1. Harley cites Arthur H. Robinson's "The Uniqueness of the Map," (*American Cartographer* 5 [1978], 5-7) and Kenneth E. Boulding's *The Image* (Ann Arbor: University of Michigan Press, 1956, 65-68) as examples of philosophical inquiries into the authority of the map.

[9] In the past is was generally assumed that the list contained both mythological and historical kings and that Gilgamesh was mythological. However, recent scholarship asserts that while many of the feats of Gilgamesh told in the tale are fantastical, Gilgamesh, like Odysseus and Agamemnon, may have been a historical figure.

[10] The most complete version is from the 7th c. BCE, however, the earliest known versions (found in partial form) date from 2150-2000 BCE.

[11] "Darmock" Episode 102. Writ. Joe Menosky, *Star Trek: The Next Generation* episode (aired 30 Sept. 1991).

John Henry Cardinal Newman

INTELLECT, THE INSTRUMENT OF RELIGIOUS TRAINING

And when He came nigh to the gate of the city, behold, a dead man was carried out, the only son of his mother: and she was a widow. (Luke 7:12)

This day we celebrate one of the most remarkable feasts in the calendar. We commemorate a Saint who gained the heavenly crown by prayers indeed and tears, by sleepless nights and weary wanderings, but not in the administration of any high office in the Church, not in the fulfillment of some great resolution or special counsel; not as a preacher, teacher, evangelist, reformer, or champion of the faith; not as Bishop of the flock, or temporal governor; not by eloquence, by wisdom, or by controversial success; not in the way of any other saint whom we invoke in the circle of the year; but as a mother, seeking and gaining by her penances the conversion of her son. It was for no ordinary son that she prayed, and it was no ordinary supplication by which she gained him. When a holy man saw its vehemence, ere it was successful, he said to her, "Go in peace; the son of such prayers cannot perish." The prediction was fulfilled beyond its letter; not only was that young man converted, but after his conversion he became a saint; not only a saint, but a doctor also, and "instructed many unto justice." St. Augustine was the son for whom she prayed; and if he has been a luminary for all ages of the Church since, many thanks do we owe to his mother, St. Monica, who having borne him in the flesh, travailed for him in the spirit.

The Church, in her choice of a gospel for this feast, has likened St. Monica to the desolate widow whom our Lord met at the gate of the city, as she was going forth to bury the corpse of her only son. He saw her, and said, "Weep not;" and he touched the bier, and the dead arose. St. Monica asked and obtained a nobler miracle. Many a mother, who is anxious for her son's bodily welfare, neglects his soul.

So did not the Saint of today; her son might be accomplished, eloquent, able, and distinguished; all this was nothing to her while he was dead in God's sight, while he was the slave of sin, while he was the prey of heresy. She desired his true life. She wearied heaven with prayer, and wore out herself with praying; she did not at once prevail. He left his home; he was carried forward by his four bearers, ignorance, pride, appetite, and ambition; he was carried out into a foreign land, he crossed over from Africa to Italy. She followed him, she followed the corpse, the chief, the only mourner; she went where he went, from city to city. It was nothing to her to leave her dear home and her native soil; she had no country below; her sole rest, her sole repose, her *Nunc dimittis*, was his new birth. So while she still walked forth in her deep anguish and isolation, and her silent prayer, she was at length rewarded by the long-coveted miracle. Grace melted the proud heart, and purified the corrupt breast of Augustine, and restored and comforted his mother; and hence, in today's Collect, the Almighty Giver is especially addressed as *"Mœrentium consolator et in Te sperantium salus"*; the consoler of those that mourn, and the health of those who hope.

And thus Monica, as the widow in the gospel, becomes an image of Holy Church, who is ever lamenting over her lost children, and by her importunate prayers, ever recovering them from the grave of sin; and to Monica, as the Church's representative, may be addressed those words of the Prophet: "Put off, O Jerusalem, the garments of thy mourning and affliction; arise, and look about towards the East, and behold thy children; for they went out from thee on foot, led by the enemies; but the Lord will bring them to thee exalted with honor, as children of the kingdom."

This, I say, is not a history of past time merely, but of every age. Generation passes after generation, and there is on the one side the same doleful, dreary wandering, the same feverish unrest, the same fleeting enjoyments, the same abiding and hopeless misery; and on the other, the same anxiously beating heart of impotent affection. Age goes after age, and still Augustine rushes forth again and again, with his young ambition, and his intellectual energy, and his turbulent appetites; educated, yet untaught; with powers strengthened, sharpened, refined by exercise, but unenlightened and untrained— goes forth into the world, ardent, self-willed, reckless, headstrong, inexperienced, to fall into the hands of those who seek his life, and to become the victim of heresy and sin. And still, again and again does hapless Monica weep; weeping for that dear child who grew up with her from the womb, and of whom she is now robbed; of whom she has lost sight; wandering with him in his wanderings, following his steps in her imagination, cherishing his image in her heart, keeping his name upon her lips, and feeling withal, that, as a woman, she is unable to cope with the violence and the artifices of the world. And still again and again does Holy Church take her part and her place, with a heart as tender and more strong, with an arm, and an eye, and an intellect more powerful than hers, with an influence more than human, more sagacious than the world, and more religious than home, to restrain and reclaim those whom passion, or example, or sophistry is hurrying forward to destruction.

My Brethren, there is something happy in the circumstance, that the first Sunday of our academical worship should fall on the feast of St. Monica. For is not this one chief aspect of a University, and an aspect which it especially bears in this sacred place, to supply that which that memorable Saint so much desiderated, and for which she attempted to compensate by her prayers? Is it not one part of our especial office to receive those from the hands of father and mother, whom father and mother can keep no longer? Thus, while professing all sciences, and speaking by the mouths of philosophers and sages, a University delights in the well-known appellation of "Alma Mater." She is a mother who, after the pattern of that greatest and most heavenly of mothers, is, on the one hand, *"Mater Amabilis,"* and *"Causa nostræ lætitiæ,"* and on the other, *"Sedes Sapientiæ"* also. She is a mother, living, not in the seclusion of the family, and in the garden's shade, but in the wide world, in the populous and busy town, claiming, like our great Mother, the meek and tender Mary, "to praise her own self, and to glory, and to open her mouth," because she alone has "compassed the circuit of Heaven, and penetrated into the bottom of the deep, and walked upon the waves of the sea," and in every department of human learning, is able to confute and put right those who would set knowledge against itself, and would make truth contradict truth, and would persuade the world that, to be religious, you must be ignorant, and to be intellectual, you must be unbelieving.

My meaning will be clearer, if I revert to the nature and condition of the human mind. The human mind, as you know, my Brethren, may be regarded from two principal points of view, as intellectual and as moral. As intellectual, it apprehends truth; as moral, it apprehends duty. The perfection of the intellect is called ability and talent; the perfection of our moral nature is virtue. And it is our great misfortune here, and our trial, that, as things are found in the world, the two are separated, and independent of each other; that, where power of intellect is, there need not be virtue; and that where right, and goodness, and moral greatness are, there need not be talent. It was not so in the beginning; not that our nature is essentially different from what it was when first created; but that the Creator, upon its creation, raised it above itself by a supernatural grace, which blended together all its faculties, and made them conspire into one whole, and act in common towards one end; so that, had the race continued in that blessed state of privilege, there never would have been distance, rivalry, hostility between one faculty and another. It is otherwise now; so much the worse for us;—the grace is gone; the soul cannot hold together; it falls to pieces; its elements strive with each other. And as, when a kingdom has long been in a state of tumult, sedition, or rebellion, certain portions break off from the whole and from the central government, and set up for themselves; so is it with the soul of man. So is it, I say, with the soul, long ago— that a number of small kingdoms, independent of each other and at war with each other, have arisen in it, such and so many as to reduce the original sovereignty to a circuit of territory and to an influence not more considerable than they have themselves. And all these small dominions, as I may call them, in the soul, are, of course, one by one, incomplete and defective, strong in some points, weak in others, because not any one of them is the whole, sufficient for itself, but only one part of the whole, which, on the contrary, is made up of all the faculties of the soul together. Hence you find in one man, or one set of men, the reign, I may call it, the acknowledged reign of passion or appetite; among others, the avowed reign of brute strength and material resources; among others, the reign of intellect; and among others (and would they were many!) the more excellent reign of virtue. Such is the state of things, as it shows to us, when we cast our eyes abroad into the world; and every one, when he comes to years of discretion, and begins to think, has all these separate powers warring in his own breast—appetite, passion, secular ambition, intellect, and conscience, and trying severally to get possession of him. And when he looks out of himself, he sees them all severally embodied on a grand scale, in large establishments and centers, outside of him, one here and another there, in aid of that importunate canvass, so to

229

express myself, which each of them is carrying on within him. And thus, at least for a time, he is in a state of internal strife, confusion, and uncertainty, first attracted this way, then that, not knowing how to choose, though sooner or later choose he must; or rather, he must choose soon, and cannot choose late, for he cannot help thinking, speaking, and acting; and to think, speak, and act, is to choose.

This is a very serious state of things; and what makes it worse is, that these various faculties and powers of the human mind have so long been separated from each other, so long cultivated and developed each by itself, that it comes to be taken for granted that they cannot be united; and it is commonly thought, because some men follow duty, others pleasure, others glory, and others intellect, therefore that one of these things excludes the other; that duty cannot be pleasant, that virtue cannot be intellectual, that goodness cannot be great, that conscientiousness cannot be heroic; and the fact is often so, I grant, that there is a separation, though I deny its necessity. I grant, that, from the disorder and confusion into which the human mind has fallen, too often good men are not attractive, and bad men are; too often cleverness, or wit, or taste, or richness of fancy, or keenness of intellect, or depth, or knowledge, or pleasantness and agreeableness, is on the side of error and not on the side of virtue. Excellence, as things are, does lie, I grant, in more directions than one, and it is ever easier to excel in one thing than in two. If then a man has more talent, there is the chance that he will have less goodness; if he is careful about his religious duties, there is the chance he is behind-hand in general knowledge; and in matter of fact, in particular cases, persons may be found, correct and virtuous, who are heavy, narrow-minded, and unintellectual, and again, unprincipled men, who are brilliant and amusing. And thus you see, my Brethren, how that particular temptation comes about, of which I speak, when boyhood is past, and youth is opening;—not only is the soul plagued and tormented by the thousand temptations which rise up within it, but it is exposed moreover to the sophistry of the Evil One, whispering that duty and religion are very right indeed, admirable, supernatural—who doubts it?—but that, somehow or other, religious people are commonly either very dull or very tiresome: nay, that religion itself after all is more suitable to women and children, who live at home, than to men.

O my Brethren, do you not confess to the truth of much of what I have been saying? Is it not so, that, when your mind began to open, in proportion as it opened, it was by that very opening made rebellious against what you knew to be duty? In matter of fact, was not your intellect in league with disobedience? Instead of uniting knowledge and religion, as you might have done, did you not set one against the other? For instance, was it not one of the first voluntary exercises of your mind, to indulge a wrong curiosity—a curiosity which you confessed to yourselves to be wrong, which went against your conscience, while you indulged it. You desired to know a number of things, which it could do you no good to know. This is how boys begin; as soon as their mind begins to stir, it looks the wrong way, and runs upon what is evil. This is their first wrong step; and their next use of their intellect is to put what is evil into words: this is their second wrong step. They form images, and entertain thoughts, which should be away, and they stamp them upon themselves and others by expressing them. And next, the bad turn which they do to others, others retaliate on them. One wrong speech provokes another; and thus there grows up among them from boyhood that miserable tone of conversation—hinting and suggesting evil, jesting, bantering on the subject of sin, supplying fuel for the inflammable imagination—which lasts through life, which is wherever the world is, which is the very breath of the world, which the world cannot do without, which the world "speaks out of the abundance of its heart," and which you may prophesy will prevail in every ordinary assemblage of men, as soon as they are at their ease and begin to talk freely—a sort of vocal worship of the Evil One, to which the Evil One listens with special satisfaction, because he looks on it as the preparation for worse sin; for from bad thoughts and bad words proceed bad deeds.

Bad company creates distaste for good; and hence it happens that, when a youth has gone the length I have been supposing, he is repelled, from that very distaste, from those places and scenes which would do him good. He begins to lose the delight he once had in going home. By little and little he loses his enjoyment in the pleasant countenances, and untroubled smiles, and gentle ways, of that family circle which is so dear to him still. At first he says to himself that he is not worthy of them, and therefore keeps away; but at length the routine of home is tiresome to him. He has aspirations and ambitions which home does not satisfy. He wants more than home can give.

His curiosity now takes a new turn; he listens to views and discussions which are inconsistent with the sanctity of religious faith. At first he has no temptation to adopt them; only he wishes to know what is "said." As time goes on, however, living with companions who have no fixed principle, and who, if they do not oppose, at least do not take for granted, any the most elementary truths; or worse, hearing or reading what is directly against religion, at length, without being conscious of it, he admits a skeptical influence upon his mind. He does not know it, he does not recognize it, but there it is; and, before he recognizes it, it leads him to a fretful, impatient way of speaking of the persons, conduct, words, and measures of religious men or of men in authority. This is the way in which he relieves his mind of the burden which is growing heavier and heavier every day. And so he goes on, approximating more and more closely to skeptics and infidels, and feeling more and more congeniality with their modes of thinking, till some day suddenly, from some accident, the fact breaks upon him, and he sees clearly that he is an unbeliever himself.

He can no longer conceal from himself that he does not believe, and a sharp anguish darts through him, and for a time he is made miserable; next, he laments indeed that former undoubting faith, which he has lost, but as some pleasant dream—a dream, though a pleasant one, from which he has been awakened, but which, however pleasant, he forsooth, cannot help being a dream. And his next stage is to experience a great expansion and elevation of mind; for his field of view is swept clear of all that filled it from childhood, and now he may build up for himself anything he pleases instead. So he begins to form his own ideas of things, and these please and satisfy him for a time; then he gets used to them, and tires of them, and he takes up others; and now he has begun that everlasting round of seeking and never finding: at length, after various trials, he gives up the search altogether, and decides that nothing can be known, and there is no such thing as truth, and that if anything is to be professed, the creed he started from is as good as any other, and has more claims— however, that really nothing is true, nothing is certain. Or, if he be of a more ardent temperature, or, like Augustine, the object of God's special mercy, then he cannot give up the inquiry, though he has no chance of solving it, and he roams about, "walking through dry places, seeking rest, and finding none." Meanwhile poor Monica sees the change in its effects, though she does not estimate it in itself, or know exactly what it is, or how it came about: nor, even though it be told her, can she enter into it, or understand how one, so dear to her, can be subjected to it. But a dreadful change there is, and she perceives it too clearly; a dreadful change for him and for her; a wall of separation has grown up between them: she cannot throw it down again; but she can turn to her God, and weep and pray.

Now, my Brethren, observe, the strength of this delusion lies in there being a sort of truth in it. Young men feel a consciousness of certain faculties within them which demand exercise, aspirations which must have an object, for which they do not commonly find exercise or object in religious circles. This want is no excuse for them, if they think, say, or do anything against faith or morals: but still it is the occasion of their sinning. It is the fact, they are not only moral, they are intellectual beings; but, ever since the fall of man, religion is here, and philosophy is there; each has its own centers of influence, separate from the other; intellectual men desiderate something in the homes of religion, and religious men desiderate something in the schools of science.

Here, then, I conceive, is the object of the Holy See and the Catholic Church in setting up Universities; it is to reunite things which were in the beginning joined together by God, and have been put asunder by man. Some persons will say that I am thinking of confining, distorting, and stunting the growth of the intellect by ecclesiastical supervision. I have no such thought. Nor have I any thought of a compromise, as if religion must give up something, and science something. I wish the intellect to range with the utmost freedom, and religion to enjoy an equal freedom; but what I am stipulating for is, that they should be found in one and the same place, and exemplified in the same persons. I want to destroy that diversity of centers, which puts everything into confusion by creating a contrariety of influences. I wish the same spots and the same individuals to be at once oracles of philosophy and shrines of devotion. It will not satisfy me, what satisfies so many, to have two independent systems, intellectual and religious, going at once side by side, by a sort of division of labor, and only accidentally brought together. It will not satisfy me, if religion is here, and science there, and young men converse with science all day, and lodge with religion in the evening. It is not touching the evil, to which these remarks have been directed, if young men eat and drink and sleep in one

233

place, and think in another: I want the same roof to contain both the intellectual and moral discipline. Devotion is not a sort of finish given to the sciences; nor is science a sort of feather in the cap, if I may so express myself, an ornament and set-off to devotion. I want the intellectual layman to be religious, and the devout ecclesiastic to be intellectual.

This is no matter of terms, nor of subtle distinctions. Sanctity has its influence; intellect has its influence; the influence of sanctity is the greater on the long run; the influence of intellect is greater at the moment. Therefore, in the case of the young, whose education lasts a few years, where the intellect is, there is the influence. Their literary, their scientific teachers, really have the forming of them. Let both influences act freely, and then, as a general rule, no system of mere religious guardianship which neglects the Reason, will in matter of fact succeed against the School. Youths need a masculine religion, if it is to carry captive their restless imaginations, and their wild intellects, as well as to touch their susceptible hearts.

Look down then upon us from Heaven, O blessed Monica, for we are engaged in supplying that very want which called for thy prayers, and gained for thee thy crown. Thou who didst obtain thy son's conversion by the merit of thy intercession, continue that intercession for us, that we may be blest, as human instruments, in the use of those human means by which ordinarily the Holy Cross is raised aloft, and religion commands the world. Gain for us, first, that we may intensely feel that God's grace is all in all, and that we are nothing; next, that, for His greater glory, and for the honor of Holy Church, and for the good of man, we may be "zealous for all the better gifts," and may excel in intellect as we excel in virtue.

Feast of St. Monica—Sunday after Ascension, 1856. Preached in the University Church, Dublin.

SPECIAL FEATURE

Christopher Coppola, Jim Fox, & Curtis Scott Shumaker

POST-MODERN MUSIC AND THE SUBLIME

> *This art of Musick is the most sublime and excellent, for its*
> *wonderful Effects and Inventions.*
> —J. Playford, 1664

Recently, I sat down with filmmaker/composer Christopher Coppola and composer/professor/ record label owner Jim Fox for a three hour discussion on the topic of the sublime in Post-Modern music. These two men share vast experience and knowledge in this genre. Coppola has studied music under John Cage, Fox, and other eminent contemporary composers. In his earlier career, his composed such ambitious works as an opera based on Plato's "Allegory of the Cave." Although he has mostly given up composing in favor of filmmaking, he has developed a special expertise for carefully and creatively selecting cutting edge music for the soundtracks of his film and video projects. In addition to being a well-received composer over several decades, Jim Fox is also the owner of the small but influential Cold Blue Music label. *The International Record Review* described his music this way: "Fox's music invites one to believe that if the stars, constellations and galaxies emitted sounds, these unearthly harmonics are what one might hear."

In defining the topic of the sublime in music, we especially considered these quotes from the *Oxford English Dictionary*:

> *Thou hast nor Eare, nor Soul to apprehend The sublime*
> *notion, and high mystery.*
> —Milton

> *The sublime Style necessarily requires big and magnificent*
> *Words; but the Sublime may be found in a single Thought,*
> *a single Figure, a single Turn of Words.*
> —Chambers

*Great and elevated objects considered with relation to the
emotions produced by them, are termed grand and sublime.*
—Anonymous

Below are several excerpts from the interview. Footnotes give
on-line links for samples of the music we discussed. Some of the
links are rather long for typing, but the same sources can more easily
be found with an on-line search using the title and composer's name.
Soon, the on-line version of this journal will include the complete
interview, with a richer selection of musical samples, with easily
navigable hyperlinks.

*   *   *

FOX: One of the more basic things to bring up is the question
of whether the sublime is innate in the work; if it's in the work or if
it's in the observer. Or is the observer just attuned to something
that's innate in the image so they both have to be alive? Think about
it culturally—with all the different world music cultures, what does
one find exciting.

SHUMAKER: I think a certain part of the sublime has to do
with perception; you see things that are sublime in a piece of work
that a writer, a musician, an artist doesn't see him or herself. So there
must be a level of perception there, a kind of creation of a nexus that
is emerging out of a relationship between what the artist has done
without realizing it and what the observer perceives without really
looking for it.

COPPOLA: There is definitely some contemporary music
examples, standards, that I think definitely the idea is there, it gives
the musician no idea what it's going to sound like. He does not have
any idea, if played for an hour, what sound he's going to have. It's a
surprise. He knows what will happen, and we'll talk about that, but
he doesn't know exactly what it will be in the end. And to me that's a
form of sublimity; you're breaking things down to such degree that it
becomes its own thing. And you can feel that in your heart more than
your mind.

For me, in my mind, if it gets into my heart, where I'm no longer thinking... Um, just to give you a crazy example: modes. I was listening to the Beatles and, you know, they're great but there's one particular song that somehow gets into me and it's Eleanor Rigby. I just discovered it's written in a mode. An ancient mode, Mixolydian, and they chose that mode specifically so that it could get in there. They were reading about the sublime and certain modes. What do you think about that? Modes are like ancient scales, Dorian, Ionic....

SHUMAKER: I certainly don't have the ear for them, but I know the definitions.

COPPOLA: Well, you would know if you're listening to something that you can't quite understand. It's not the normal progression of scales that we're used to. And I was just thinking about modality as an ancient thing and yet somehow it still affects us. So is there some kind of history to this sublime, even though you're saying it changes? Is there some kind of history that affects us, like how the same person in ancient Greece might be affected?

SHUMAKER: There has to be. I think there has to be, because otherwise this stuff wouldn't hold up for so long, century after century, or thousands of years. At least in the case of literature, why would we still listen to it, why would we still be moved by it unless it resonates with something in the—I don't know what to call it, psyche or brain structure—the human way we perceive?

COPPOLA: Jim doesn't think so, so let's hear what he has to say.

FOX: I think there's something funny to how things come down through history. I used to like to joke how, if our world were to blow up now and everything would be buried in rubble for thousands of years and then they start digging up the literature, what would they find? What kind of stuff would be most frequently disseminated? It might be the worst. So his thought is, well, perhaps that's what we really have in ancient Greece. It's the equivalent at least. But if there's some other...

SHUMAKER: I know. There were so few people literate in those days that the cream of the crop is all that's really written down and recorded.

COPPOLA: It would probably be plastic. Non-literature would be plastic. Anyways, before we get into music theory and just Jim talking about different interpretations, I just want to read quickly this guy's interpretation of the sublime in the modern world and where it's going.

Jim was my electronic music teacher; that's where we met, University of Rhodes. And so I'm just reading this in that sense. And there are some standard pieces in terms of electronic music that maybe are things your readers should listen to. And I thought Jim could talk about them. I'm playing Beethoven and stuff, but there are standards in contemporary music—both Avant Garde European and in American—that act as starting points but have also gone in many different directions. Which Jim will get into.

Let me just read this account about the sublime in the technological world. Edmund Burke—he's a key figure in this techno-aesthetic movement.

SHUMAKER: Who else is in it?

COPPOLA: I'll tell you right now…Mario Costa. It comes in the postmodernist period along with the Frenchman Leotard. And now, everyone's talking about Mario Costa, who says: "The concept of the sublime should be examined first of all in relation to the epochal novelty (okay, novelty is interesting) of the digital technology and the technological artistic production: new media art, computer-based generative art, networking, telecommunications. New technological means allow for a new kind of sublime, the technological sublime. The traditional categories of aesthetics—beauty, meaning, expression, feeling—are being replaced by this notion of the sublime which, after being natural for the older centuries and are now mechanized and industrial in a modern era, have now become technology."

There has been some resurgence of interest in the sublime in analytical philosophy in the last fifteen years. The occasional article in the journals of aesthetics and art criticism…in the British journals as well as monographs by writers such as Malcolm Bud, James Curran, and Kirk Pillow.

As in the postmodern in our critical theory tradition, analytical studies often begin with the work of Kant. You know, I just thought it was interesting; this guy starts by talking about a new form of sublime created by digital technology, maybe because the "0s" and "1s" are not analog? And that's what makes it a new form?

FOX: I'd have to live with that one a while before I accept it. To read more about it before I know exactly what he means.

COPPOLA: Whatever he's saying, a lot of that makes me think of electronic music. Even though it's different, it somehow overlaps our background...

Now we're moving onto some stuff, but I just want to say that our relationship, in terms of electronic media, music: Jim was my teacher. I remember you made me listen to something by Morton Subotnick. What was the piece? It was a standard...

FOX: Oh, "Silver Apples of the Moon."[1]

COPPOLA: Right. What would you say to give a description to people about that period in what electronic music was like? Was it tape loops? Was it the Moog synthesizer?

FOX: Yeah. It was all of that. It was coming out of a tape-based thing from the fifties and then moving into synthesizers and now the digital world has replaced the wonderfully-tactile tape loops and stuff that people used to make. Weird machines and threading through doorknobs and everything else that they did. Fifty-foot loops or something.

COPPOLA: I started that with you, but you do not seem like somebody now, knowing your musical taste, who would be in electronic music, for some reason. Why is that? Why even teach it?

FOX: Because it was fun. It was fun to play around with and I used to enjoy making weird pieces of music at that time.

COPPOLA: See, I think that's kind of what contemporary is. There's a playfulness to it.

FOX: Yes, but there's a playfulness to every period.

SHUMAKER: Yeah and I think there's an angle here, the technological angle, that allows us to go beyond the limitations of the human body. We can do more than the human voice can do, what ten fingers can do. And also the instruments had to be workable...I mean, you can't pluck a 500-foot long string physically. You can do all kinds of interesting things with electronics that simulate things well beyond the capacity of human bodies or physical instruments.

FOX: Well, look at pianos. When you take the player piano, [early mechanical pianos programmed by a punch card type of technology] you have certain ways you can play. Then you take the work of Conlon Nancarrow, and it's all work that can't be done on a regular piano. That's why he did it.

COPPOLA: Then there's also John Cage's altered piano, "Prepared Piano," [where objects such as paper clips and rubber bands are attached to certain strings to alter their timbre] made some incredible sounds.

FOX: But the direct analog to electronic music's expansion of the palette or fingers, or what have you, of an artist would be the earlier innovation of the electronic piano, or any similar instrument. I mean, there are pieces that have been done for 100 metronomes. I just saw a fella who's local the other day. He did some things, beautiful, made a box—some forty or fifty music boxes—he had some sort of a clutch you could put in and they would all hold stable until he wound them all up. It was a beautiful, beautiful business. Good woodworking, too. And he had all these things you could wind up, and you pull out the clutch and they all go at once. And it makes sort of a lovely...

COPPOLA: But did he have control over it when they all went at once? He didn't know exactly how...I mean, there was some point where he didn't have control over it, right?

FOX: Well, they spin at roughly the same speeds, but it wasn't like one device would hit this note, then the one next to it would trigger. They were each either programmed or punched by him, and he just set the metronomes in motion.

*   *   *

COPPOLA: Moving on with the history of what you're calling contemporary music. Avent Garde being, more European, and new music and experimental music, being more American. In the Avant Garde, the Germans we got our Arnold Schoenberg, Veburn, and later Karlheinz Stockhausen. I don't find anything sublime in that music except some Berg and some Veburn. There is a romantic element there that I like. Then with the French, we have Stockhe and the Statics, I find a lot of sublime and I don't know exactly why, but there is something about emotion. Most people universally would rather hear Stockhe then Stockhausen percussion.

FOX: I suppose that's true in Western culture, sure.

COPPOLA: I think even it is even in Eastern culture. If you listen to simplicity, I've traveled in Japan and Vietnam and the stuff that really puts you in the realm is it's simple and unexplainable. Drones and all that stuff. There are certain things that we all draw from when we write music. I don't write music any more, but there is stuff that comes out of style. With you and your chord of twenty, doing things with mathematical twos, threes, and triplets in that, is so difficult for me to hear, so I don't even listen to that aspect of it and it takes me to a state.

FOX: Well that's the point of using it. It's a way of moving it out of sight of time, moving it out of time.

COPPOLA: To me, that is more sublime because there is some simplicity and depth to it that I can't explain. You can hear that and if you slow it down to a quarter note ten, do you hear that or is it a surprise to you in the performance of it?

FOX: No, it's just that I don't take it so religiously. It is what it is as long as it's down to roughly the right kind of thing. It's not like, oh my gosh, you're twenty-one not twenty. We are talking about tempo. The end of the metronome is normally forty, the slowest, with sixty meaning one beat per second on the metronome. Minute is divided into forty parts. Twenty means there are three seconds between beats.

COPPOLA: To me, it's not a gimmick, but they are talking about the idea of the 500 long string. You can kind of get an idea, but there are certain types of styles with a note of universal sublimity. If you play it in Vietnam they would respond to it more than something else.

FOX: I just don't know if there is any point in making pronouncements like that.

SHUMAKER: Is there some sort of underlying experience of the sublime that cuts across all of these cultural barriers of what music is? All these technical definitions of what music is (scales, tempos, and everything else you do in music)? I know there is something going on that moves me, regardless of my whether we have the same cultural background or if I understand what is going on technically.

COPPOLA: And how many does it move at once? But also, the readers don't know a lot about contemporary music. Maybe a starting point is to prick up their ears softly first or make them get out of the easy chair, to get them ready for an exploration.

SHUMAKER: What people think of when they think of orchestral music or classical music is oh, this is symphonic music with a tonal aspect where you return to the key note and it sounds nice and pretty. In the 20th century music, there are a lot of experiments to get beyond those rigid forms. Start off with an example that separates contemporary or Post-Modern, modern music from the Beethovens and the Mozarts as a jumping off point.

COPPOLA: For me, the king of what we call contemporary music is Charles Ives. Maybe we should start with him. What he did was before people like Stravinsky did it and nobody knew it. Now we know it. One reason why he went into music is he would sit there and listen to two bands playing different things while marching at each other. He would listen to that and he would find the microtones or tones between the tones. It was an experimentation that he had no control over that fascinated him and caused him to compose echoes or his own interpretations.

FOX: He had a predilection to it because he had that in his ear as a child. That doesn't always take. Daughter said her father was cruel and all he would play were twelve tone rows from when she was in the cradle. He never played any nice cradle music. He had a kind of future sensibility that is a troublesome thing to do is to say there is a direct trajectory in various arch fields. You are always shooting for the next improvement or advancement on the previous and that will always be there.

COPPOLA: There is one piece though that affects many people at once in a deep way by Charles Ives and that's the "Unanswered Question." Every time I play that to anybody, they are affected by it. Maybe Jim can describe why it has an effect on everybody.

FOX: I don't know that I can because I know some people that it would not have an effect on.

COPPOLA: Maybe those not affected already have that disposition.

FOX: No, no, no.

COPPOLA: How do you feel about that piece of music?

COPPOLA: I think it's a lovely piece of music.

COPPOLA: I play it to people of different walks of life, even a plumber, and that one piece isn't difficult for anyone to digest. Maybe that's why some people dislike it. It's simple.

FOX: I'm talking about people that have problems with classical language. I did lectures when I was living in Chicago about contemporary music and if the nun hadn't been in the room they would have been throwing stuff at me. So that's what I'm talking about. I suppose that one through background and training could come to like it. Maybe that plumber you were talking about was an opera buff on the side and it wasn't as much of a leap.

COPPOLA: I'm just trying to bring out certain pieces that some of these readers can listen to as building blocks to move on. It's interesting that Charles Ives who said "get your ears out of the easy chair" had this piece of music.[2]

If you listen to all of his music, there is some really heavy stuff to digest that you might not like or the reader's may not like. But this piece of music, even though it has some of that stuff going on in it, is accessible. It must be something about the accessibility that has to do with the sublime.

SHUMAKER: As a music lover, what I find compelling about this, even before I knew the title, are these long drawn out tones, the rising ones, and the trumpet coming in a little lower. To me, that gives a sense of longing and questioning I understood even before I knew the title. That is a highly anecdotal example, but there must have been something within the structure of the music that connected with me that I got the sense of what he was aiming for, at least in the broadest idea.

COPPOLA: The only reason I bring this up is he is one of the founding fathers of contemporary music for his day and it's an interesting piece out of his body of work.

FOX: But he is also a person who is out of that trajectory. He stood alone. There was no one preceding him or immediately following him. Many of his works were not performed. He was very old before people like Bernstein started championing him. He was not part of that iconic class of he studied with this composer, and then he taught the next one, he is completely out of that lineage. Carl Ruggles is another of the New England transcendentalists like Ives. His Sun Treader is another piece I would consider sublime.

COPPOLA: Here's a piece called "Tiger Balm," it was composed by Annea Lockwood, and this is interesting—it's a cat purr with music on top of it. It's simple, and the purr is sublime in my opinion because it's an animal thing.[3]

What I'm talking about is the idea of dissonance with the reverse of that—how they went back and forth to a precursor state which is, in my mind, sublime.

FOX: It is trance music, trance-inducing music. It's universal around the world. You could actually say that the big liturgical works in Western culture are actually, when performed in those echoic cathedrals, sublime and put you in that trance world.

COPPOLA: What's interesting to me is that if you listen to that period of music, and if you listen to Jez Waldo--who murdered his wife and child because he thought his child wasn't his--his music has a real darkness and dissonance to it for that day, which transports you, well, me, even more.

FOX: It's hypnotic. You hear that and it's terrifying.

COPPOLA: What I like about that is that the cat purr has a universal symbol of sound to it, and Annea Lockwood creates a dissonance with it that I like.

FOX: I don't hear any of the dissonance though…

COPPOLA: Do you? [to Shumaker]

SHUMAKER: Can there be dissonance between natural sounds and instrumentation? I might call it antithetical contrast, if I wanted to talk like a literature professor. I was just going to ask you about this particular piece and if you would consider it to be a mimetic piece of music, imitative of the natural sound? That's what I was expecting—we have a cat purr and the music is going to somehow model it, but I didn't really hear that happening myself.

FOX: I think it is just another instrument, you know? I don't think the point was that…

SHUMAKER: That would certainly be the goal of the early 20th century music, and before. It would be mimetic—we're going to imitate the sounds of nature...

COPPOLA: Exactly. And this is the perfect place to go to these next two pieces that started with ideas. She had an idea starting with the cat purr.

FOX: And the cat purr is hypnotic.

COPPOLA: But she started with an idea. I don't like to use the word "gimmicky," but it is a different concept idea. Like Alvin Lucier's "I'm Sitting in a Room." His voice is very hypnotic, he has a speech impediment, and his idea was to record his voice, play it back in the room and play that back in the room...

FOX: Record it being played back in the room?

COPPOLA: Yeah—record it playing until you have no more sense of his voice but the rhythm. You have to be patient and listen through several cycles for the effect to materialize.[4]

FOX: You end up with resonance. You record it and play it back so you get the ringing, like when you go into a room and you clap and hear a kind of tone...and you get these dancing pictures because of the room.

COPPOLA: What I'm saying is that it is, to me, sublime because it started out with an idea—an unanswered question—but I had no idea where this was going to go. When you hear it in its raw element, it's kind of like going to the Alps and seeing something.

FOX: This is one piece that I would play in my electronic music class. Steve Reich's *Come Out* is the other one.

COPPOLA: We're going to talk about that too . . .Now we're giving you standards of a type, but Steve Reich's "Come Out" was a kind of music called Phase Music. Would this also be considered Phase Music? [Two instruments playing the same piece but gradually shifting out of tempo; enhanced by electronic components where the composer sets off several copies of the same tape loop simultaneously on different machines with slightly varied tempos.]

FOX: No, this is different.[5]

This is again charged verbally the way that one was charged with his speech impediment. This one is charged because of the youth picked up by the drag note of Cops in the New York riots. And it's his speech.

COPPOLA: Phillip Glass' violin—was that before this or after? Phillip Glass and Steve Reich, they were both...?

FOX: They came up kind of together doing similar things. They play in each other's ensembles.

COPPOLA: Music in similar motion. There are two different styles: this is one that is a standard. What I find interesting about this is the idea of the terror—it's destruction. Destruction and creation. Starting with something, and then obliterating it, and even he says "destroy it"; that is something that is different in contemporary music than your standard music. That's what makes it experimental, because that's not what you would normally hear in classical: the idea, and then changing it by destroying it.

SHUMAKER: In regards to the last two pieces you showed me, ["I'm Sitting in a Room" / "Come Out"]... The first one, I was thinking about how you take a very human voice—it's more human because it has the impediment, you know you're not going to design a machine that speaks with an impediment—so it's this very natural thing which, because the machine technology is slowly absorbed, is obliterated by the machine aspect of the prospect. Halfway through you can still hear the speech elements with these winding and feedback type things, and by the time you get to the end the voice is totally gone. Here you have the idea of a very profound moving experience, and it soon went from being personal to having many voices that multiply to the point where you can no longer hear it. It's the way we react when we see people shot down in a crowd in Tiananmen Square: we don't react as personally as when we see the murder of a single person. The multiplicity both magnitudes the scale of the tragedy, but at the same time impersonalizes it.

COPPOLA: I found that one has a rhythmic thing, coming out of that anger, and the other has a harmonic thing, coming from smoothing out. It's different outcomes, but there's another one…I just want to give Jim some examples and then I want to get into what he does. He represents a whole new style—well, not new, it's been around with Harold Bug's stuff—but he's a champion of this style of music.

FOX: This is another look on something which could be considered as sublime.

COPPOLA: This is another "standard"—although there's actually two more "standards" which they should listen to as an early contemporary art which does this kind of stuff. This one's called "Jesus' Blood Never Failed me Yet" by Gavin Bryers. They recorded an old man who is clam digging or something and made a movie of it. He was on the beach and he sings this song which is completely out of tune but his heart is there. Gradually adds a melodic…well, it's a melody, right?

FOX: Well no…the guy's singing the melody and Galvin said he was doing the sound for a film. He picked this guy up, the sound of this fellow, and he found it was so beautiful that all he had to do was add accompaniment to the voice. With the accompaniment, the odd faltering in the man's voice when he was acapella now became sort of like Frank-Sinatra, behind the beat moments. So much of this is tied to the same concept of process—so much music is systemic in process. They're adding an instrument or two per repetition and ends up with a nice size chamber orchestra accompanying this fellow.

COPPOLA: It builds and builds and builds, but the interesting aspect is…

FOX: Not that there was anything wrong with the man's singing.

COPPOLA: No no—but the interesting thing is that he does become like Frank Sinatra. It was a change, a transformation, and I think it's kind of interesting to put it into the category of those kind of pieces—each one having a different effect.

I was the one who played this to Tom Waits and that's why he did his thing. He did a version of this and you can blame me for that. He was asking me because I came out of the School of Modern Music…

FOX: I tell you, for a classical music, between this and his other piece I love so much, on the flip side of the LP, they sold a quarter of a million copies. At least he has to date.

SHUMAKER: Was Tom Waits' song the same as here or…?

FOX: It's the same piece, it's just that he used his own voice rather than this lovely voice.

COPPOLA: But it's because of me.[6]

LINKS TO MUSIC CLIPS

1. http://www.youtube.com/watch?v=EelvKqhu1M4

2. http://www.bing.com/videos/search?q=charles+ives+unanswered+question&mid=3E53F5171D0D535DC5A93E53F5171D0D535DC5A9&view=detail&FORM=VIRE1

3. http://www.youtube.com/watch?v=sV5Gr3tkr-8

4. http://www.youtube.com/watch?v=sCgicEWD1Nc

5. Not freely available, legally: can be downloaded on itunes.

6. http://www.youtube.com/watch?v=ta-uxOT9uXA

CONTRIBUTORS

Ned Balbo received the 2010 Donald Justice Prize for *The Trials of Edgar Poe and Other Poems* (Story Line Press). His previous books include *Lives of the Sleepers* (Ernest Sandeen Prize, ForeWord Book of the Year Gold Medal) and *Galileo's Banquet* (Towson University Prize). *Something Must Happen*, a chapbook, appeared from Finishing Line Press. He has received three Maryland Arts Council grants, the Robert Frost Foundation Award, and the John Guyon Literary Nonfiction Prize. He was featured poet in the Fall 2011/Winter 2012 *Valparaiso Poetry Review*; other recent poems appear in *Iowa Review, River Styx, Sou'Wester,* and elsewhere.

William Coleman teaches literature and composition at Northfield School of the Liberal Arts, in Wichita, KS. A former teaching fellow at Harvard University, he has worked as managing editor of *Image* and executive editor of nonfiction of *DoubleTake.* His poems have been published in *Poetry, The Paris Review, The New Criterion, Image,* and other publications. His book and music reviews have been published in *Image* and *The Martha's Vineyard Times,* respectively.

Christopher Coppola is a seasoned film and television director who is also founder and chairman of Project Accessible Hollywood (PAH), a non-profit organization that brings digital empowerment to underserved communities and individuals worldwide. To date, Coppola has held 38 digital media festivals, called PAH-FESTS, across the U.S. and abroad. He is also known as Biker Chef and the DigiVangelist. His cat Otto is the world famous BIKER CAT.

Matthew Eck's debut novel *The Farther Shore* was the winner of the Milkweed National Fiction Prize, was a Barnes and Noble Discover Great New Writers Selection, and won the Fiction Award from the Society of Midland Authors. He is Fiction Editor at *Pleiades* and lives in Kansas City.

Jim Fox is a Los Angeles-based composer. His music—usually quiet, slow, unassuming, and often described by critics as "austere" and "sensuous"—has been commissioned and performed by ensembles and soloists throughout the United States and released on a half-dozen different record labels, including Cold Blue Music, a new music label which he directs.

Lise Goett is the winner of the 2012 Robert H. Winner Memorial Award from the Poetry Society of America for her manuscript-in-progress, *Leprosarium*. She received the Pen Southwest Book Award in Poetry in 2005 and the 2001 Barnard New Women Poets Prize for her first collection, *Waiting for the Paraclete* (Beacon 2002). Her other awards include the James D. Phelan Award in Literature, the Capricorn Prize from the Writer's Voice of West Side Y, postgraduate fellowships from The Milton Center and from the Creative Writing Institute at the University of Wisconsin-Madison, and *The Paris Review* Discovery Award.

Merrick Rees Hamer, born August 29th, 1950, is a native Californian who has spent much of his creative life as a dramatic and musical storyteller. A formal education in music and an introspective nature led to an early fascination with legend and with ideas that "were not," but that "could be." This background, with a speculative perseverance and the library settings in which he has spent a portion of his professional life, ultimately has seen him embrace metaphysical doctrine, and he has more than occasionally lifted the pen to jot down his own ideas as a mystical Christian.

Wes Jackson, President of The Land Institute, holds a B.A Biology, an M.A. in botany, and a Ph.D. in genetics. His most recent works, *Nature as Measure* (2011) and *Consulting the Genius of the Place: An Ecological Approach to a New Agriculture* (2010), were both published by Counterpoint Press. Author of many books, Jackson has published in *The Atlantic Monthly*, *Audubon*, *National Geographic*, and *Time Magazine*. Named by *Life* magazine as one of 18 individuals they predict will be among the 100 "important Americans of the 20th century," Jackson is also a recipient of the Pew Conservation Scholars award, a MacArthur Fellowship, the Right Livelihood Award, and the Louis Bromfield Award. He has received four honorary doctorates. In 2007 he received the University of Kansas Distinguished Service Award and was one of the 2011 recipients of the University of Kansas College of Liberal Arts & Sciences' Distinguished Alumni Awards.

Laura Kopchick is a graduate of the MFA program in Fiction at the University of Michigan, where she was a Colby Fellow and where she received the Roy W. Cowden Award in short fiction as well as the Hopwood Award in short fiction. She is also the recipient of the 1998 First Place National Award (with a $10,000 prize) in short Fiction from the National Society of Arts and Letters. Her stories have appeared in the *Santa Monica Review, Ascent, Pleiades,* and others. Currently she teaches creative writing at The University of Texas at Arlington. She is also General Editor of the Katherine Anne Porter Award in short fiction from the University of North Texas Press.

David Lunde is a poet and translator whose work has appeared in such journals as *Poetry, The Iowa Review, TriQuarterly, Kansas Quarterly, Chelsea, Confrontation, Hawai'i Review, Chicago Review, Seneca Review, Cottonwood, The Literary Review, Renditions,* and *Northwest Review.* His work has been included in 40 anthologies, and he is the author of 11 books of poems and translations, the most recent being: *Nightfishing in Great Sky River* (1999); *The Carving of Insects* (2006), Bian Zhilin's collected poems co-translated with Mary M.Y. Fung, which won the 2007 PEN USA Translation Award; *Instead* (2007), a collection of poems; *Breaking the Willow* (2008), and *300 Tang Poems* (2011), translations of classical Chinese poetry.

Maureen McCoy is the author of four novels: *Walking After Midnight, Summertime, Divining Blood,* and *Junebug.* Recent short fiction and personal essays are included in *Antioch Review, Epoch, Mississippi Review,* and forthcoming elsewhere. *Antioch's* "Vickie's Pour House: A Soldier's Peace" was a finalist for a National Magazine Award. Maureen is a professor at Cornell University.

John Henry Cardinal Newman (1801-1890) was a writer, educator, and theologian in England and Ireland during the nineteenth century. Newman began his career as an Anglican priest and a fellow of Oxford's Oriel College. In 1845, he converted to Catholicism and was ordained to the Catholic priesthood. As the first rector of the Catholic University of Dublin, Newman wrote and published *The Idea of a University* (1854) which outlines his influential theory of liberal education and intellectual development. His book *Apologia Pro Vita Sua* was read widely in Great Britain and America and was instrumental in decreasing anti-Catholic prejudices throughout the

English-speaking world. Pope Leo XIII made Newman a cardinal in 1879. In 2010, Pope Benedict XVI beatified Cardinal Newman in a ceremony in Birmingham, England.

Timothy Richardson's poetry has appeared in *The Paris Review, Western Humanities Review*, and *The North American Review* (among others). He is currently Associate Professor of English at the University of Texas at Arlington, where he directs the Creative Writing Minor and teaches in poetry, rhetoric, and critical theory. He has always wanted to be a DJ, but has no skills.

Vicky Santiesteban grew up on the outskirts of the Florida Everglades where she learned to ride a horse, catch reptiles, and suck sugar from cane. Her work has appeared in *Alaska Quarterly Review, River Styx*, and *The Best of Writers at Work*.

Curtis Scott Shumaker was born in Oklahoma, received his B.A. from the liberal arts college of USAO, and earned his Masters and Doctorate in English at Iowa State University and Texas A&M Commerce, respectively. He now lives in Hollywood California and teaches at California Polytechnical University. He is a 32 Degree Freemanson, a member of various esoteric and Hermetic orders, and has publications in various scholarly, Masonic, and creative venues.

C. Jason Smith is Professor of English at LaGuardia Community College of the City University of New York and the co-author, with Ximena Gallardo C., of *Alien Woman: The Making of Lt. Ellen Ripley* (Continuum 2004). He lives and writes in The Twilight Zone, Astoria, Queens, New York.

Sonya Taaffe's poems and short stories have won the Rhysling Award, been shortlisted for the SLF Fountain Award and the Dwarf Stars Award, and appeared in anthologies such as *The Moment of Change: An Anthology of Feminist Speculative Poetry, People of the Book: A Decade of Jewish Science Fiction & Fantasy, Last Drink Bird Head, The Year's Best Fantasy and Horror, The Alchemy of Stars: Rhysling Award Winners Showcase, The Best of Not One of Us*, and *Trochu divné kusy 3*. Her work can be found in the collections *Postcards from the Province of Hyphens* and *Singing Innocence and Experience* (Prime Books) and *A*

Mayse-Bikhl (Papaveria Press). She is currently on the editorial staff of *Strange Horizons*. She holds master's degrees in Classics from Brandeis and Yale and once named a Kuiper belt object.

Frederick Turner, Founders Professor of Arts and Humanities at the University of Texas at Dallas, was educated at Oxford University. Poet, critic, translator, philosopher, and former editor of *The Kenyon Review*, he has authored 30 books, including *Natural Classicism, The Culture of Hope, Genesis: An Epic Poem, April Wind, Hadean Eclogues, The New World, Shakespeare's Twenty-First Century Economics, Paradise, Natural Religion,* and *Two Ghost Poems*. With his colleague Zsuzsanna Ozsváth he won Hungary's highest literary honor for their translations of Miklós Radnóti's poetry. He has been nominated for the Nobel Prize for Literature internationally over 40 times.

Albert Wendland is Director of the Master of Fine Arts in Writing Popular Fiction at Seton Hill University. He has written on science fiction, graphic novels, popular fiction, and the sublime in literature. His interests include Romanticism, science fiction of the 50s, astronomy, the history of landscape painting, writing poetry, geology, and film studies. He has completed a science-fiction novel and he is currently working on a book about descriptive writing in popular fiction.

Mary Jane White is a poet and translator who practices law at her home, the O. J. Hager House in Waukon, Iowa. Her poetry and translations have received NEA, Bread Loaf, and Squaw Valley awards. She taught briefly at the University of Iowa and Luther College, and has practiced law for the last 33 years. Her work has appeared in *AGNI, The American Poetry Review, The Iowa Review, Crazyhorse, The Black Warrior Review, The Louisville Review, Nimrod, The New England Review,* and many others. Her first book *Starry Sky to Starry Sky* (1988) is still available from Holy Cow! Press.

OUR MISSION

Archaeopteryx: The Newman Journal of Ideas exists to provide a space for meaningful academic and creative work that investigates the true, the beautiful, and the good. We welcome faith, we welcome reason, we welcome the sublime. Named for the first bird—ancient, fossilized, frozen as if in the act of flying through shale—*Archaeopteryx* is intended to shake free stone and set the soul free to soar.

SUBMISSIONS

Archaeopteryx: The Newman Journal of Ideas accepts submissions year-round and is published annually in both print and online versions. All work that is accepted for publication will receive a payment of two year's subscription to the magazine (worth 20 dollars). Contributors will be given the option to purchase, at a reduced rate, additional copies of the volume in which their work appears. *Archaeopteryx* maintains the right to publish and reproduce all accepted submissions in both print and online versions. Rights to reprint the work are returned to the author upon publication. Writers may send poetry, short stories, creative non-fiction, and essays to either of the following addresses:

Archaeopteryx
c/o Bryan D. Dietrich
Newman University
3100 McCormick
Wichita, KS 67213

Archaeopteryx2012@gmail.com.

While the magazine welcomes unsolicited manuscripts, it cannot accept responsibility for their loss or damage. Rejected manuscripts will not be returned unless accompanied by a self-addressed, stamped envelope. All submissions must be in English and previously unpublished. Please submit no more than six poems at a time. Please submit only one story or essay manuscript at a time. Essays should be submitted in endnote style (no parenthetical citations).

Simultaneous submissions are also acceptable as long as we are notified immediately if the manuscript is accepted for publication elsewhere. Be sure to include phone and (if possible) e-mail contact information. We suggest to all who submit that they read several issues of *Archaeopteryx* to acquaint themselves with material the magazine has published. Back issues may be obtained through Amazon.com or by writing to either of the addresses above.

ARCHAEOPTERYX

12092109R00150

Made in the USA
Charleston, SC
11 April 2012